To the memory of Thomas Evan Whitton

(1891-1966)

soldier and newspaper proprietor,

who stowed away on the *Beltana*

to join his mates at Gallipoli.

The Cartel

Lawyers and
Their Nine Magic Tricks

Evan Whitton

Herwick Pty Ltd 1998

Herwick Pty Ltd
Locked Bag No 2018, P.O. Glebe NSW 2037 Australia
Phone: + 61 2 9566 4121   Fax: + 61 2 9552 6755

Distributed in Australia by Tower Books Pty Ltd
19 Rodborough Road, Frenchs Forest NSW 2086
Phone: (02) 9975 5566   Fax: (02) 9975 5599

Available worldwide: www.ewhitton.com
Updates and additional information: info@ewhitton.com

First Published 1998

Copyright © Evan Whitton, 1998

National Library of Australia
Cataloguing-in-Publication Data
Whitton, Evan
The Cartel: Lawyers and Their Nine Magic Tricks
ISBN 0-646-34887-6

1. Evidence (law) history. 2. Justice, miscarriages of.
3. Law, comparative. 4. Sociological jurisprudence. I. Title.

Cartoons by Patrick Cook

Printed by Griffin Press Pty Ltd
Production and design ABC Graphics Glebe NSW
Typeset in Serifa

Contents

Acknowledgements

I have to thank many people who directly or indirectly through their writings pointed me in the right direction: Mel Barnett, Dr Edward de Bono, Bob Bottom, Justice Ian Callinan, Vic Carroll, Richard Coleman, Nicholas Cowdery QC, Ian David, Justice Geoffrey Davies, Helen Deller, Quentin Dempster, John Dobies, Bruce Donald, Commodore Michael Dunne, Dr John Forbes, Brian Gallagher, Bruce Grundy, Commander James Goldrick, Brett Jackson, Hon David Jackson QC, Dr. Peter James, Matthew Kelly, Sir Ludovic Kennedy, Justice Michael Kirby, Dr John Langbein, Anthony Lennon, Jane Lennon, Susanna Lobez, Rick McDonell, Bron McKillop, Ken Marks QC, Bob Mulholland QC, Claire O'Brien, Elizabeth O'Brien, Hugh O'Brien, Stephen Odgers, Ian Pike, Adrian Roden QC, Andrew Rogers QC, Jeffrey Shaw QC, John Slee, Jim Staples, Max Suich, Terry Hanley and the Veech Library of the Catholic Institute of Sydney, John Wareham, Ross Wilson, Anthony Whitton, Margaret Whitton, Thomas Whitton, Spiro Zavos, Dr Alex Ziegert.

For his brilliant illustrations, Patrick Cook, Australia's leading satirist and cartoonist for two decades, and a colleague from happy days at *The National Times*.

And, as ever, my astonishingly multi-skilled wife, Noela Whitton, for being the great Lazare Carnot of this and other enterprises, and for her love and coffee.

"... You and I both do the same thing,
he would chide me, "sleight of hand –
making things appear to be what they're not."

– Alan M. Dershowitz, US defence lawyer,
writing of his son, a professional magician, 1991

"... you really feel you've done something
when you get the guilty off."

– Stuart Littlemore, QC, 1995

INTRODUCTION

I don't think it's a justice system as such; it's a legal system.

— Mel Barnett, common lawyer, 1997

A new millenium offers a chance to reflect on many things, including the law. Citizens of English-speaking common law countries, some 1600,000,000 in all, might urgently debate whether they want a justice system or a legal system, what sort of judges and lawyers they want, and indeed whether their system has ever been legitimate.

Mr Barnett is not wrong; the position of the common law is quite untenable. Law exists to protect the community, but the result of common lawyers' nine magic tricks is that about one per cent of people in prison are innocent, and about 80 per cent of fairly serious criminals are found not guilty.

By contrast, a 1992 study on inquisitorial pre-trial procedures in France and Germany for Viscount Runciman's inquiry into the criminal justice system found it was unlikely that miscarriages such as the Guildford Four and the Birmingham Six would occur in France and Germany.

And Justice James Burchett, of the Australian Federal Court, says French courts are fair and their verdicts are generally accurate. But French and German trials convict about 90 per cent of fairly serious criminals against the common law's 20 per cent.

How did the cartel which has run the common law for eight centuries allow it to get into this parlous situation? What is the solution? Lawyers don't ask these questions, let alone answer them. Perhaps they should try the Greenpeace approach: What is the problem? What is the solution? What am I doing about it? What are you doing about it? Who should do what?

PROBLEMS

Ignorance. Ignorance of the origins of the magic tricks is profound; law schools teach how to use them but not where they came from. How do you make a lawyer stutter? Ask him: Who decided that truth is not important to justice? When was the adversary system invented? Much of what follows will thus be new and surprising – and I trust alarming – to judges and lawyers.

The English Disease. I apologise in advance to non-lawyers for the Dick and Dora prose, but I have to keep the malady in mind: common lawyers and judges have always seemed to find clarity of thought and utterance difficult, a phenomenon known as *la maladie Anglais*. The magic tricks may be seen as manifestations of the malady in the 13th and 18th centuries, but lawyers and judges stubbornly and consistently refuse the cure, a truth serum; further manifestations are reported daily.

13TH CENTURY

Accusatorial Systems. Legal systems in England and Europe in the Dark and early Middle Ages believed in the Judgment of God, i.e. that the facts were gathered and the verdict delivered by an inscrutable deity. The procedure was accusatorial: one person accused another; the trial took various forms, including trial by ordeal and the judicial duel, or trial by single combat (trial by battle), in which an armed champion could stand in for accuser and accused.

An Inquisitorial System. After a conference in Rome in November 1215, European courts decided to drop the deity as the fact-gatherer and to use a judge instead. The judge questioned everyone, including the suspect, who might help him find the truth. This is called an inquisitorial, or investigative, system. European judges, like English judges, sometimes resorted to torture.

The Cartel. In 1216, the English monarch, Henry III, was aged nine; the decision on whether to follow the European courts was left to a recently-formed cartel of some two dozen lawyers and untrained and ignorant judges. A problem with such an incestuous connexion is that lawyering is lawyering and judging is judging.

There is a disobliging view that those in the cartel were primarily interested in money, status and power; Judge Richard Posner, a US economist and appeal court judge, said this of the cartel in 1995: "... self-interest has played as big a role in legal thought as in medical thought ... The history of the legal profession is to a great extent, and despite noisy and incessant protestation and apologetics, the history of all branches of the profession, including the professoriat and the judiciary, to secure a lustrous place in the financial and social-status sun ... the profession was [until recently in the US] an intricately and ingeniously reticulated though imperfect cartel."

Self-interest was no doubt at times a factor in the shambles that is the common law, but Judge Posner may be overly harsh as to motive. Apart from the malady, "noisy and incessant protestation" about its supposed merits probably convinced many that it is a great system, and that they were properly furthering the interests of justice; those who relentlessly obstruct reform may well believe they know better. A question is: when does invincible ignorance shade into culpable ignorance?

The First Magic Trick. At all events, the 13th century cartel decided that investigating the truth was not the way to go. The "wogs begin at Calais" posture seems to have been a factor; Dr R.M. Jackson, an English legal historian, says they persisted with the accusatorial system partly because of "an insular dislike of things foreign".

The ludicrous notion that truth is not relevant to justice is the first and greatest magic trick; it is the fundamental problem from which all others flow. The 1600 million groaning under the yoke of the common law might reasonably ask why they should still be at the mercy of a few racist buffoons in the 13th century. One answer is that the rule of precedent means that judges must abide by the decisions of earlier judges even though they were probably wrong, confused or had a secret agenda.

A Defective Jury System. Dr Jackson says the other reason for not adopting the inquisitorial system was that England was experimenting with a jury system. Perhaps not unexpectedly, the system was, and is, fatally flawed: the cartel merely replaced an inscrutable deity with an inscrutable jury; a German maxim says: without reasons there can be no valid judgment. The jury system is the second magic trick: it eventually gave defence lawyers the excuse to invent a series of rules that help keep guilty clients at large.

Meanwhile, for five centuries judges alleviated the jury problem to a degree by informally discussing the case with the jurors. They helped them with the weight they should give certain types of evidence, e.g. hearsay. They sought jurors' views on the way they were heading; asked them their reasons; and put them right if they got it wrong, at least as the judge saw it.

Unfair Criminal Trials. Lawyers in the cartel appeared for the parties in civil actions, but were remiss in not persuading judges to allow them to represent accused in criminal trials; perhaps there was little money, status or power in it. The judge was supposed to watch the accused's interests, but must have been fairly perfunctory; trials were said to be nasty, brutish and short.

The judge did not conceal evidence but did not look for it either; he was not an investigating fact-gatherer in the European sense. He was not briefed beforehand on the accuser's case; he took the evidence as it came from the accuser, and he alone questioned the witnesses, including the accused.

The Legislature. Citizens wonder why, if the law is so bad, the cartel has managed to prevent reform for eight centuries. One reason may be that lawyers got control of Parliament in the 14th century, and they retain a powerful influence in legislatures. In the United States, where there is one lawyer for every 350 persons, being a lawyer is almost a condition of entry into politics.

Exporting the Malady. England began exporting the common law (and the malady) in the 17th century: Jamestown, Virginia, in 1607, Cape Town, South Africa in 1652, Bombay, India, in 1661, Canada in 1670, Sydney, Australia, in 1778, to New Zealand in 1792.

18TH CENTURY

Legal Academics. Membership of the cartel was tightly held; legal academics were excluded for five centuries. William Blackstone was the first admitted; despite "his freedom from excessive learning" he began to teach common law at Oxford University in 1753. He accepted the law without question and was a hugely successful apologist for it in England and America. With exceptions, academics tend to follow the Blackstone line.

He appears to have invented the "rotten apple" defence, thus anticipating corrupt police forces. *The Westminster Review* reported in 1826: " ... so successful have been the artifices of lawyers that Englishmen have hitherto almost universally believed the assertion of Sir William Blackstone that these inconveniences are the price we *necessarily* pay for the benefits of legal protection."

A Mafia Ode to the Common Law. Blackstone's panegyrics were echoed two centuries later by the US Mafia. Judge Giovanni Falcone and other Palermo investigating magistrates laid on a maxi-trial of 475 members of the Sicilian Mafia in 1986. The Sicilian Mafia's response, apart from assassination, was to bribe Italian legislators to change from an inquisitorial system to one more like the common law. Joe Gambino, a major US heroin supplier who got his product from Sicily, discussed the new system with an anonymous colleague just back from Sicily in 1988. Their ode (in Sicilian dialect) to the common law and its magic tricks was taped at the Cafe Giardino, Brooklyn:

Gambino: Oh, so it's like here, in America?

Anon: No, it's better, much better. Now those bastards, the magistrates and cops, can't even dream of arresting anyone the way they do now.

Gambino: The cops will take it up the ass! And that other one [Judge Falcone] won't be able to do anything either? ... They'll all take it up the ass!

Anon: Yeah, they'll take it in the ass.

Joe Gambino's metaphor is not one I would care to use for what happened to 18th century judges and to police in common law countries ever since, but the following may explain his ringing endorsement of the common law.

A Quantum Lurch. Members of the cartel claim that a great strength of the common law is that it can adapt and change. Indeed it can, and for the worse. Towards the end of the 18th century it made a quantum lurch: from extreme injustice to the accused to extreme injustice to the victim and the community. Defence lawyers persuaded dubious judges to accept an unjust and unfair form of adversary system and rules which conceal evidence and get the guilty off.

Even more remarkably, lawyers persuaded judges to surrender control of civil and criminal trials to people whose obligation is to win, i.e. lawyers.

Judges who allowed this to happen included Lord Chief Justice (1756-88) Mansfield, a politician who sat with corrupt Whig oligarchs in Cabinet, and Justice (1770-80) Sir William Blackstone, the academic spin doctor. The kindest thing to say about them is that they must have been in a terminal phase of the malady.

Adversary Systems. It should be noted that any legal system which purports to be fair has an adversary system. In inquisitorial versions, the defence lawyer can protect his client's interests in every way up to the point where he might interfere with the truth. That point is cross-examination: in the hands of a fact-gathering judge, it is a great engine for discovering the truth; in the hands of a defence lawyer, it a great engine for obscuring it.

Hijacking the Trial. What happened in the 18th century may be seen as happenstance or as a series of brilliantly executed manoeuvres by lawyers to take over control of criminal and civil trials. Either way, the result is a gravely flawed legal system. The steps took place so gradually over a century that few noticed what was happening. I have relied largely on work by Professor John Langbein, of Yale University, for the process. The steps were:

Step 1. Parliament offers rewards for information on criminals in 1692. Constables and criminals begin to fabricate to get the blood money.

Step 2. Defence lawyers get their toe in the door of the criminal courts via the Treason Act of 1696.

Step 3. Defence lawyers use the constables' oppression and fabrication to persuade judges to let them cross-examine along with the judge. Since it crosses the truth boundary, such an adversary system may be termed excessive.

Step 4. Defence and prosecution lawyers persuade judges to retire from examination and cross-examination altogether. This gives lawyers control of criminal trials.

Step 5. Lawyers persuade judges to also surrender control of civil trials. With little to do, Lord Coleridge took up sleeping on the bench; Lord Thankerton took up knitting.

A Grossly Excessive Adversary System. Count Dracula now had control of the blood supply: lawyers decided what witnesses will be heard and what evidence they will give in criminal and civil trials. This grossly excessive adversary system is magic trick number 3. It builds in miscarriages both ways; the verdict is likely to go to the better legal team. A strong prosecutor and a weak defence lawyer can put innocent people in prison, and vice versa, as recent high profile US cases demonstrate.

Trial by Battle Reinvented. The wheel had gone full circle. Those racist buffoons in the 13th century may have turned their backs on truth and substituted an inscrutable jury for an inscrutable deity, but at least they gave up trial by battle. Now defence lawyers and Justices Mansfield, Blackstone *et al* had contrived to reinvent it. This inevitably led to an attitude articulated, apparently quite properly, by an Australian lawyer, Stuart Littlemore, in 1995: "You really feel you've done something when you get the guilty off."

Those who fund legal aid for the new judicial duel may not be amused, but novelists and film and television makers are desperately in the debt of Mansfield and the others. The dread Erle Stanley

Gardner, the lawyer who invented fictional defence lawyer Perry Mason, was perhaps an even greater apologist than Blackstone; he probably convinced many of the 1600 million that truth is sought and found in a common law court.

On the other hand, televising the O.J. Simpson criminal trial had the virtue of revealing the truth; Professor David Luban, of Georgetown University, said: "The O.J. Simpson trial has persuaded most Americans that the adversary system is at best grotesque."

Step 6. Rules for Concealing Evidence. But the invention of this grotesque system was not the end of it; defence lawyers were just getting into their stride. A wedge had been driven between judge and jury. The now passive judge could no longer informally discuss the case with jurors, and judges agreed that they were of dubious mental calibre. Defence lawyers said it was only fair to protect their clients from jury error by concealing certain relevant evidence.

Prophylaxis for Cure. Instead of finding a way to solve the jury problem, the judges accepted the rules for concealing evidence. In a startling image, Professor John Langbein observed: "Prophylaxis substitutes for cure." But prophylactics are notoriously unsafe; innocent men have gone to the electric chair and the gallows, and, as noted, there are figures to suggest that one per cent of inmates of common law prisons are not guilty.

The new system also increased the vices it was supposed to prevent: oppression and fabrication were now used by defence as well as prosecution, and it did make it much easier for defence lawyers to get their guilty clients off.

The rules for concealing relevant evidence (Magic Tricks 4 to 9) are:

● **A Privilege against Self-incrimination/Right of Silence**. This is brilliant; it protects the guilty only.

● **A Rule against Similar Facts**. This is particularly brilliant for organised criminals outside the US and for sex criminals everywhere: it conceals evidence of their patterns of criminal behaviour. It thus causes wholesale miscarriages in favour of the guilty: when the US RICO (Racketeer-Influenced and Corrupt Organisations) legislation made an exception for organised criminals, the previously untouchable heads of virtually every Mafia family in the US went to prison.

● **Rule Against Hearsay**. This conceals evidence from witnesses not available for cross-examination which might show they were wrong, confused or had a secret agenda., e.g. O.J. Simpson's murdered ex-wife. The rule may be usefully contrasted with the rule of precedent; as noted, it obliges judges to adhere to the decisions of judges who were wrong, confused or had a secret agenda, e.g. certain clowns in the 13th and 18th centuries.

● **A Confusing Standard of Proof**. The confusingly negative formula for the standard of proof, beyond a reasonable doubt, is one of the better cards for keeping guilty clients out of prison. Jurors can feel a doubt about anything, but judges cannot tell them what reasonable means. If the lawyer can get a hung jury, the prosecutors may not put taxpayers to the expense of a retrial. In jurisdictions requiring unanimous verdicts, hung juries can run as high as 25 per cent of trials.

● **The Christie Discretion**. This gives judges the power to conceal virtually all admissible evidence. The grounds for applying the discretion require a degree in metaphysics rather than law. Error is inevitable, but there can be no appeal against wrong decisions.

● **The Exclusionary Rule**. This can conceal evidence said to have been improperly obtained by police. It doesn't hurt the police, but it does hurt the victim and the community. The US version was invented by a judge who may effectively have been appointed to the Supreme Court by a Mafia fixer, Murray (The Camel) Humphreys. Eliminating police evidence via this rule was fundamental to the strategy of O.J. Simpson's defence team.

Charles Dickens observed in 1852: "The one great principle of English law is to make business for itself." Apart from everything else, the rules for concealing evidence enable lawyers and judges to engage in endless technical discussion on whether evidence can be admitted.

Presumptions of Innocence and Guilt. A reasonable approach to suspects is agnostic: they may or may not be guilty. But defence lawyers persuaded judges to presume they are innocent. We could be more persuaded of the judges' good faith if they had not also invented a presumption of guilt for anyone who might expose corruption in high places; Lord Mansfield's final solution for the problem of journalism was the brazenly ludicrous dictum: the greater the truth the greater the libel.

Corrupt Cops. We can now see why hard-headed organised criminals in police forces are as grateful to the cartel as the Mafia's Joe Gambino. They know that if they brazen it out at an inquisitorial proceeding the common law's nine magic tricks will probably save them from prison if charges are subsequently laid. At the Wood Royal Commission on police corruption in New South Wales (hereafter NSW) Justice Wood offered amnesty to officers in the endemically corrupt detective section of the NSW police service, but only a handful accepted. A Sydney detective, Craig (Snidely Whiplash) McDonald, explained to a (wired) colleague on December 5, 1997: "The only thing that caused a problem at the Royal Commission was blokes under pressure shitting themselves."

The United States. The Preamble to the 1787 Constitution states: "We, the people of the United States, in order to form a more perfect union, establish justice, insure domestic tranquillity, provide for the common defence, promote the general welfare, and secure the blessings of liberty to ourselves and our posterity, do ordain and establish this Constitution for the United States of America."

Amendments in 1791 (and Supreme Court interpretations of them) entombed in the Constitutions the right of silence (Fourth and Fifth Amendments), the adversary system (Sixth Amendment), and the common law itself and any further rules for concealing evidence that might be invented (Seventh Amendment).

Notorious cases, Bruno Hauptmann, O.J. Simpson, the Menendez boys, Lorena Bobbitt, the English nanny, merely confirm that the Amendments do not deliver justice; the Supreme Court could probably eliminate them by invoking the overrider about justice in the Preamble. It has not happened, perhaps because the court is not immune to a malady *Americain*; that at least seems to be the view of Judge Harold Rothwax, of the New York State Supreme Court.

Cartel Eulogies. In England, the cartel apparently judged that a massive public relations campaign would be needed to get citizens who fund the law to accept the new rules' wholesale assault on the truth. Justice David Ipp, of the West Australian Supreme Court, notes that "the 19th century opened upon a legal system which inspired the most extravagant eulogies from the Bench and Bar. There was a startling degree of smugness and self-satisfaction".

It was not totally successful; Justice Ipp reports: "The press and the general community did not share this sense of wellbeing. There was considerable tension between the public and the courts". Nonetheless, in 200 years the common law adapted and changed only at the margins.

End of Blood Money. The blood money, which started the whole catastrophe, was abolished in 1827, but by then most had probably forgotten it was an excuse for inventing the extreme adversary system.

Truth. In view of the above, it is idle for common lawyers and judges to claim that a criminal or civil trial is a "tribunal of fact". In criminal trials, one nominal fact-gatherer, the prosecutor, is impeded by the rules for suppressing evidence, and the defence lawyer is often impeded by his obligation to his client. In civil actions, the lawyers gather only those facts which help their case and try to hide those which don't. A US Judge, Marvin Frankel, says: "It is the rare case in which either side yearns to have the witnesses, or anyone, give *the whole truth*." (Judge Frankel's emphasis.)

The Result. To repeat, figures are available to suggest that in 100 fairly serious common law criminal cases 80 guilty get off and one innocent person goes to prison. Costs to the state can be $100,000 a week and up. Costs in civil cases can be higher.

SOLUTIONS

Melbourne lawyer Mel Barnett told Susanna Lobez on Radio National's *Law Report* in November 1997 he had "very much" lost faith in the adversarial system. He said: "I feel that we do have to change the way in which we look at a criminal trial and perhaps search more for the truth. And this may well be done through an inquisitorial system."

Barnett presumably agrees that what happened in the 13th and 18th centuries were aberrations. Solutions thus involve accepting that truth is important, winding the adversary system back to the point where it does not obscure it, reverting to the system in which the judge was in charge of civil and criminal trials, and adding a few wrinkles on fairness and justice borrowed from inquisitorial systems used by some 1000,000,000 people in Europe, its former colonies and Japan.

Inquisitorial Systems. European inquisitorial systems are not without flaw, but they do accept that truth is relevant to justice; their adversary system is designed to help find the truth, not obstruct it. *Anatomy of a French Murder Case* (1997) by Sydney University's Bron McKillop, is a major contribution to understanding inquisitorial methods; law Professor Ian Dennis, of University College, London, says he knows of "no comparable study in this detail". McKillop traces a French case from investigation to trial to appeal, and contrasts it with common law procedures not necessarily to the latter's advantage.

There is of course little need for organised criminals to corrupt passive common law judges, but safeguards are necessary to protect the fact-gathering inquisitorial judge from temptation.

Pre-Trial Investigation. The pre-trial investigation is the key to justice in Europe. The method is superior to those in common law countries for several reasons. It is an inquiry into the truth; every detail, including material favourable to the suspect, goes into a dossier; an adversary system operates; the suspect's lawyer can inspect the dossier at any time and suggest other lines of inquiry; professional judges supervise the police and question the suspect and witnesses; this tends to eliminate oppression and fabrication. Hence the rarity of miscarriages against the innocent.

The Trial. The major figures at an inquisitorial trial are the fact-gathering judge and the suspect. The judge does not accept a guilty plea; that would prevent him from finding out the facts for himself. He has studied the dossier beforehand; he calls the witnesses, including the accused, and questions them in a neutral way. The jury, if there is one, is on the bench with him; there are no magic tricks for concealing evidence.

The adversary systems strikes the right balance; lawyers appear for the accused, the victim and the community. The accused's lawyer can do everything to protect his interests, including suggesting questions for the judge to ask and making submissions, except obscure the truth by cross-examining. The judge and jurors work in a collegial way: the jurors supply the common sense; the judge supplies the weight to be given to evidence. They work out the verdict and penalty together and the judge writes their reasons.

Civil Litigation. In Germany, civil litigation is more like a conference than a trial. Putting fact-gathering into the hands of truth-seeking judges would reduce the cost and many of the problems of civil litigation.

The Cartel. Inquisitorial systems do not have a cartel; the cartel can be dismantled by training judges separately from lawyers. This was recommended by the Australian Law Reform Commission in 1997.

Judges. It seems reasonable to compensate active professional judges rather more generously than passive amateur judges; for the first time, they will be doing the work of fact-gathering and investigating the truth; say an average of $200,000 per annum.

In 1983, West Germany had 17,000 judges in a population of 61,306,700, one judge for every 3606 persons. Rough estimates of the number of judges needed for an inquisitorial system in some common law countries are thus: India: 210,000; United States: 70,000; United Kingdom: 16,600; South Africa: 11,000; Canada: 8,300; Australia 5128; Ireland: 1150; New Zealand: 1100.

In November 1997, Australia had 863 judges, including magistrates. It would thus require a six-fold increase in judges.

Costs. The cartel, heavily represented in legislatures, will say that governments will not pay for the extra judges. More research is needed, but it is not at all clear that an inquisitorial system would cost more than a common law system. It does not have committal hearings and its trials cost one-third to one-half the cost of common law trials. One reason is that lawyers and judges do not spend weeks and months discussing what evidence will be concealed; there is nothing to discuss. In civil actions, a judge gathering all the facts at $4000 a week is less costly than a clutch of lawyers gathering some of the facts at $100,000 plus a week.

The common law also has hidden costs. Crime is estimated to cost a small country like Australia $13,000,000,000 a year, and what is laughingly called the criminal justice system costs $6,000,000,000, much of it obviously wasted; as one of Joe Gambino's Mafia colleagues observed, common law prosecutors may as well "go pick beans".

In any event, what is the price of justice? As Mel Barnett says, the common law is not a justice system, only a legal system.

Appeals. Quality control is maintained by having serious cases automatically reviewed by a higher court. (In Germany jurors help appellate judges on the meaning of facts.) The prosecutor has equal rights with the defence lawyer in arguing that the verdict was wrong, and the appeal court can overturn not guilty verdicts and ask for a re-trial.

That cannot happen in common law countries; the inscrutable jury (and a judge when sitting alone) is held to be capable of error when they find someone guilty but incapable of error when they find him innocent. This nonsense prevents retrials in such apparently worthy cases as the O.J. Simpson criminal case.

WHO HAS TO DO WHAT?

Judges. Judges insist that they have the right to make bad law, and that only the community, i.e. the legislature, can change bad law "entrenched" (however recently) by judges in the common law, e.g. the excessive adversary system and the right of silence.

Lawyers. There are some three million lawyers and judges in the common law world, many desperately trying to produce justice from a system fatally infected eight centuries ago. Lawyers like Mel Barnett and judges likes Harold Rothwax and Geoffrey Davies are speaking out for change, and it was certainly a giant step for lawyers at the Australian Law Reform Commission to effectively recommend that the cartel should be dismantled.

But there is a view that real change will have to come from the community; most lawyers are not interested; Nicholas Cowdery QC, Director of Public Prosecutions in NSW, says: "To a lawyer love of justice is, or should be, the love of a lifetime. Is it being spurned?"

The Community. The giant is stirring; among the common law's 1597 million non-lawyers some in the US are joining such organisations as Justice For All, People Before Lawyers, UCLR (United Citizens for Legal Reform) and FLAC (For Legally-Abused Citizens). In 1997 FLAC was considering a march on Washington to demand reform; UCLR was planning to use the RICO legislation in a class action seeking US$100 billion on behalf of victims of the American judicial system. An Australian chapter of FLAC was formed in November 1997.

Those organisations tend to focus on ever-abundant legal horror stories, e.g. FLAC Australia's case of a dispute over $230 that generated $20,000 in legal fees. But the cartel has long absorbed such punishment – if never in such concentrated form – by reference to Blackstone's brilliant line that the inconveniences are a tiny price to pay for the protection their grand legal system affords.

The organisations should thus have subsidiaries called something like GLARA (Genuine Law Reform Association), NELSA (New Legal System Association) or TILA (Truth in Law Association). The subsidiary should have a programme of positive and costed reform based on: 1. An understanding of how the common law went wrong; and 2. The better aspects of the common law and inquisitorial systems. May I modestly suggest that this book provides the basis of such reform programmes? Chapters 33-40 provide data on criminal pre-trial and trial procedures in France, Germany and Italy, and on civil litigation procedures in Germany.

The Legislature. Law-and-order politicians tend to focus on the wrong end of the system: long sentences for the few relatively minor criminals the law manages to convict. A more persuasive deterrent is the degree of certainty of going to prison if caught. A real law-and-order programme would focus on putting more major criminals into prison and keeping the innocent out.

The fundamental reform is a commitment to truth; no reform will succeed without it. The words: "The object of justice is to find the truth" at the head of a new Crimes Act should wind back the adversary system to acceptable levels. The rules for concealing evidence can be abolished by a simple change in the layout of the court room: moving the jury from the side of the court to the bench. A pre-trial system of investigating judges and defence lawyers' access to the dossier can be instituted by a stroke of the legislative pen.

Arranging for people to be trained as professional fact-gathering judges in charge of police investigations and criminal and civil trials will effectively abolish the cartel.

If judges refuse to co-operate on some spurious ground, e.g. that the new system is unfair to the accused, or that fact-gathering leaves no time for knitting, the community's representatives will sadly have to take the iron fist out of the velvet glove and remove them from office for misconduct, i.e. effectively refusing to sit.

Legal Academics. As will be apparent, I have relied on legal academics for much of the material in this book, but Judge Rothwax says: "Even in law journals, arguably the centre of legal learning and dialogue, there has been little attempt to view the system as a whole." It is ridiculous that *Trial by Voodoo* and *The Cartel* are the only books in the language which offers a critical examination of the law as a whole; legal academics should apply the weight of their knowledge and authority to the big picture.

Law Schools. Law schools will be left behind if they continue to mindlessly assert that the common law is the best system and that's all there is to it. They will have to learn the origins of both systems, how inquisitorial systems work, and how to teach students to be professional fact-gatherers. Dare I say that, until a better one comes along, *The Cartel* is unfortunately the obvious, and indeed the only, text?

High Schools. The law is critical to society; high school teachers should teach how it actually works and what can be done about it. Again, *The Cartel* is sadly the only text. Any civics class could compile a book supplementary to this by cutting and filing data from the Press in a number of folders: The Cartel, The Malady, The Unimportance of Truth, The Adversary System, the Right of Silence and the other magic tricks.

Civil Libertarians. It is surprising that civil liberties groups do not agitate to stop torture and fabrication, i.e. by judicial supervision of police and for trials that are fair to accused, victim and community. Is it because they tend to be lawyerised?

The Media. A traditional function of journalism is to expose wrongdoing, in particular corruption, which defeats democracy. The common law has been doing wrong for eight centuries; libel law has been protecting the corrupt for nearly three.

Obstructing Reform. The cartel is the only impediment to reform; it has been obstructing it for eight centuries. One technique is to assert that the law is a great mystery and that only its priesthood can know how it really works. But ignorance is recycled; the priests don't know either.

Judge Richard Posner says: "'Legal Theory' is the body of systematic thinking about (or bearing closely on) law to which non-lawyers can and do make important contributions, and which lawyers ignore at their peril." Nonetheless, it may confidently be surmised that elements of the cartel will seek to dismiss *The Cartel* as the work of a mere scribbler.

In a sense, however, scribblers have an advantage over lawyers. The rule against similar facts makes lawyers nervous of context and pattern but they are a reporter's stock-in-trade. This is confirmed by a psychologist; he said of a remark that a journalist needs a mind like a corkscrew: "The technical term for corkscrew mind is *divergent intelligence*. This correlates highly with the pattern approach to evidence espoused by RICO.

"English law seems to me to be a determined attempt to limit divergent intelligence and to promote its opposite, *convergent intelligence*. Divergent intelligence is right-brained, convergent left-brained. One point of promoting women judges is that fewer are so totally left-brained."

The great masters of contextual or pattern journalism are *The Philadelphia Inquirer's* Jim Steele and Donald Barlett. Steele described the technique in 1976: "The challenge is to gather, marshal and organise vast amounts of data already in the public domain and see what it adds up to."

Ending the Magic. The data gathered for *The Cartel* shows why it is inevitable that the common sense will replace the common law. Some lawyers and judges won't like it, but the cartel has had a splendid innings.

Note: Unless otherwise stated all dollar signs indicate dollars Australian

Part I

Fundamental Problems:
The Cartel, Truth,
The Jury, The Malady

I

The Cartel

Let [the laity] once clearly perceive that [the common law's] grand principle is to make business for itself at their expense, and surely they will cease to grumble.

– Charles Dickens, 1852

A cartel is a syndicate formed to prevent competition and to maximise benefits, including profits, via a monopoly. In a sense, the legal cartel may be seen as a giant bureaucracy in which the needs of the members – power, status, money, winning – may supersede the ostensible mission of the organisation, justice.

"The one great principle of the English law," Charles Dickens wrote in *Bleak House*, "is to make business for itself. There is no other principle distinctly, certainly, and consistently maintained through all its narrow turnings. Viewed by this light it becomes a coherent scheme, and not the monstrous maze the laity are apt to think it. Let them once clearly perceive that its grand principle is to make business for itself at their expense, and surely they will cease to grumble."

The Rules of the Game. Dr Edward de Bono* says: " ... in Europe a certain [company] division shared a lawyer with another division. In the USA the equivalent division had 50 full-time lawyers ... if you can get more profit out of a lawsuit than out of industrial production then that is the way the rules of the game are written".

Judge Richard Posner has been Chief Judge of the US Court of Appeals for the Seventh Circuit (Illinois, Wisconsin, Indiana) since 1981. He is also an economist, and is thus inclined to subject the law to useful economic analysis. He says the "law" to which the title of his book, *Overcoming Law*, refers "is a professional totem signifying all that is pretentious, uninformed, prejudiced, and spurious in the legal tradition".

Self-interest. "The history of the legal profession," Judge Posner says, "is to a great extent, and despite noisy and incessant protestation and apologetics, the history of efforts by all branches of the profession, including the professoriat and the judiciary, to secure a lustrous place in the financial and social-status sun." And: "Self-interest has played as big a role in legal thought as in medical thought ... the [legal] profession was an intricately and ingeniously reticulated though imperfect cartel" until competition began to weaken it [at least in the US] about 1960.

* Sources mentioned in the text are listed at the end of the book.

Power. I note in chapter 41, How the Cartel Obstructs Reform, that a Sydney lawyer, Kerrie Henderson, reported the Australian High Court as stating in 1988 that "there is a paramount interest in the administration of justice which requires that cases be tried by courts on the relevant and admissible evidence".

Henderson commented: "The call to 'the interests of justice' asserts the primacy of the legal system as a social institution – the High Court's 'paramount interest in the administration of justice' – and in so doing also reinforces the standing of the courts and the judiciary as the organs through which that paramount interest is expressed. Such powerful tools are rarely voluntarily weakened ..."

Origins of the Cartel. The legal cartel seems to have first been formed by some two dozen lawyers and judges in Westminster Hall, London, early in the 13th century. A contemporary, Judge Henry de Bracton (d. 1268), says some of the judges of this period were ignorant and corrupt.

Truth. Euroscepticism, if not provincial narcissism, was a factor in the English psyche then as now. One of the cartel's first decisions was perhaps its most significant: it declined to follow European courts in their new method of making a judge responsible for finding the truth. (see chapter 2: The Unimportance of Truth.) In discounting the importance of truth, the cartel left the way open for defence lawyers to invent a series of truth-defeating devices in the 18th, 19th and 20th centuries.

An Inner Cartel. What may be termed an inner cartel, equivalent to modern senior barristers and appellate judges, was formed about the middle of the 13th century. This was the lucrative order of Serjeants-at-law. Theodore Plucknett says: "The Serjeant's emoluments ... must have been enormous ... The creation of a Serjeant obliged him to provide a feast comparable to a king's coronation, to distribute liveries and gold rings in profusion, and to maintain the proceedings for seven days."

The Serjeants had a monopoly of inventing the common law. In a remarkable statistic, J.H. Baker says: "[The] refinement [of the common law] as a body of rational principles in the 13th and 14th centuries was chiefly the accomplishment of the elite body of judges and advocates who belonged to the order of Serjeants-at-Law; a body which, in over six centuries of history, numbered less than 1000 members." Depending on death rates, the inner cartel may thus at times have consisted of as few as a dozen or twenty lawyers and judges.

Isolation. Legal academics were not admitted to the outer cartel for five centuries. Baker says: "The strength and unity of this profession explain how the reasoning of a small group of men in Westminster Hall grew into one of the world's two greatest systems of law. For this peculiarly English professional structure was wholly independent of the university law faculties, where only Canon law and Roman Civil law were taught, and this factor as much as any other ensures the autonomous character of English law and its isolation from the influence of continental jurisprudence."

In short, the cartel protected the common law from the notion that truth is important to justice; to this day, many lawyers and judges are blissfully ignorant of continental jurisprudence.

Intimacy. There is no cartel in Europe; European lawyers and judges appear to understand that lawyering is lawyering and judging is judging, but common law legal academics don't seem to be troubled by the "intimate" relationship between common lawyers and judges.

Theodore Plucknett says the 13th century "saw the rise of a group of practitioners before the King's courts ... In such a state of affairs there must arise the question of the relations between bench and bar. Not only is there the purely formal relationship to be settled, but there is the even more fundamental psychological attitude of bench and bar to be considered. When the same half-dozen judges are constantly being addressed by the same score or so of practitioners, these two small groups cannot help influencing each other ... In the middle ages ... the Serjeants during term time lived together in their inns and discussed their cases informally together simply as Serjeants, without distinction between those on the bench and those at the bar ... In the course of the 14th century the Serjeants [became] a close guild in complete control of the legal profession ... By the close of the 14th century the judges are all members of the order of Serjeants, and Serjeants alone can be heard in the principal court, that of Common Pleas" (civil cases). They kept that monopoly until 1846.

Complexity. Plucknett says common lawyers were the "dominant interest" in Parliament by the 14th century. He says: "Bench, bar and Parliament, therefore, were alike under the influence of the conservative, professionalised lawyer to whom the complexities and technicalities of the law were a peculiar and valuable learning." Indeed it was. In ambiguity lies power. And money. The more complex and technical the law could be made, the greater the fee the lawyer-priest could charge to interpret it. The roots of modern lawyers' fees and the high cost of law go deep, back to the self-interested cartel in the 13th century.

Opposition to Reform. Plucknett continues: "What is more, these very men also acquired control of legal education as well. The inevitable result was the disappearance of a liberal outlook upon law, and the loss of contact with other systems ... instead of this broad learning they turned to the narrow and tangled studies of procedure and pleading.

"It was the common lawyers who were mainly instrumental in making parliamentary supremacy a fact, but, as Maitland has said, 'the supremacy of Parliament may have been worth the price paid for it; nonetheless, the price was high'. The price consisted in the extreme centralisation of justice, the decline of old local institutions, the subjection of custom to the common law, the growth of immense quantities of technicality, opposition to reform, and the rejection of the broader and more liberal attitude towards law that showed so clearly in Bracton."

Elements of the cartel thus controlled the law and Parliament. They achieved another quantum leap in technicality in the 18th century, when defence lawyers invented the extreme adversary system and five rules for concealing evidence. How the cartel continues to obstruct reform is examined in the final chapter.

Tyler and Cade. Lawyers' technicalities and perhaps the activities of a few psychopaths may partly explain why, historically, lawyers have never enjoyed great public acclaim. Resentment against lawyers is said to have been a cause of Wat Tyler's revolt of the peasants in 1381, and a breakdown in the administration of justice was a cause of Jack Cade's rebellion in 1450. Shakespeare (c. 1592) has Cade saying he had once signed a document and "was never mine own man since", and agreeing that the first thing to do is "kill all the lawyers".

Royal Courts. The royal courts, which operated from the late 15th century, used the European inquisitorial method rather than the English accusatorial method. They thus represented a threat to the common law courts in power and method and also in money: the common law judges got a share of the fines they levied. The cartel thus sought supremacy over the royal courts as well as over the monarch. It won the battle in the 17th century; Parliament arranged to axe the royal courts in 1641 and the king himself in 1649.

Exporting the Law. Except for accidents of geography and history, the oddities of the common law would be no more than mildly quaint tourist attractions in a small island off the coast of Europe. England's isolation, instrumental in the stand against truth in the 13th century, enabled it to look beyond Europe in the 17th; 1607 saw the start of a maritime empire; the common law was exported to its colonies.

Godbolt and the Witchfinder-General. The quality of legal thinking in the 17th century may perhaps be gauged by a resumption of trial by ordeal in the period between the cartel's triumph over the royal courts and the killing of the king. In 1645-6 a judicial commission under a lawyer-MP, John Godbolt, "swam" and hanged scores of alleged witches. Godbolt's Witchfinder-General, Matthew Hopkins, had such a nose for witches that he was suspected of being one himself. He was tried by cold water in 1647, floated, and was hanged, but the cartel looked after Godbolt: Parliament appointed him judge of common pleas in 1647.

Hale. Sir Matthew Hale (1609-76) was a flexible type of lawyer. He had no difficulty in accommodating himself to the republic when Charles I was executed, nor to the monarchy on its restoration. He contrived to be an MP, Serjeant-at-law, and a Justice of the Common Pleas in the one year, 1654. Magnus Magnusson says he was "a believer in witchcraft", and the *Concise Dictionary of National Biography* (CDNB) notes that he presided at the conviction of two witches in 1662. He became Chief Justice of the King's Bench in 1671.

Highway Thieves in the Inner Cartel. The diarist, Sir John Evelyn (1620-1706), was a Serjeant and, from 1685 to 1687, a commissioner of the Privy Seal. In a speech on legal ethics in August 1997, Nicholas Cowdery QC, Director of Public Prosecutions in NSW, (pop. March 1997 6,260,900), from 1994, quoted Evelyn's entry for 26 November 1686. It apparently concerns civil rather than criminal matters. Thus: "I din'ed at my L.Chancelors, where being 3 other Serjants at Law, after dinner being cherefull and free, they told their severall stories, how long they had detained their clients in tedious processes, by their tricks, as if so many highway thieves should have met and discovered the severall purses they had taken: This they made but a jeast of: but God is not mocked:"

Cowdery commented drily: "It would seem, however, that God has been a little slow to address the problem and the community has run ahead of him or her." But Evelyn's sinister document goes rather further than mockery, or lack of it, of an inscrutable deity. The Lord Chancellor was (and is) the highest judicial functionary in England; his apparent acceptance of theft from clients by members of the inner cartel suggests that their criminal behaviour was known and condoned at the highest level of the cartel late in the 17th century. Within a century, judges had allowed these "highway thieves" to take over control of criminal and civil trials.

More Tricks. Six years later, in 1692, Parliament legislated to curtail the activities of actual highway thieves. This had extraordinary consequences; it enabled defence lawyers to invent a grossly excessive version of the adversary system and to invent magic tricks 3, 4, 5, 6, 7, 8, and 9.

The Legislature. The cartel retained its power in legislatures. In the US being a lawyer is almost a condition of entry into politics. In England, the Lord Chief Justice was a politician for several centuries. The last, and typical of the genre, was Tom Inskip, Viscount Caldecote (1876-1947). He was a Conservative MP 1919, Solicitor-General 1922-28 and 1931-32, Attorney-General 1928-29 and 1932-36, Minister for Defence Co-ordination 1936-39, Secretary of State for Dominions 1939-40, Lord Chancellor 1939-40, and Lord Chief Justice 1940-46. The CDNB notes that when [the sexually depraved] Lord Goddard succeeded him as Lord Chief Justice in 1946, he was the "first non-political holder of the office".

David Rose noted in 1996 that "there are more than a hundred barrister MPs" among some 600 members of the House of Commons. He said "the influential Tory Chairman of the Commons Select Committee on Home Affairs, Ivan Lawrence QC MP ... believes English criminal justice is 'democracy at work', and thus 'streets ahead of any other system'."

The Inner Cartel. The inner cartel today approximates to appellate judges and senior lawyers, e.g. constitutional lawyers and Queen's Counsel in former English colonies. I of course write as an honorary member of the inner cartel, appointed thereto as "Whitton QC" in 1983 by the then Premier of NSW, the Hon Neville Kenneth Wran QC, for sterling work in reporting every trivial, irrelevant and footling detail of a Royal Commission in which he was embarrassingly accused, falsely as it happily turned out, of colluding with a corrupt magistrate to fix a case for a sporting identity.

Advocates and Judges. Plucknett says the system of choosing judges "from among the Serjeants" has persisted with little modification in common law countries, and that "its great characteristic is the **intimate connection** between bench and bar … This co-operation … is of the utmost importance for the working of the common law system". Not to mention the cartel. (Emphasis added.)

As noted, the trouble is that lawyering and judging are fundamentally different. Advocates are partisan; judges are supposed to be detached, disinterested, impartial. The advocate seeks to win. Socrates (469-399 BC) said casuistry (intellectual dishonesty) is a knack; Judge Posner says bright law students pick it up very quickly. In civil law countries, aspiring professional judges are trained from the beginning in the judicial function, separately from lawyers. Common law judges are amateurs; as advocates elevated, they have no training to speak of.

Sir Garfield Barwick (1903-97, Chief Justice of the High Court of Australia 1964-81), was the quintessential advocate. After his death, Clyde Cameron, who became Barwick's friend after he left the court, said: "I'd never known anyone who is able to so easily explain in a way that is so uncontroversial that a piece of white paper is jet black and a piece of black paper is snow white." Barwick appeared to continue his advocacy of tax avoidance when he became Chief Justice; his decisions cost the revenue and people not in a position to avoid tax hundreds of millions.

Dismantling the Cartel. Michael Mansfield QC, who represented five of the Birmingham Six at their successful appeal, apparently believes the inner cartel should be dismantled. He said in 1993: "I would like to see a system in which judges are not culled almost exclusively from the ranks of the Bar but come from all walks of life. Being a judge should be a normal career structure like any other which you decide on when you leave school. It should be no different to deciding to become an engineer, a doctor or a social worker and judges should be open to public scrutiny and accountable, subjected to the control of a Ministry of Justice. Of course, that is precisely what many of the Law Lords want to avoid because there will be no guarantee that they are the ones who finish up with the power and the jobs. However, we shouldn't have to wait for even more miscarriages before these people begin to feel the wind of change on the back of their necks ... Such a proposition as mine is neither outrageous nor unique. In France a similar system already operates and it operates well." Mansfield noted that French advertising hoardings carry an invitation:

WHY NOT BE A JUDGE?

The Australian Law Reform Commission effectively recommended in July 1997 that, after eight centuries, the cartel be dismantled, i.e. law students planning careers as judges should be trained separately from advocates. However, Justice Murray Gleeson, Chief Justice of NSW, appears to believe that judges should continue to be appointed from the Bar and that senior judges should control whatever training they may then get. Speaking of judicial education in October 1997, he said: " ... this is a relatively new area of activity for judges and administrators and its implications are still being worked out. In England, where there is a Judicial Studies Board, there has been debate about the possibility of both formal training and performance review, and the implications that may have for judicial independence which entails, amongst other things, the independence of judges from one another. Both in England and in New South Wales the issue of independence has been handled by an insistence that the senior judiciary should control judicial training and education ... The judiciary should insist upon maintaining control of judicial training, but it should be prepared to state its case, publicly, for financial support [from the executive government]."

There are a number of problems with Justice Gleeson's view that senior judges should have a monopoly of training judges. Senior judges are themselves untrained in judging and are probably largely ignorant of the origins of the common law. And what would they teach? That the common law is the best system? As noted in chapter 4, Justice Gleeson's colleague on the NSW Court of Appeal, Justice Michael Kirby, said in April 1994: "People tend to forget that criminal trials do not involve a search for the truth." But a month later, as noted in chapter 5, Justice Gleeson said the administration of justice does involve a "search for the truth". Justice Kirby was right, but Justice Gleeson was the senior judge.

The argument from independence also appears to have no legs: as members of the inner cartel, judges have never been independent of lawyers. Training them in judicial training schools separately from lawyers would give them that independence.

2

Magic Trick I

The Unimportance of Truth

Great is truth, and mighty above all things.

— Esdras, Apocrypha, Old Testament

The entrance to the building that houses the law school at the University of Queensland is inscribed with the words of Esdras. I told them they could be done for false advertising.

Is truth important? Esdras thought so; so did the ancient Egyptians; the feather in the cap of Maat, goddess of justice, stood for truth, justice, order. So does European law. And so does Judge Harold Rothwax, of the New York State Supreme Court. He says: "... truth must be a primary goal of criminal procedure. Indeed, truth must be the goal of *any* rational procedural system ... Suppressing evidence is suppressing truth ... Without truth there can be no justice ... Our system is a maze constructed of elaborate and impenetrable barriers to truth. Criminals are going free."

English common law has never been based on truth. On Judge Rothwax's analysis, it has never been a legitimate legal system. It appears to follow that it is unconscionable to ask citizens to pay legal aid to lawyers for such a system. And further that any trade or profession based, however nominally, on truth, e.g. selling used cars, is sadly but necessarily a higher calling than the law and the judiciary.

Illogical. But Justice Ron Sackville, of the Australian Federal Court, cautions against transplanting elements of the truth-driven European system to the common law without proper research. He says: "... great care must be taken to understand the social and historical context in which a legal system has developed." We can help him there. So might Dr R.M. Jackson, Professor of the Laws of England, Cambridge. He says: "... the machinery of justice in England has to be seen in its peculiar historical setting. It must not be regarded as a logical structure designed round basic principles. Procedures and practices led to a 'contest' conception of trial ... but this gives it no special sanctity."

Insularity. Professor Jackson says the common law is partly the product of an insular dislike of Europe. To be fair, the English had (and have) every reason to be nervous; every five centuries or so someone from Europe had invaded England: Celts from Germany and France in the 5th century BC; Italians in the first century BC;

33

Saxons in the 5th century; Danes and French in the 11th century. (Bonaparte tried it in the 19th, and Adolf Hitler in the 20th.)

The Judgment of God. In the Dark Ages European and English legal systems presumed that God delivered the verdict. The procedure was accusatorial; A accused B. The trial was often some form of ordeal. One form of ordeal was "swimming a witch". The suspect was trussed and thrown in a part of a river that had been blessed. If the blessed water "received" her, i.e. if she sank, she was not a witch; if she floated, she was a witch and was burned or hanged.

Trial by Battle. In the judicial duel, or trial by battle, the accuser and accused swore oaths before a judicial officer that they were telling the truth and then fought a duel. The winner got the verdict; the loser, if still alive, was hanged.

The Inquisitorial Concept. The church was always opposed to the Judgment of God on the ground that it was wrong to tempt the deity. Pope Stephen VI tried to stop the ordeal in 877 AD. About 1190 AD, Cardinal Lotario di Segni, a lawyer, invented a rational method of investigating the truth of alleged monkish misbehaviour: a trusted person was sent to the monastery to question everyone who might have information. "This founded the inquisitorial concept of a trial," says Dr R.M. Jackson, "whereby the judge is expected to find out for himself what has happened, and he will do this by examining all persons, including the accused or suspect person, who may be able to enlighten him." Inquisitorial means investigative. The term carries some baggage, and the cartel makes much of that, but in their present refined form inquisitorial systems are far less subject to the miscarriages of justice either way that plague the common law system.

Magna Carta. As interpreters of the law, the cartel got a sniff of power in June 1215; the magnates (the great men of the realm) obliged King John to guarantee, via Magna Carta, that freemen would only be imprisoned by "the law of the land", whatever that might mean. However, the charter only lasted eight weeks. England was then a fiefdom of Pope Innocent III (as Cardinal di Segni had become in 1198), and in August he declared the charter null on the ground that his vassal, King John, had signed under duress and without the knowledge of his overlord, the Supreme Pontiff.

The Lateran Council. Three months later, in November 1215, Innocent III held a "brilliant" ecumenical council at the Lateran Palace, the fourth held there. Justice Ken Marks says it was attended by 412 bishops, 800 abbots and ambassadors of many temporal rulers. The council endorsed the Pope's concept of the inquisitorial procedure and banned clergy from taking part in trial by ordeal. We can hear the Pontiff and the others (and Judge Rothwax) chanting:

All we are saying,

Is:

Give truth a chance.

European courts followed; the truth-seeking, fact-gathering no-magic-tricks judge remains the basis of criminal and civil justice in countries which use the inquisitorial system.

The Fork in the Road. The Lateran Council was the fork in the road for European and English law. The cartel, after a period of hesitation, refused to adopt the inquisitorial concept of rational investigation of the truth. This appears to have been bad for common lawyers' sleep patterns. Henry Evans, a Chicago psychiatrist who has many lawyers on his couch, said in April 1996 that truth is good for the soul. He said: "It's a cliche to ask what it takes to sleep at night, but honesty is most often the answer." The solution to their torment is to change to a system that has truth and justice as the goal.

An Insular Dislike of Things Foreign. Professor Jackson says: "The English kept to the accusatorial theory, partly because of an insular dislike of things foreign, and partly because of the emergence of jury trial. Jury trial simply replaced trial by ordeal, the verdict of the jury having the same finality and inscrutability as the Judgment of God." (See Chapter 6: A Defective Jury System.) Apart from possibly being in retrospective breach of the Racial Discrimination Act, some of the judges of the time were ignorant and corrupt, according to Bracton, that "flower and crown of English jurisprudence". Perhaps a motive was sloth; the decision absolved judges of the task of investigation. It certainly did not help defence lawyers; they were barred from criminal trials until the 18th century.

The judges continued dubious. In 1289 the Lord Chancellor, Bishop Robert Burnell, investigated claims that judges engaged in corruption, witchcraft and murder. The Chief Justice of Common

Pleas [civil cases] fled the country; the Chief Justice of the King's Bench [criminal cases], although found guilty of tampering with a record and heavily fined, was made Chief Justice of Common Pleas. Seven centuries later, Sir Garfield Barwick, Chief Justice of the High Court of Australia, was accused of tampering with a document. He found himself innocent.

The notion that truth is not relevant to justice was the cartel's first and greatest magic trick; the others could not exist without it. Truth is of course more than a goal; it is a brake on spurious argument, intellectual dishonesty, sophistry (ingenious but falsely deceptive argument), injustice, self-delusion, folly, muddle, madness. But no common law judge can ask a lawyer: "How does this help us find the truth?"

3

What is Truth? Said Jesting Pilate

One that loved not wisely but too well.

– W. Shakespeare, 1604

If Lotario di Segni is a patron saint of European law, the patron saints of the common law include Pontius Pilate, the cruel and rapacious Roman procurator of Judaea and Samaria 26-36 AD, and Sir James Lewis Knight-Bruce (1791-1866).

St John recorded (18.38): "Pilate saith unto Him: 'What is truth?'" Francis Bacon, later a corrupt Lord Chancellor, knew the quibble was merely an attempt to shift the goalposts. In Of Truth (1597), he wrote: "'What is truth?' said jesting Pilate, and would not stay for an answer." Pilate was sent to Rome in 36 to answer to the Emperor Tiberius for wretched behaviour. His end is uncertain; he either suicided, or was beheaded, or was exiled to Vienna.

Sir James Knight-Bruce was J.L. Knight until September 1837, MP 1831, vice-chancellor and knighted 1841, chief judge in bankruptcy 1842, lord justice of appeal 1851. His remarks in *Pearse v Pearse* (1846) are much-quoted by common lawyers, but they hardly bear examination.

Knight-Bruce said: "The discovery and vindication and establishment of truth [!] are main purposes certainly of the existence of Courts of Justice ... Still for the obtaining of these objects [truth], which, however valuable and important, cannot be usefully pursued without moderation, cannot be either usefully or creditably pursued unfairly or gained by unfair means, not every channel is or ought to be open to them ... Truth, like all other good things, may be loved unwisely – may be pursued too keenly – may cost too much."

There is certainly something in what Knight-Bruce says, particularly about being fair, but the essential hollowness of his utterance is exposed by reference to Magic Trick 3, the grossly excessive adversary system; it virtually obliges defence lawyers to use all the zeal they can muster in cross-examination to **obscure the truth**. If he had had any real sense of justice, the learned chief judge in bankruptcy might also have said: "Obscuring the truth, like all other bad things, may be loved unwisely – may be pursued too keenly – may cost too much: the guilty may escape justice."

4

Admissions that the Common Law Does Not Seek the Truth

... perhaps we should be restoring truth as a central goal of a criminal trial.

— Mel Barnett, common lawyer, 1997

Elaborating the Obvious. A legal system that has upwards of a dozen "barriers to truth" is not trying to find the truth, whatever else it might think it is doing. This elaboration of the obvious is unfortunately necessary because, as noted in chapter 5, significant elements of the cartel, including the US Supreme Court, assert that the common law does seek the truth, even in the face of such decisions as *Coolidge* (see chapter 18, The Exclusionary Rule). Apart from Judge Rothwax, others who understand that the common law does not try to find the truth include:

Samuels. The Hon Gordon Samuels, Governor of NSW and formerly a Justice of the NSW Court of Appeal, said in November 1996: "Sometimes a suggestion that neither the criminal nor the civil procedures of our system of justice is essentially designed to find the truth strikes both lay and professional persons as profoundly shocking, almost to the degree of blasphemy. But there are statements of authority in the High Court that seem to me to adopt that view."

Callinan. Hon Mr Justice Ian Callinan, who was appointed to the Australian High Court in December 1997, said in 1987 that in adversary litigation "the object of the parties is simple, to win the case. If in the course of winning the case, the whole truth is unmistakably ascertained and all relevant facts exposed, then a desirable, but nonetheless no more than incidental, result will have been achieved". The term "parties" may seem to mean non-lawyers involved in the litigation, but in practice it means their lawyers.

Roden QC. The Hon Adrian Roden QC, a former Justice of the NSW Supreme Court, said in 1989: "The right to silence, the caution, the right to make an unsworn statement at trial without being cross-examined, and the common advice 'to say nothing' combine to frustrate many police investigators and courts alike, as under the common law system they are frequently obliged to proceed without the assistance of those who are likely to know more than anyone else about the matter under enquiry. Clearly that is not the best way of getting at the facts.

"Common lawyers however are at pains to explain that under our system courts are not concerned with getting at the facts, it is not their function to search for the truth. Their aim in criminal proceedings is to determine whether, after a trial conducted in accordance with the rules of procedure and evidence, at which a fair trial has been had according to law, the accused's guilt has been proved beyond reasonable doubt. The rights of accused persons in and leading up to such are not to be judged by their effect on the fact-finding process. They must be seen as part of a total body of rules designed to protect citizens from oppression, and to redress the imbalance in power between the State with all its resources and the otherwise very vulnerable individual."

(The common law's claims of fairness and prevention of oppression are risible. Trials may be "fair" according to law but are unfair in fact. The rules do not protect citizens from oppression by the State, but they do allow lawyers to oppress witnesses. Judges oppress alleged offenders in criminal contempt trials by presuming their guilt, by refusing to allow them trial by jury; and, uniquely, by convicting them although the error was inadvertent, i.e. there was no *mens rea*, guilty mind.)

Six years later, when the Wood Royal Commission on police corruption in NSW heard police admit to routinely fabricating evidence, Roden QC said it came as no surprise to anyone who worked in the judicial system. He said the adversarial nature of the system gave police a feeling, "with some justification", that the defence side was being unduly favoured. He said no-one really claimed the system was well designed to get at the truth; a review of the rules was long overdue.

Roberts-Smith QC. On Roden's 1989 analysis, defence counsel Len Roberts-Smith QC accurately stated the common law position to a Supreme Court jury in Perth, Western Australia, in March 1996. It was alleged that Ronald Joseph Buckland, 45, murdered his wife at common law, Victoria Robinson, 18, mother of their one-month-old son, during an argument in their bedroom in May 1993, buried her, and claimed she walked out on him and the baby.

A witness said she heard Robinson's screams and dragging sounds on the carpet of her bedroom; another said Buckland told him he had to snap Robinson's legs to get her body into the boot of his car because *rigor mortis* had set in. Detectives said Buckland told them Robinson was at peace and rest; they denied Roberts-Smith's suggestions that they made up their minds from the start that Buckland was guilty and fabricated conversations with him to support their belief.

Roberts-Smith QC told the jury its role was not to work out what had really happened to Robinson, but to judge whether the Crown had proved beyond reasonable doubt its claim that Buckland had killed and buried her.

Ducker. Judge Thomas Ducker said in the Sydney District Court in March 1994 that the truth "is being hidden from juries at times in circumstances which are productive of injustice and unfairness".

Hasluck. Lawyer-novelist Nicholas Hasluck wrote in his aptly-titled novel about the law, *A Grain of Truth* (Penguin, 1994): "That's the great irony about the law. The public sees a widely respected advocate in action, mouthing noble sentiments, and believes he stands for morality and justice: the traditional values of society. But actually most of his techniques are aimed at subverting rational argument – constantly interrupting, confusing witnesses with nit-picking questions, blocking the presentation of crucial facts, shaping the truth to suit his client's case. Deep down, the professional advocate has to be something of an anarchist."

Kirby. The Hon Mr Justice Michael Kirby, then President of the NSW Court of Appeal (he was elevated to the High Court of Australia in 1996), said in April 1994: "People tend to forget that criminal trials do not involve a search for the truth."

Dobies. John Dobies, an Australian lawyer, said in 1996: "Court procedure has little to do with truth or justice."

Police Speak. In March 1995, three senior English police officers protested against the common law's attitude to truth. Sir Paul Condon, chief of the London Metropolitan Police (Scotland Yard), said: "Many police officers feel the criminal justice system is almost nothing to do with establishing the truth." David Phillips, Chief Constable, Kent, said: "The search for truth is not an objective; rather, the trial often turns on clever argument testing the prosecution case." Charles Pollard, Chief Constable, Thames Valley, said: "I have lost my faith in Britain's justice system. Many trials are not concerned to search out the truth. They are about one side winning and the other losing."

Inspector John Riley, investigator of child abuse in Queensland for 20 years, said in November 1995: "Our legal system is not set up to have the truth come out in court ... The court system is not set up to seek the truth."

Yearning for Truth. As psychiatrist Henry Evans said, truth is good for the soul. I take Mel Barnett to be representative of thousands of lawyers desperately trying to make the common law work, but sufficiently troubled by it to yearn for a truth-based system.

Barnett spoke to Susanna Lobez on *The Law Report* on Australia's Radio National on November 11, 1997. I include the interview in full because it brilliantly traverses a fundamental problem of the common law: how lawyers try to resolve the unresolvable conflict between, on the one side, their relatively new adversary system and rules for concealing evidence, and on the other, truth and justice:

Susanna Lobez: Lawyers are often asked, How do you represent a guilty person? The wider issue is, What's the emotional cost of acting for a person charged with bashing a 12-day-old baby, or a corporation which disregards the environment? Over my years of talking with lawyers, I've wondered whether there might be a condition I'll call 'ethical fatigue'. In our system, even the bad guy is entitled to legal representation. Think of the lawyer who daily has to put the best side forward for clients charged with horrible anti-social acts. And let's face it, some of them are guilty.

Mel Barnett in his years as a lawyer represented many criminal defendants. He is also the President of the Victorian branch of VOCAL, a victims' rights group. I wondered how he copes with switching teams so often. Does fighting for both sides in the criminal justice system cause him ethical fatigue?

Mel Barnett: It does cause a degree of frustration, but I try to look at it in a way that as a lawyer it is my function and my duty to do what's best for my client and that's what I do within the scope of the law. What is one of my concerns, working with victims of crime, is that to a large extent the victim of crime has been shut out of the criminal justice system in the past.

Obviously the way in which a criminal trial is designed is to give it the best possible defence and the best possible opportunity to the offender or the person acccused of the offences. And as such you have to give their counsel every opportunity to properly defend them. But what happens in that situation is that the victim has no place in that system, other than to be a human exhibit. They are called by the prosecution, they are called to support the prosecution's case, but they have no other role, and the protection given to the victim in the past has not been all that great. They're not properly represented in the sense that they have separate representation. Fortunately, judges in recent years have recognised this and are helping and perhaps protect them against very unfair cross-examination. But you have a conflict there which is very difficult to resolve if you are going to give the accused the best possible defence. [**Author's note**: In European systems, the victim is represented by a separate lawyer. See Part III, There Are No Fox-Hunters in Europe.]

Lobez: Well of course the defence tactics on behalf of the accused invariably involve discrediting the prosecution witness. It might be the memory of the person, it might be their reputation, it might be their truthfulness.

Barnett: That's so. I mean the case has to be proven against the accused beyond reasonable doubt, and I think in that comes one of the basic problems for a victim, because if the accused or his counsel or her counsel can prove that there is any element of doubt – and this is often established through the lack of credibility of a witness – then the accused is given that benefit. And that's how the system works.

Lobez: How do you as a lawyer acting for an accused person, a defendant, go into court, knowing that you may hurt the feelings of a prosecution witness or victim, knowing that the truth may not be told, the complete truth may not be told? How do you mentally and emotionally get yourself in a position where you can do that?

Barnett: Well, I think you have to log yourself into a sense of duty, which is to do what's best for your client, what's best for the accused. And if you don't do that then you're certainly not going to do your job as a lawyer properly.

Lobez: So you put aside any doubts that you might have about your client?

Barnett: Well, a lot of lawyers certainly don't want to know whether their client has committed the offence. They work on the basis of the instructions they have, which may in many cases be somewhat incomplete. And they feel that that will enable them to work perhaps with a great deal of vigilance and determination that they might not have if they were aware of too many details of the truth.

Lobez: Isn't it true that the most common question asked of lawyers at cocktail parties is: "How can you act for someone that you know is guilty?" What do you say?

Barnett: Well, one answer is: "Do you always know they're guilty?" And certainly in many cases you're not sure. But the point is, the system of law as we have it requires people to be properly defended. If they're not properly defended, then as we say justice can't take place. So you are part of that system. What I, as a personal individual in this situation, have reservations about is that lawyers tend to overstate their place in the justice system. I don't think it's a justice system as such; it's a legal system.

Lobez: So in that whole process what perhaps the ordinary person might think is an integral part, namely truth, is not really the ultimate destination of the court process is it?

Barnett: Unfortunately, lawyers tend not to talk very much about this, but I think it's a reality, and I was very pleased to hear Michael Rozenes, a former Director of Public Prosecutions, a few years ago make it quite clear that the function of a criminal trial is not a search for the truth, and he was being completely honest with this. It is something lawyers feel a bit uncomfortable about, but it's something they live with. What I'm concerned about is that perhaps we have lost the way a little, and perhaps we should be restoring truth as a central goal of a criminal trial.

Lobez: Wouldn't that give the lawyer a dilemma though? Because if you're defending an accused person there may sometimes be the suspicion, depending on how detailed your instructions are, that if the truth in its entirety were to come out, your client would be convicted and quite possibly jailed. So isn't there a conflict between duty to the truth and duty to the court versus your duty to the client?

Barnett: Absolutely, and I think in the adversarial system that will be a difficulty that lawyers would face, and I guess their duty to

42

their client would be paramount, and for that reason the truth, as it often is perhaps, I won't say distorted, but certainly swept under the carpet. It is not the function, for instance, of a defence counsel to expose elements of the truth that are going to be detrimental to his or her client. So the truth is to some extent set aside quite knowingly by the defence counsel, and quite properly by him or her. I feel that we do have to change the way in which we look at a criminal trial and perhaps search more for the truth. And this may well be done through an inquisitorial system.

Lobez: So, are you losing a little bit of faith with the adversarial system as serving society's ends?

Barnett: Very much so. I feel that we have to some extent distorted the notion of justice. It's always interesting when you look at the courts of law. They're known as courts of law in Australia; in some countries they're known as palaces of justice. We're a long way short of calling them palaces of justice.

* * *

Mel Barnett's suggestion that perhaps we should have an inquisitorial system to "restore" truth as a central goal of a criminal trial would necessarily involve the abolition of the nine magic tricks.

5
Claims that the Common Law Does Seek the Truth

The basic purpose of a trial is the determination of the truth.

– US Supreme Court, *Tehan v Scott,* 1966

As Melbourne lawyer Mel Barnett observes, lawyers are "a bit uncomfortable" about the fact that truth is not the goal of a common law trial. But some assert that in fact truth is the goal.

US Supreme Court. Justice David Ipp, of the West Australian Supreme Court, noted in September 1995: "The United States Supreme Court has expressed itself consistently in favour of the proposition that the discovery of the truth is the ultimate purpose of the legal system. In *Tehan v Scott* [1966], the court affirmed that 'the basic purpose of a trial is the determination of the truth'." But if trials are really trying to determine the truth they would not have magic tricks which conceal it. *Tehan v Scott* thus seems to confirm the malady and that appellate courts should have lay judges, as in Europe, to explain the facts to the judges.

O.J. Simpson. During the O.J. Simpson criminal case, Christopher Darden, prosecuting, said to Judge Lance Ito: "This is supposed to be a search for the truth, and we shouldn't be trying to trick witnesses to get them to say something that might affect their credibility." Simpson's lawyer, Johnny Cochrane, standing next to Darden, allowed himself a faint smile.

Zuckerman. A.A.S. Zuckerman, Praelector in Jurisprudence at University College, Oxford, had his book on criminal evidence read by several legal authorities before it was published. The second sentence reads: "When a court of law sets out to decide whether a disputed event took place ... the court is concerned to find the truth about the event."

Adversary System. Justice Ipp says that according to Applegate (*Witness Preparation*, 1989), it is now generally accepted in the United States that "ascertaining the truth is the paramount goal of the adversarial system and the primary basis for its legitimacy". But Justice Callinan says the paramount goal of the adversary system is not truth but winning; it appears to follow that the adversary system is not legitimate.

Lord Eldon. John Scott, Lord Eldon (1751-1838) was a member of the cartel who straddled politics and the law: MP 1783-96, Solicitor-General 1788, Attorney-General 1793, Serjeant-at-Law 1799, Lord Chief Justice of Common Pleas 1799, Lord Chancellor 1801-1806 and 1807-27. As a politician, Lord Eldon opposed political reform and religious liberty and vigorously pursued a policy of subjugating Bonaparte. As a lawyer, he is famous for two things. In the Leeds Grammar School case (1805) he found that a grammar school is "for reading grammatically the learned languages", and hence that modern subjects, including French and German, could not be taught without changing the statutes.

And in *ex parte Lloyd* (1822), Lord Eldon proclaimed: "Truth is best discovered by powerful statements on both sides of the question." Members of the cartel frequently repeat this claim, but Justice Ipp says: "Lord Eldon's aphorism is not necessarily accurate." Indeed, it is doubly false: the law is not trying to find the truth, and lawyers are not equally powerful. The truth will not be found if the lawyer effectively trying to conceal it has the more powerful voice in thuggish cross-examination or in casuistical submission.

The Bar Speaks. In 1995, the Australian Government gave the Australian Law Reform Commission a reference to examine the adversarial system in civil litigation. The commission produced an issues paper in 1997. Richard Ackland, editor of *Justinian*, reported (*The Sydney Morning Herald*, October 24, 1997) that the NSW Bar Association submitted that the adversary system "is based on a common law system of orality which is by far the best method yet discovered of ascertaining the truth and delivering justice". "Orality" is a lawyer's term for oral evidence subject to cross-examination by lawyers. It appears to imply that inquisitorial systems rely overmuch on the paper and are less likely to find the truth because judges, not lawyers, question the witnesses.

Ackland also reported that the Bar Association believes the system of parliamentary democracy is the model for the adversary system. As noted, self-interested advocates in the cartel got control of the legislature in the 14th century and have maintained their influence; parliamentary democracy may thus approximate to government by self-interested lawyers. In chapters on the adversary system, it is noted that defence lawyers "captured" criminal trials in the 18th century and then invented more magic tricks that made it increasingly easy to get the guilty off.

The Bar Association went on to claim: "Control of the legal process by the parties is as important to them as control of the political process is to citizens in our political culture." It seems reasonable to translate that as: "Control of the legal process by lawyers is as important to them as control of the political process is to lawyers in our political culture."

Ackland put it slightly differently. He said: "In other words, litigants, and by extension their lawyers, should control this publicly-funded machine through which citizens can endlessly enforce their rights and lawyers take their rewards. The judges should not control it. It is there for the parties to litigation to do with what they will. For a Bar Association to serve up this sort of tripe in this day and age is deeply unsettling, or amusing."

Shaw. Responding to some mild animadversions about the adversary system, the Hon Jeffrey Shaw QC, first law officer of NSW, wrote (*The Australian*, January 20, 1997): "Evan Whitton's criticism of the adversary trial in our criminal justice system is finely argued and well-intentioned iconoclasm. It is true that the criminal trial is not a search for ultimate, historical truth. But it is an inquiry into truth in a very important sense: has the prosecution proved that the defendant is guilty, beyond reasonable doubt, of the charge brought against him or her based upon the admissible evidence put before a jury?"

Bar Rules. Rule 20 of the NSW Bar Association's rules states: "A barrister appearing for the Crown in a criminal case is a representative of the State and his function is to assist the court in arriving at the truth."

Gleeson. The Hon Mr Justice Murray Gleeson, Chief Justice of NSW and widely expected in December 1997 to be the next Chief Justice of the High Court of Australia), said in May 1994: "The way we go about administering justice is an enormously labour-intensive search for the truth."

"Zeal". The view that the common law and the adversary system seek the truth seems at odds with the attitude, at least in Australia, of common lawyers and law courts to tribunals that are charged with actually seeking the truth, e.g. commissions of inquiry and standing commissions on corruption such as the NSW Independent Commission Against Corruption (ICAC). No doubt following Knight-Bruce, the common law code for being overly interested in the truth is "zeal".

The Bar Speaks Again. The NSW Bar Association excoriated a Royal Commissioner, Justice Philip Woodward (1912-97), for stating the simple truth that Bob Trimbole, a leader of the Griffith cell of the Calabrian Mafia, was complicit in the assassination of a politician, Donald Mackay, in 1977. The Bar Association said it was "outrageous to the basic principles of British justice that a finding of guilt ... by a Royal Commissioner should be published to the world at large."

ICAC. ICAC is an inquisitorial body established in 1988 following nearly two decades of journalistic disclosures of corruption in Sydney (pop. June 1996: 3,879,400), and criminal charges laid against magistrate Murray Farquhar in 1983 and the Hon Mr Justice Lionel Murphy, of the High Court, in 1984. Judges shortly claimed that a body set up by the Parliament to seek the truth about corruption should not say it had found it. The parliamentary committee on ICAC reported in September 1992: "In June 1990 the High Court brought down a decision in *Balog and Stait v ICAC* which restricted the ICAC's reporting powers. The High Court found that the ICAC could not make a finding that a person had engaged in corrupt conduct because to do so would be tantamount to finding that a person had committed a criminal offence, and questions of guilt or innocence should be left to the courts."

The High Court ruling overlooked the fact that common law courts are demonstrably not competent to deal with corruption; that an inquiry into the truth is different from a common law court; and that the evidence heard by jurors may be only a fraction of that heard by an inquiry. The committee reported that Parliament amended the ICAC Act "to overcome the High Court's decision" and to enable "the ICAC to find that individuals had engaged in corrupt conduct".

Goldring. Professor Jack Goldring got his Master's degree in Laws at Columbia University. Now at Wollongong University, south of Sydney, he responded thus (*The Australian*, October 2, 1996) to a query on how universities reconcile their obligation to search for the truth with the law's belief that it has no such obligation: "Our law is certainly not neutral. It embodies the values of those who have power. Most law students learn this very quickly. But it is also concerned with fairness, facts and truth. Our system is an adversary system. The courts themselves, as former Justice Roden pointed out, do not themselves seek facts. But they do decide impartially between versions of the facts presented by the parties. Above all, they are concerned with facts. Undoubtedly those able to hire more competent lawyers better present their versions of facts. But the courts are concerned with facts and truth."

And to a reference to Sexton and Maher's 1981 quote suggesting that law schools operate in a trade school sort of way, Professor Goldring wrote: "In 1981, law schools were generally 'trade schools'. That is no longer true, especially in newer law schools. Students learn not only the rules but how those rules affect, and are affected by, the social context. For lawyers, unlike journalists, context is vital."

Indeed it is, except perhaps for the legal rule against similar facts and for contextual or pattern journalism. Professor Goldring is also an acting District Court judge; would he let in pattern evidence against an organised criminal or a rapist?

6

Magic Trick 2

A Defective Jury System

Without a statement of reasons there can be no valid judgment.

Professor John Langbein, of Yale University, says: "In Continental legal systems it is regarded as a fundamental requirement of due process that the court disclose the grounds of its decision. [This] is designed both to deter abuse and to facilitate review for error". He quotes a German maxim: "*Ohne Begrundung kein Urtreil*, that is, without a statement of reasons there can be no valid judgment."

The Jury Debacle. The cartel's truth debacle was thus compounded by a jury debacle; in eight centuries common law juries have never given reasons. As Dr R.M. Jackson noted, apart from an insular dislike of Europe, the cartel rejected the inquisitorial method in the 13th century because England was experimenting with a jury system. By the 14th century it was decided to leave the verdict to the inscrutable jury.

"Jury trial simply replaced trial by ordeal," Dr Jackson said, "the verdict of the jury having the same finality and inscrutability as the Judgment of God." Likewise Theodore Plucknett: "... a jury was just a newer sort of ordeal ... the jury states a simple verdict of guilty or not guilty and the court accepts it, as unquestionably as it used to accept the pronouncements of the hot iron or the cold water."

Juries Fraught with Danger. Dr Langbein says: "Despite its merits, jury trial has always been fraught with danger. Jurors are untrained in the law, they decide without giving reasons, they have no continuing responsibility for the consequences of their decisions, and their verdicts are quite difficult to review. The risks of error and partiality in this system of adjudication are ineradicable ... From the Middle Ages to our own day, the driving concern animating the Anglo-American law of evidence has been to protect against the shortcomings of trial by jury."

A Partial Solution. Judge and jury got round the problem to some extent for five centuries; they operated in a manner rather similar to the way the French judge and jury work today, i.e. they sorted things out together. Langbein says: "... the judge could influence and correct jury verdicts in advance of accepting them ... we see routine informal communication between judge and jury, the judge's awesome power of comment and instruction, and the jurors' enthusiasm for following the judge's professional guidance. Jury verdicts were collaborative products, impounding deep judicial involvement on the merits."

Thus, he says: "In *Ash v Ash*, decided in 1697, Chief Justice Holt explained that jurors were expected to disclose their thinking to the court in order that the court could assist them to amend their verdict. He reversed what he deemed to be a grossly excessive award of damages (£2000 for an incident of false imprisonment involving the detention of a youth for a couple of hours), saying: "'The jury were very shy of giving a reason for their verdict, thinking that they have an absolute, despotic power, but I did rectify that mistake, for the jury are to try cases with the assistance of the judges, and ought to give reasons when required, that, if they go upon any mistake, they may be set right ...'"

Ryder. Langbein shows that this procedure continued until the later 18th century in his 1996 review of "a novel historical source, the judge's notes of Sir Dudley Ryder, Chief Justice of King's Bench during the years 1754-56". Ryder (1691-1756) straddled the law and politics during the high noon of the corrupt Whig oligarchy. (see chapter 9. The 18th Century: Oligarchy, Corruption and Lord Mansfield's Final Solution for the Problem of Journalism.) Ryder was a barrister from 1725, MP from 1733, the corrupt Sir Robert Walpole's Solicitor-General 1733 and his Attorney-General 1737, Lord Chief Justice of King's Bench 1754. He was succeeded in 1756 by the dread Lord Mansfield, who persisted, to the disgust of the London mob, until 1788.

Langbein says: "Ryder's notes supply an exceptionally detailed narrative of the trials over which he presided. They cast a shaft of light into the mid-eighteenth-century courtroom, allowing us to glimpse what actually transpired in the conduct of civil and criminal trials".

Later in the 18th century, however, defence lawyers invented a grossly excessive adversary system which isolated the judge from the jury; defence lawyers then used the "fraught with danger" notion to invent several more magic tricks.

The Scrutable Judge. The common law appears to recognise that reasons should be given; a judge has to give his reasons when he sits on a criminal case without a jury. This may seem an advance, but the judge still has to conceal the same evidence from himself as he would from a jury. And no judge enjoys being overturned; a higher court can overturn his verdict of guilty, but not his verdict of innocent. This may subconsciously exert pressure for a not guilty verdict. Janet Fife-Yeomans reported (*The Australian*, August 27, 1994): "Figures from the NSW District Court show that the jury convicted in half the cases while the judge, when hearing a case alone, convicted in only a quarter."

The Inscrutable Jury in Action. In 1994, a Sydney judge delivered a speech, *Complex Criminal Trials*, to law enforcement agencies. On juries, he said: "At the moment, unfortunately, the best qualified by training and experience to understand the evidence and issues are almost always excluded, and as Professor Glanville Williams has said, it would be an understatement to describe the persons empanelled as jurors as a 'group of people of average ignorance' ... The recent report of the AIJA [Australian Institute of Judicial Administration] *Jury Management in NSW* merits some attention by those who wish to present a prosecution brief to a jury, and by judges who are expected to preside over the trial. This study exposes something of the dynamics of the jury process, the problems they have, and the assistance they need.

"One of the most interesting if not disturbing responses came from a juror who had served on a nine-month trial, and became so incensed with the experience as to keep a diary in which she described the conflicts between the jurors. She reported that by the end of the first day, a majority of the jury were agreed that the accused must be guilty:
  – one because he was wearing an earring
  – one because he looked too glitzy
  – one because he was ugly, probably because he was bad, and
  – one because his lawyer looked positively evil.
"From that point, the juror said, this group only listened to evidence or argument which reinforced their conclusion of guilt. She was personally ostracised and marginalised from the start, being described as a 'pinko lezzo". Another juror suffered the same fate because, despite being intelligent, he was very badly groomed with poor personal hygiene.

"Our reporter was informed by one juror that she would be put on a hit list if she went against a verdict of guilty, and another tried to persuade her to stay at home. One juror, a bank manager who was confident and handsome, emerged as the leader, and had a number of followers who agreed with everything he said. On the final day, when it became clear that our reporter and her ally were not going to go along with a guilty verdict, the bank manager changed his mind and was followed by the rest because, she said, it was clear he had expected an early verdict and had made plans for golf which he did not want to break.

"This may be a horror story, but it has the support of other jurors who reported on their experiences in similar terms. You can imagine the frustration of those who investigated and presented those cases, and that of the judge who carefully marshalled the evidence and law, and directed the jury, if they were to learn that was the way their work was received."

The judge said that, on the basis of the AIJA study, fewer than 20 per cent of juries will have a clear understanding of complex facts. He said other points to emerge from the study were: "While jurors can cope with directions of law, and a reasonable amount of evidence, they have problems with special terms and placing the evidence into the context of issues ...

"There are real difficulties experienced in maintaining concentration and recalling a large volume of evidence over any length of time ... All jurors need to feel that they are being involved, since there is a real risk of the foreman or the loudest dominating them in the jury room. A verdict in a long and complex trial is likely to be given out of frustration or boredom as out of a considered appreciation of the merits of the case ..."

It would thus be useful to know the jurors' reasons in some famous guilty verdicts: Timothy Evans, Derek Bentley (both of whom were hanged), Rupert Max Stuart, the Birmingham Six. And in some not guilty verdicts: O.J. Simpson; Said Morgan, a Sydney policeman who admitted to executing a paedophile; Lorena Bobbitt, who sliced off her husband's penis while he was asleep; Dean Waters, a Sydney boxer who admitted to taking part in a murder on his father's instructions; four Los Angeles police caught on video tape bashing Rodney King; and three men filmed bashing a truck-driver, Reginald Denny, during riots in Los Angeles after the Rodney King verdict.

Solutions. Two things seem obvious. Questions of guilt and innocence may more usefully be placed in the hands of semi-professional lay judges. And putting the jurors on the bench with the judge and making them both responsible for the verdict would tend to eliminate verdicts based on the accused's earring or the really evil visage of his lawyer.

7

The Malady:

Why Judges Can't Seem to Think Straight

Justice is too important to be left to the judiciary.

– Ludovic Kennedy, 1989

The English Disease. The cartel's 13th century decision not to pursue the European path of truth may have been a factor in the condition known as Common Law Mind, i.e. judges sometimes seem to find clarity of thought difficult. The French might call it *la maladie Anglais*, or even, if feeling seriously Gallic, *la vice Anglais* (pron. veesonglay). Judges were surely in the grip of the malady when they agreed to defence lawyers' requests for an extreme adversary system in the 18th century. That system and the rules for concealing evidence that followed seem to have exacerbated the condition.

I am not saying that judges (and lawyers) cannot think straight. In court I have two reactions: 1. Awe at the clarity and rapidity of their thought. And 2. Raymond Chandler was wrong: advertising is not the greatest waste of human intelligence ever devised. What does seem beyond argument is that judges sometimes appear to feel obliged to speak and write **AS IF** mentally crippled by the law.

A 500-Year Problem. Sir William Holdsworth (*A History of English Law*, 1927) offers what may perhaps be seen as a startling example of the malady. As quoted by Justice Ken Marks, of the Victorian Supreme Court, he said "it took the common law 500 years to arrive at the obvious answer" to a particular problem. In fact, judges never found the answer; Parliament did. The problem was that a trial could not begin until the accused indicated, by pleading one way or the other, that he consented to be tried. He had a motive to refuse: conviction meant his goods were forfeited; his family would be destitute, particularly if he was hanged. The judge had a motive to get the trial under way; he got a share of the proceeds, but even that did not induce clarity of thought.

To force a plea, judges tried prison in the 13th century and crushing the accused with boulders in the 15th. Nothing worked. It was not until 1827 that Parliament found the "obvious" answer: a refusal to plead would be taken as a plea of not guilty. The English Parliament likewise took two centuries to correct the cartel's error concerning the right of silence.

Many decisions that go to make up "the rule of law" may seem explicable only in terms of the malady. This has serious implications for those who go to law in the belief that the judge will probably produce the right decision in commercial cases and correct rulings on admissibility in criminal cases.

FLAC. The US FLAC (For Legally Abused Citizens) organisation receives some 200 "horror" stories each week, some apparently to do with aspects of the malady. Thus: A curfew breach in Virginia carried a maximum fine of US$10. A girl, 12, was arrested for being out 20 minutes past the curfew. The judge found her guilty, took custody away from her single mother and put the girl in the care of social services. She was in the juvenile penal system for 19 months, deprived of her education and raped. She was returned to her mother before giving birth. FLAC organised a protest; 40 people testified against the judge's reappointment before the Courts of Justice Committee. The judge was not reappointed, a first in Virginia's history.

Curran. In *Curran*, (1974), eminent judges on the Australian High Court, Chief Justice Sir Garfield Barwick and Justices Sir Douglas Menzies and Sir Harry Gibbs said that an apparent profit of $2782 was a loss, for purposes of tax avoidance, of $186,046. Justice Sir Ninian Stephen strongly disagreed; he said a profit had obviously been made. In 1978, John Howard, then Treasurer (he became Prime Minister in 1996), legislated to recoup losses to the revenue caused by the High Court's tax decisions. Lawyers were not happy. Sexton and Maher report: " ... a number of lawyers opposed retrospective amendments to the tax laws in 1978 – amendments designed to counter one tax avoidance scheme that had been estimated to involve $941 million in deductions claimed – as being a threat to the 'rule of law'..."

The Lawyer-Priest. In view of the malady, other remarks by Sexton and Maher take on a new poignancy. They specifically concern Australia but can relate to any common-law country. Sexton and Maher state: "In non-judicial roles lawyers, through their involvement in parliaments, the bureaucracy, the business world, and in the profession itself, have a direct bearing on the outcome of many, if not most, political issues. In addition, lawyers have long been treated, by virtue of their legal training, as the community's principal source of fact-finding skills. ... Why is it then, that lawyers, in addition to pre-eminence in their own field, have been considered more competent than any other group in the community to consider problems that are outside that field? ... The answer seems to lie in the way law and lawyers are perceived by the rest of the community. To a large extent the law is seen as a set of immutable principles that have always and will always exist, and lawyers as the priests who reveal these principles to laymen, always with a remoteness and neutrality, especially in the case of judges, that transcend any question of personal value or interests."

Inquiries. The problem is that the common law is not a fact-finding system in the sense that a European inquisitorial system is.

This becomes apparent when the trade of authority finds it necessary to find the truth about some grave social problem, and has to turn to the methods of European law (and, as it happens, journalism), and appoints a Royal Commission or similar commission of inquiry. The procedure is inquisitorial; common law rules for concealing evidence are supposed to be suspended, but Callinan said: "Commissions of inquiry are supposed to be different. They are supposed to be designed to investigate and expose the truth [but] most lawyers do not readily translate from the court room to the inquiry room, and in saying this I intend to include judges."

I suspect that what happens is that the lawyers or judge suspends the rules for concealing evidence during the hearing, but they are so ingrained that they tend to reimpose them in making their findings, and so tend to be unable to say what the truth is. This seems to confirm that truth is not the common lawyer's *metier*. The solution is to provide them with lay assessors to advise on what the facts mean or to have trained historians run such inquiries, with of course a lawyer to ask the questions. The following may illustrate the problem:

Gibbs. Callinan noted Mr Justice Harry Gibbs's "formalism" at a 1963 inquiry on police corruption at Brisbane's National Hotel. He said "judicial conservatism and restraint ... are capable of producing inhibitions in the performance of inquisitorial work ... the Inquiry was rather unlikely to be very effective". Justice Gibbs reported that in general he adhered to the rules of evidence. His associate at the inquiry, the Hon David Jackson QC (as he now is), said in 1992 that Justice Gibbs had had a good idea of the truth of the matter, i.e. that the Police Commissioner, Frank Bischof, and others were corrupt. But on his view of the evidence he did admit, Justice Gibbs felt obliged to make a positive finding that no police were corrupt.

Matrix-Churchill. Lord Justice Scott used the full inquisitorial procedure in the Matrix-Churchill inquiry in 1995, i.e. he did not allow cross-examination by lawyers other than himself and his counsel assisting, Ms Presiley Baxendale QC. However, the tenor of his final report suggested he may have subconsciously reimposed the rules for concealing evidence.

Lanfranchi. A Coroner's inquest is supposed to be an inquisitorial proceeding. In 1981, an inquest was held into Detective Sergeant Roger Rogerson's fatal shooting of Warren Lanfranchi in Sydney. Rogerson and other detectives said Lanfranchi menaced them with a gun. The coroner and all the lawyers, including those for Lanfranchi's family, agreed that the evidence disclosed no ground for common law charges against anyone. The coroner told the jurors they could find, if they wished, that Rogerson killed Lanfranchi in self-defence. They specifically refused to do so, but, as with all common law juries, they did not give their reasons. This left their view as to whether Lanfranchi was armed open to speculation.

ICAC. The NSW Independent Commission Against Corruption is supposed to be an inquisitorial procedure. It suspends the rules for concealing evidence but it is not inquisitorial in the sense that it allows lawyers for suspects to cross-examine. In 1994, I asked ICAC commissioner Ian Temby QC if he had reimposed the rules in his *Milloo* report on Arthur Stanley (Neddy) Smith's claims of police corruption. He said: "No, but we are all the products of our background and training." His report showed he had reimposed the rule against hearsay in a particular matter.

Askin. A Sydney newspaper, *The Sun-Herald*, asked a former coroner, Kevin Waller, to look at material relating to the corruption of former NSW Premier Sir Robert Askin. Among a mountain of direct and circumstantial evidence pointing to corruption was the fact that Askin was a bank clerk until he became a member of Parliament in 1950 and was a professional politician until he retired in 1975. David Hickie, author of a book about Askin, researched his year-by-year salary from 1950 to 1975. From 1950 to 1965 he got a total of $99,550. For the 10 years from 1965 he was Premier, he got a total of $275,180. He died in 1981 and left a declared estate of $1,957,995, mostly to his widow. On her death 2 1/2 years later, she left a declared estate of $3,724,879.

A woman who worked at a large illegal bookmaking firm said Askin extorted bribes. She said: "Sir Robert Askin bet as 'RWA' by this method: he took an each-way bet on Race One for $80; if that didn't win, he bet $160 each way on his choice in Race Two; then, if that didn't win he bet $320 each way on Race Three. We worried if his first choice didn't win. He never paid any money. We always paid him his winnings."

Waller reported that his duty to the law prevented him from finding that Askin was corrupt, but said privately he might say something different in a pub. This suggests that the common law rules of evidence may have prevented him from finding on the facts he had reviewed what an ordinary person may have found.

The US Grand Jury. It should be noted that the US inquisitorial procedure, the grand jury, has its defects but it does avoid the problem of Common Law Mind: it consists of one lawyer and 23 non-lawyers. I touch on the techniques of the grand jury in chapter 36.

Courts of Appeal. The malady sometimes seems to be a major problem in a court of appeal. Judge Harold Rothwax is severely critical of some of the US Supreme Court's decisions; he believes they cause justice to miscarry. Ludovic Kennedy is likewise critical of the English Court of Appeal's difficulty in coming to grips with obvious miscarriages. In 1989 he asked how Appeal Court procedure could be improved to "ensure that in future the Courts arrive at more realistic judgments? ... justice is too important to be left to the judiciary ... their record in recent cases, both in Court of Appeal judgments and in the findings of post appeal inquiries, shows this to be so ... It is the jury, not the judge, who are interpreters of the facts, the jury, not the judge, who determine the fate of the defendant. Why therefore exclude this lay element from the Court of Appeal?" German appeal courts have lay assessors.

8

Precedent:
Abiding by the Decisions of
Judges Who Were Probably Wrong,
Confused or Had a Secret Agenda

*There are many things wrong with the English legal system.
A large proportion of them can be explained by our reverence for
the doctrine of precedent. We do things not for any rational
reason but because they have previously been done that way.*

— David Pannick QC

The legal principle, *stare decisis* (the decision stands), means abiding
by precedent. It seems to be another factor in the malady. Pannick
gives some jokey examples:

● Sir Orlando Bridgeman, Chief Justice in the 1660s, resisted
change to the location of the court on the ground that it would
contravene Magna Carta.

● An 18th century judge, Samuel Lovell, was "overtaken by the
tide" but refused to escape drowning unless a precedent could be
quoted for judges mounting the coach-box.

● Wigs, once a gentleman's fashion, caused scalp-itch; all except
bishops, judges and barristers stopped wearing them at the end of
the 18th century. Bishops discarded them in 1832; some members of
the cartel persist.

Secret Agenda. The rule of precedent and the rule against
hearsay (Magic Trick 6) are mutually contradictory. Hearsay evidence
is concealed because the original speaker is not available for cross-
examination, which may show he was wrong, confused or had a
secret agenda. Equally, cross-examination might show that 13th
century and later judges were wrong, confused, or had a secret
agenda, e.g. Lord Mansfield on libel law (see chapter 9). They are not
available for cross-examination, but their decisions stand.

Mansfield. Lord Mansfield said in 1780 that property matters
needed the certainty of fixed rules, so much so that "if an erroneous
or hasty determination has got into practice, there is more benefit
from adhering to it, than if it were to be overturned."

Lord Eldon. Lord Eldon, who famously found that grammar
schools should teach grammar, said bad law should be retained. He
said in *Sheddon v Goodrich* (1803) that "it is better the law should
be certain than that every judge should speculate upon
improvements in it".

Carter. In *Carter* (1995), the Australian High Court likewise decided that legal privileges that are "firmly entrenched in the law", e.g. the right of silence (Magic Trick 4), can only be curtailed by the legislature; they cannot "be exorcised by judicial decision" even if that might produce evidence to show an accused is innocent, and hence assist a fair trial.

McHugh. Judges thus seem to be claiming they have no obligation to correct legal error and injustice, even if the Parliament takes centuries to do it for them. In *Lange* (1997), Justice Michael McHugh said in the Australian High Court: "Anyone who does not believe judges make law is not living in the real world." It seems to follow that judges are free to make bad law, but are not free to unmake it. Thus is injustice perpetuated.

Pontius Pilate. Pontius Pilate thus seems an appropriate common law symbol: he was not interested in truth, and he washed his hands of any responsibility for justice.

9

The 18th Century:
Oligarchy, Corruption and Lord Mansfield's
Final Solution for the Problem of Journalism

*[Seditious libel is] written censure upon any public man whatever for
any conduct whatever, or upon any law or institution whatever.*

– 18th century definition of libel.

Having got truth and the jury wrong in the 13th century, the cartel
laid the foundation in the 18th for getting everything else wrong.
The main game was defence lawyers' successful attempt to take
over criminal trials, but the details remain obscure; either the
lawyers and judges involved covered their tracks too well, or legal
and historical scholarship has been wanting. We do know that a
lawyer-politician, William Murray, first Earl of Mansfield (1705-93)
must have been a key figure in the process. A brief sketch of that
thoroughly corrupt century – and Lord Mansfield's role in concealing
its corruption via libel law – may give us a glimpse, as in a glass
darkly, of some of the forces at work.

Oligarchy. Lawyer-politicians had been prominent when
Parliament won the contest for power with the monarch in the
middle of the 17th century. The two great power blocs at the start of
the 18th century were thus politics and the law, and the cartel
straddled both. Oligarchy is government by a few; England was
governed by Whig oligarchs; their method was an all-encompassing
corruption; politicians bought their seats in Parliament, and sold
their votes. Neither they nor the cartel took kindly to a new
institution, modern journalism.

The Press. Journalism antedates the common law and the cartel
by perhaps a thousand years. Rome's *Acta Diurna*, a sort of
government gazette chipped in stone, began about 132 BC; Plutarch
(c. 46 AD-c. 120 AD) and Suetonius (75 AD-160 AD) were among the
first, and finest, practitioners of the anecdotal (joke) approach to
journalism. Technology, or lack of it, restricted the market; journalism
was not a threat to the power of the cartel or the trade of authority
until the 15th century: Johann Gutenberg (1397-1468) invented
moveable type about 1436; William Caxton (c. 1421-1491) introduced
the printing press into England in 1477.

Censorship. Printing troubled those with things to hide; it was
soon followed by pre-publication censorship. In 1501, a dubious
Borgia pope, Alexander VI (c. 1431-1503, pontiff 1492-1503) issued a
Bull requiring printers to submit copy to church authorities

beforehand; in 1534, King Henry VIII invented the Church of England and laws to license the Press. The licensing laws were in force for 161 years, and only lapsed because of a trick.

Ignorance. Before we get too pompous about lawyers' and judges' ignorance of the origins of their trade, we should note that probably not a huge number of journalists are aware of the role of pamphleteer Charles Blount and lawyer Edmund Bohun, or even Daniel Defoe, journalist and secret agent, in the origin of the modern version of their trade, the tercentenary of which will, or should, be celebrated in 2004.

1688. Parliamentarians and others reasserted their power in 1688: they got rid of King James II and imported a Dutch person, William III, and his wife Mary to sit on the throne. However, James Sutherland says Lord Macaulay reported that Edmund Bohun (1645-1699) "succeeded in convincing himself that William and Mary reigned by right of conquest."

1692. By chance, events in the same year, 1692, created an excuse for the adversary system and the conditions for the emergence of journalism proper. Chapter 13 notes that legislation in 1692 offering rewards for information leading to the conviction of criminals was a factor in lawyers' later takeover of trials.

End of Licensing Act. Bohun was appointed Licenser of the Press in 1692. Charles Blount (1654-1693) anonymously produced a pamphlet he knew Bohun would be foolish enough to license: *King William and Queen Mary Conquerors*. It caused grave offence to their Majesties' political masters, and Bohun got the blame. The common hangman was called in to formally burn the offending document in the yard at Westminster Palace; Bohun was called before the Bar of the House and imprisoned in 1693; the Licensing Act was renewed for two years only, and allowed to lapse in 1695. (Bohun made a comeback in the colonies; he was appointed Chief Justice of Carolina in 1698.)

The Press was now allegedly free, and in the 18th century the English were inclined to claim that the freedom of its Press demonstrated the superiority of their civilisation over that of European countries. But the Press was never likely to be free; in 1704, the very year that modern journalism was invented, Chief Justice Sir John Holt ruled: "It is very necessary for all governments that the people should have a good opinion of it."

Defoe. Daniel Defoe (1660-1731), who also invented the modern novel (*Robinson Crusoe*, 1719-20) invented *The Review* and modern journalism in 1704. Whatever the flaws of its practitioners, journalism has a natural bias in favour of truth, democracy and honest government; its traditional function, in addition to interesting and amusing the customers, is to serve the community by exposing wrongdoers, in particular those who subvert democracy by corruption. The Press was thus instantly seen as a purveyor of new and dangerous sentiments, and as a threat to the cartel's power to and the oligarchs' power and corruption. That would never do.

Taxation, Bribery etc. Hypocrisy prevented the reintroduction of the Licensing Act, but censorship was reimposed by the back door. Several methods were tried: secrecy, always the bottom line on corruption, (it was made a crime to report Parliamentary debates), the ever-popular bribery, and taxation. In 1712, Defoe's *Review* and numerous other organs, including Addison and Steele's *The Spectator*, were taxed out of business.

Wild. Jonathan Wild (1682?-1725) and Sir Robert Walpole (1676-1745) were seen as typical 18th century figures, notably by John Gay and Henry Fielding, who was a lawyer, journalist, playwright and novelist. Wild, the century's most notorious organised criminal, was the head of a large corporation of thieves. He received stolen goods and profited from the 1692 legislation: he got rewards for informing on his own criminals. He was hanged at Tyburn in 1725.

Walpole. Walpole ran a corrupt Whig oligarchy from 1721 to 1742. In the last 10 years he paid bribes of £50,000 (some $15 million of our money) to newspaper proprietors. In 1728, John Gay produced *The Beggar's Opera*, a thinly-disguised satire on Walpole's government: Peachum, a receiver of stolen goods, represents Walpole and Wild; Macheath, a highwayman, is a member of Peachum's organisation. In 1731, Fielding promised another satire on corrupt government, *Grub Street Opera*, but Walpole bribed him to desist. It eventually appeared as a novel, *The History of Jonathan Wild the Great*, in 1743, the year after Walpole's fall, with Wild again representing Walpole.

Newcastle. Thomas Pelham-Holles, Duke of Newcastle (1693-1768), was the most celebrated bagman (collector and distributor of bribes) in the history of the English trade of authority. He became Walpole's designated bagman in 1724 and was thereafter secretary of state for 30 years. His younger brother, Henry Pelham (1693?-1754), was a corrupt Whig Prime Minister from 1743 to 1754. The great bagman himself was then Prime Minister 1754-56 and 1757-62. The Pelhams' record tells us much of what we need to know about Lord Mansfield, seen to have been the pre-eminent jurist of the second half of the century.

Macclesfield. But first we glance at the "silver-tongued counsel", Thomas Parker, first Earl of Macclesfield (1666?-1732, Lord Chancellor 1718-1725) and some of the Masters in Chancery. The record suggests that there were at least pockets of corruption in the judiciary in the 18th century. CDNB reports: "In 1724 a committee of the Privy Council was appointed to inquire into the funds of the suitors in the hands of the Masters in Chancery. They reported not only that there were considerable defalcations in some of the Master's offices, but that there was a case of grave suspicion against the Lord Chancellor. In consequence he resigned the seals in Jan 1725, though he still continued in favour at court. In May he was impeached, found guilty, and fined £30,000." The fine was fairly stiff:

about $9 million of our money. More than a century later, the Chancery Court was still a fit subject for Dickens's scorn.

The Press. Despite bribery and taxation, some independent newspaper proprietors remained; a final solution was needed to silence them. Judges had been guaranteed their independence in 1701, but Francis Williams says in *Dangerous Estate* (Longman 1957) that 18th century judges were only too willing to do the bidding of the politicians, and in any event the cartel had an interest in keeping power out of the hands of the Press.

The Final Solution. The final solution was a neat switch in the function of libel law, from protecting the peace of the realm to protecting reputation, however vile the character of the person protected. Libel law went back at least to 1275, when Edward I made it a crime, *Scandalum Magnatum* (libelling the magnates), to utter a slur, true or false, about the great men of England. The statute was not concerned with reputation; it was designed to keep the peace of the realm: the magnates had private armies and were quick to take offence. By the 18th century, the magnates did not need private armies; they WERE the government, and as we have seen their method was an all-encompassing corruption.

Mansfield. William Murray, Lord Mansfield became a lawyer in 1730 and an MP in 1742, Solicitor-General in Henry Pelham's government from 1743 to 1754, Attorney-General in the Duke of Newcastle's government in 1754; and Serjeant-at-Law and Lord Chief Justice in 1756. He sat in corrupt Cabinets from 1757 to 1765 and adhered to the policy of coercing America in the 1760s and 1770s. He remained in politics until age 79 in 1784 and as Chief Justice until age 83 in 1788.

Like the Australian High Court's Justice Lionel Murphy (see chapter 18: Magic Trick 4: A Rule that Protects the Guilty Only), Mansfield seems to have been a Jekyll and Hyde figure. On his record, there can be no doubt that, at the least, he had guilty knowledge of the corruption of the oligarchy of which he was a leading member. It follows that part of his agenda as first law officer and Chief Justice was that oligarchy is preferable to democracy, that corruption is acceptable in an oligarchy, and that anyone, including the journalists, who disagrees with them must be silenced and/or imprisoned.

Seditious Libel. The criminal offence of seditious libel was defined in the 18th century as "written censure upon any public man whatever for any conduct whatever, or upon any law or institution whatever". The "whatever" obviously does the work; it means that disclosure of oligarchs' or judges' corruption is a crime. Hence Reyner Heppenstall's remark: "Libel law exists for the protection of rogues in high places." Mansfield insisted that the only role for the jury in cases of seditious libel was to decide if the accused had published the offending material. If he had, a presumption of guilt, i.e. the definition of seditious libel, took care of the rest.

Ambiguity. To repeat, in ambiguity lies power. John Almon (1737-1805), bookseller and journalist, was imprisoned and fined in 1770 and tried for libel in 1786 and went to France in financial difficulties. He noted: "A man had better make his son a tinker than a printer. The laws of tin he can understand but the law of libel is unwritten, uncertain and undefinable. It is one thing today, another tomorrow. No man can tell what it is. It is sometimes what the King or Queen pleases, sometimes what the Minister pleases, sometimes what the Attorney-General pleases". And sometimes what Lord Mansfield pleased; presumably to silence the Press and protect corrupt oligarchs, he invented a brazenly ridiculous dictum: the greater the truth the greater the libel.

Democracy. Libel law thus encourages corruption, and corruption defeats democracy. In America, democrats passed the First Amendment to the Constitution in 1791. It said Congress shall make no law "abridging the freedom of speech or of the Press". But in England libel law was an invention of the 18th century, whereas democracy is an invention of the 19th, the Reform Bill of 1832 being the first move in that direction. Libel law in England and other colonies was, and is, still infected by Lord Mansfield, the 18th century, and a presumption of guilt for those who seek to speak the truth.

10

Court Seeks to Raise the Quality of Journalism.
But How Can the Quality
of the Court be Raised?

I am far from confident that I have succeeded in finding my way through the labyrinthine complexities of the defamation law of [NSW]. It is an unpleasant feeling to know that one is lost; I am not sure that it is not equally unpleasant to be unsure whether one is lost or not.

– Justice Richard Blackburn, 1977

In Australia democracy may be seen to have started with *Theophanous* (1994). In that judgment, Chief Justice Sir Anthony Mason and Justices Sir William Deane, John Toohey and Mary Gaudron bravely gave citizens who want to discuss politics a constitutional guarantee of free speech. They took the view the people who wrote the Australian Constitution (1901) were trying to invent a democracy and hence must have believed in free access to information about politicians. Justices Sir Gerard Brennan, Sir Daryl Dawson and Michael McHugh did not agree. McHugh was the only judge on the court who had specialised in libel law at the Bar.

Brennan. By 1996, Justices Mason and Deane had left and Gerry Brennan was in charge. I should have known he was destined to be Chief Justice: at Downlands College I heard him tell Bill (Pickles) Breen, after some minor altercation in the locker room: "Henceforth, let all communication between us cease." I mentally filed this splendid formulation for later use, but sadly an appropriate moment never seemed to come. I sent him a note when he became Chief Justice. He kindly replied: "I imagine I read you more often than you read me but that is my advantage!"

The Brandeis Brief. The court now revisited libel law in *Lange* and a duck-shooting case and various governments submitted that *Theophanous* should be overturned. I noted (*The Australian*, October 14, 1996) that this would give the court the chance to decide whether the minority in *Theophanous* – Brennan, Dawson and McHugh – were right to deny Australians even that smidgin of democracy, and that "media organisations will pay lawyers vast sums – perhaps half a million – to argue that Mason *et al* were right. They might also usefully hire a history student and a law student – who happily work for about a 20th of silks' rates – to research libel law from the beginning. The aim would be to work up a brief of the sort invented by the great American jurist, Louis Dembitz Brandeis, in *Muller v Oregon* (1908); his 113 pages of 'social facts' and two pages of argument persuaded the Supreme Court to unanimously uphold Oregon's 10-hour law for women workers. Our student researchers should likewise find some social facts that may be both new and of compelling interest to the High Court."

Having noted some of the history traversed above, I observed: "The rule of precedent tends to bind judges to the rulings of earlier judges who may have been wrong or, like Lord Mansfield, had a secret agenda [protecting corrupt Whig oligarchs] ... The obligation to rely on precedent also tends to deprive judges of excessive knowledge of the origins of law. Our High Court judges might thus find the students' Brandeis Brief very helpful".

McHugh. During the *Lange* hearing, Justice McHugh claimed that when he advised a large media corporation [Mr Rupert Murdoch's] on libel he had never noticed that libel law had a "chilling" effect on reporting. With very great respect, that may seem, in a hotly-contested field, one of the more grotesque appellate remarks in legal history. Perhaps he was just not very observant.

In the event, democracy in Australia lasted three years; in *Lange* (1977), the court, now consisting of Justices Brennan, Dawson, Toohey, Gaudron, McHugh, Bill Gummow and Michael Kirby, unanimously overturned *Theophanous* and removed the constitutional defence. It was opined that McHugh, the specialist, had the major voice in crafting the court's view of libel law.

Ambiguity. It appeared that neither the Chief Justice nor any of the other learned judges had found any advantage in my suggestion that they examine Lord Mansfield; so far from examining the origins of libel law in the 18th century, it seemed they had largely restricted their research to the 1974 NSW Defamation Act. That monument of ambiguity was invented, as it happens, by the government of a famously corrupt elected oligarch, Sir Robin Askin. Sydney is said to place only third to New York and Los Angeles in medical negligence litigation, but to be the contempt and libel capital of the world. Perhaps Justice Richard Blackburn, of the Australian Capital Territory Supreme Court, got an inkling of the reason when he had to try to come to grips with the NSW Act in *Renouf v Federal Capital Press* (1977). In words that echo John Almon 200 years earlier he said: "I am far from confident that I have succeeded in finding my way through the labyrinthine complexities of the defamation law of [NSW]. It is an unpleasant feeling to know that one is lost; I am not sure that it is not equally unpleasant to be unsure whether one is lost or not."

Reasonableness. From the NSW Act, the High Court judges imported the notion of "reasonableness". There might be a defence, they said, if it was reasonable to have believed the offending material. The judge, not the jury, was to decide what is reasonable. But, as every juror knows, nobody, including judges, knows what reasonable means. Are 30 telephone calls reasonable, but not 29? And how often would judges find reporters' actions reasonable? A libel lawyer, Richard Coleman, pointed out that in hundreds of NSW libel cases in the 23 years since 1974, judges had effectively found the organ's conduct was "reasonable" only four times. They would certainly never find it reasonable for journalists to report with reckless indifference to the truth, although they daily have to accept it is "reasonable" for lawyers to proceed with reckless indifference to the truth in cross-examination. That is just another of the common law's inconsistencies they have to swallow.

False Presumptions. And while insisting that reporters be "reasonable", it appeared, with very great respect, that the learned judges imposed no such obligation on themselves. In a Sydney seminar on *Lange* put on by a law firm, Minter Ellison, Peter Bartlett, a Melbourne libel lawyer, said *Lange* retains the previous presumptions of libel law. But the presumptions are all false, as may be seen by inserting the name of any organised criminal, say Sir Robert Walpole, Sir Robin Askin or John Gotti, as the object of the slur in the list of presumptions:

A slur is always false.

The author of a slur is always guilty.

The subject of a slur is always innocent.

A slur always causes damage.

Appearance (reputation) is always preferable to reality (character).

The private right to reputation is always to be preferred to the public right to information.

The seventh false presumption is that a slur is always deliberately intended to cause damage. But any libel lawyer knows that at least 80 per cent of alleged libels are inadvertent.

Was it "reasonable" for the judges to leave those false presumptions in libel law? The presumptions must surely operate unfairly and unjustly in the libel courts, and hence operate against disclosure of important public information. Is that "reasonable"? What excuse did the judges have for leaving them in the law? After all, they were members of Australia's highest court, not a few fatigued lawyers asleep at the wheel on a warm afternoon in a Massachusetts courtroom (see Epilogue, How to Get a Frottist off Murder and other Jokes).

Bartlett said the judges will be really pleased with *Lange*; they will feel their unanimous decision means they have settled libel law in Australia for 50 years. That means they have set back democracy in Australia for 50 years. I asked Bartlett who would gain from *Lange* other than corrupt politicians, organised criminals and libel lawyers. He did not address himself to the corrupt and organised criminals, but conceded it would mean more work for lawyers.

He also said that in *Lange* the judges are trying to raise the quality of journalism. We can all drink to that, but the more pressing question, with very great respect, is surely: how can we raise the quality of the law? Not to mention the court.

Brill. Incidentally, the only suggestion on libel damages that ever made sense to me was put forward in 1984 by Steven Brill, then editor of *The American Lawyer*. He said damages should be restricted to actual pecuniary loss plus a maximum of three times the cost of a full-page advertisement in the offending organ: two-thirds to be kept as a solatium, one-third to be used to trumpet to the world that the organ got it wrong. (US citizens are in Brill's debt: as the inventor of Court TV, he showed them in the O.J. Simpson case how the grossly excessive adversary system actually works.)

11

Perpetuating Lawyers' and Judges' Ignorance: What Law Schools Don't Teach

First year students are simply given our system as the right way, coached in its strengths, and that is that.

– New Zealand law lecturer, quoted by Robert Mannion, 1997

Universities are supposed to seek the truth wherever it may lead; it is a continuing puzzle that they give space to a subject which effectively denies that truth is important. It is also a puzzle that university law schools do not interest themselves in a legal system that does seek the truth. Since 1753, law students have been getting the false impression that English common law is the greatest legal system ever devised by the mind of man, and that a few minor inconsistencies – the "rotten apple" theory – are a small price to pay for that. But the inconsistencies to be swallowed are not of the gnat variety, more like a ton of old iron; law students (and lawyers and judges) need the digestive system of a crocodile.

In the unreal world of the common law, the lawyer's working life becomes at best a sort of Gullible's Travels; he must try to simultaneously believe that truth is important and not important, i.e. everyone except lawyers must adhere to the truth. Citizens are asked: do you swear to tell the truth, the whole truth and nothing but the truth? (The correct answer probably is: I will if you will let me.) But the lawyer questioning the citizen can immediately proceed on the basis that the truth is not his concern.

Blackstone. Legal academics were not admitted to the cartel until the 18th century. A failed barrister, William Blackstone (1723-80) was the first; he started teaching common law at Oxford University in 1753, and became the first Professor of English Law in 1758. By then, the cartel had long since decided that truth is not important and it had invented a fatally defective jury system, and was on the way to inventing a procedure, the grossly excessive adversary system, that gave control of trials to people with little or no interest in truth or justice. Yet Blackstone not only accepted the common law as it stood, he also claimed it was virtually beyond improvement.

Ostrichism. At best, Blackstone seems to have been the first, but not the last, legal academic to suffer from what Judge Posner defines as "ostrichism, sometimes called the avoidance of cognitive dissonance, whereby a person in a bad situation, rather than taking steps (which he could do) to ameliorate it, convinces himself that it

68

actually is a good situation". Thus afflicted, Blackstone fatally persuaded the American revolutionaries to retain the common law against their inclination to adopt the European law's rational investigation of the truth. The problems of cases such as O.J. Simpson's can thus be ascribed in large part to Blackstone.

Temperate Curiosity. Blackstone published his lectures as *Commentaries on the Laws of England* in four volumes from 1765 to 1769. Damning Blackstone with faint praise, Theodore Plucknett says he "regarded our legal history as an object of 'temperate curiosity' rather than exact scholarship. His equipment in jurisprudence was also somewhat slender, but his freedom from excessive learning was an actual merit; he found explanations that seemed adequate, clear, and above all interesting ... [*The Commentaries*] leave the impression of almost indiscriminate praise for the great bulk of the old law ...

"Blackstone's work [was] particularly useful in 18th century America. *The Commentaries* had a tremendous sale there, for not only did they contain some very useful matter on public law, but also served as the principal means of the colonists' information as to the state of English law in general".

Bentham. Plucknett notes that at Oxford Jeremy Bentham "had heard Blackstone lecture, and deemed his matter unsound ... The publication of Blackstone's *Commentaries* ... drove him to fierce criticism expressed in his *Fragment on Government* (1776) ... Much of Bentham's savage attack still haunts us ..."

Julien Benda (1867-1956) wrote a book called *La Trahison des clercs* (The Treason of the Intellectuals). Was Blackstone guilty of intellectual treason? Or could he plead, as Bentham seemed to believe, the defence of bottomless stupidity? Or was he merely suffering from the malady? Or did he just want to be accepted into the cartel? He was made a judge in 1770, and presumably had a role, along with his hero, the dubious Lord Mansfield, in allowing defence lawyers to cement the grossly excessive adversary system into English law and in allowing lawyers to take over criminal and civil trials.

New Zealand. Legal academics, with exceptions, have tended to follow the Blackstone line. Robert Mannion quotes a New Zealand law lecturer: "First year students are simply given our system as the right way, coached in its strengths, and that is that."

Australia. Michael Sexton and Laurence W. Maher see a trade school mentality. They say: "Australian law schools have, overall, accepted a role of supplying lawyers to the legal profession. Many law teachers have accordingly adopted the myth of neutrality and put forward the law as it stands, without any comment as to how it developed, what effect it is having on society or where it might be going next. It is an approach that teaches skills but makes no mention of the goals to which they might be directed."

Ziegert. Professor Alex Ziegert, head of the Department of

Jurisprudence at Sydney University, notes the Mallory Argument. (See chapter 15) He says: "Law, as lawyers see it, does not need an explanation: they apply it because it is there. There is no gain in understanding in great detail where law comes from, or for that matter, in knowing precisely what law achieves or what it does not achieve, or how the legal system at home is different from other legal systems, as long as one knows 'the law'."

ICAC. The NSW Independent Commission Against Corruption was a noble, but failed, attempt to use inquisitorial procedures to get at the truth about corruption in NSW. This was a necessary task; the opening words of a book I wrote in 1986 called *Can of Worms* were: "It has been said, and not entirely in jest, that Sydney is the most corrupt city in the western world, except of course for Newark, New Jersey and Brisbane, Queensland." Section 17 of the ICAC Act (1988) stated:

1. The Commission is not bound by the rules or practice of evidence and can inform itself on any matter in such manner as it considers appropriate.

2. The Commission shall exercise its functions with as little formality and technicality as is possible ... and hearings shall be conducted with as little emphasis on an adversarial approach as is possible."

Ignorance of European Law. The Hon Michael Manifold Helsham QC, former Chief Judge in Equity in the NSW Supreme Court, had conducted an ICAC inquiry and had been part of an inquisitorial proceeding which found that Mr Justice Angelo Vasta should be removed from the Queensland Supreme Court. Helsham says he probably represents the level of common lawyers' knowledge of European law, which is apparently close to zero.

He told the ICAC parliamentary committee in 1990: "I am very interested to know how they do things elsewhere. We have this court system with adversarial procedures in the minds of our lawyers. Very few lawyers can think sideways. When we go into a proceeding like this we think along conventional lines. They do it differently elsewhere. The old judge gets involved in the thing right from the start. How much involved and what he does and how much help he has and how he conducts hearings and for what purpose is something about which I know nothing. I beg to say that there are very few people in the commission, and certainly in the ranks of lawyers, who do know anything about it. It is worth sussing this out in my view to see whether we can get something that is apposite to an inquiry. This is not a court case; it is an inquiry. I do not think we know enough about handling inquiries. That is why I have suggested that somebody should do a study to see what would emerge."

Trade School Approach. The trade school approach to legal education thus perpetuates ignorance of European law and of the origins of the common law. Academic debate on the legitimacy or otherwise of the common law has been muted since legal academics were first admitted to the cartel two-and-a-half centuries ago. As noted, they even tend to slide round the fact that it does not seek the truth. Nor, as Judge Rothwax notes, do they examine the system as a whole, [as this book does].

Rothwax. Judge Rothwax says: "It is my opinion that many of our laws and statutes are illogical and arbitrary. We need some straight talking about these issues, but it's hard to find the forum where honest dialogue can take place. Even in the law journals, arguably the center of legal learning and dialogue, there has been little attempt to view the system as a whole. A law review article might discuss the Fifth Amendment, or the Fourth Amendment, or the Sixth Amendment, but there is no attempt to integrate these various standards – to make a fair, honest, and just *whole* out of a painfully fragmented system."

Davies. Justice Geoffrey Davies, of the Queensland Court of Appeal, says the first remedy for the adversary system's unfairness and injustice is "to change the way in which lawyers, judges and law students are educated". If law schools do not change, the community, which helps to fund them, might reasonably ask whether funding should be continued for institutions which send young persons out to be lawyers, judges and legal academics armed with little more than ignorance, casuistry, and thousands of cases in which the judges were probably wrong, confused or had a secret agenda.

Part II

We Are All Fox-Hunters Now:
The Grossly Excessive Adversary System
and Its Consequences

12

The Anti-Oppression Defence of the Common Law

Our accusatory criminal procedure has, it is true, weaknesses and faults. But its great strength is that it has defended us from the oppressive state.

– Justice Michael Kirby, 1995

"Where is the defence of the law written down?" I asked an eminent lawyer when I was researching *Trial by Voodoo*.

"Nowhere," he said.

Blackstone. A defence of a sort is Sir William Blackstone's claim that it is better for 10 guilty persons to get off rather than for one innocent person to go to prison. In fact, as I note elsewhere, in 100 fairly serious cases, some 80 guilty get off, and one innocent person goes to prison.

Kirby. The Hon Mr Justice Michael Kirby, then President of the NSW Court of Appeal, made an eloquent stab at formulating an anti-oppression defence in a 1995 speech, *Crime in Australia*. He seemed to agree with Judge Posner's view that non-lawyers can and do make important contributions to legal theory, and that lawyers ignore such contributions at their peril.

A kindly man, Justice Kirby began: "Evan Whitton's book, *Trial by Voodoo* ... is a book by an experienced and distinguished journalist who takes to task the mode of trial which we have accepted for the proof of criminal accusations. Drawing upon decades of observing criminal trials and Royal Commissions, Mr Whitton is clearly unimpressed by many of our legal rules. Amongst his special targets are the right to silence, the accusatory and adversarial trial system, the hearsay rule and the limitation on the proof of similar facts. He does not much like the judicial discretion to exclude unduly prejudicial evidence ... Those who become impatient with the rules which our criminal justice system has established have their reasons of course. They must be listened to with care, especially if they have the experience in our courts as Mr Whitton does. Outsiders often see error more quickly because they are without preconceptions."

We are but the humble messengers; I was pathetically grateful that his Honour had noticed my little work. But his next word will surprise nobody. "But," he went on, "we who know what the criminal justice system is **really** about must try to explain its ultimate justification. It is to strike the balance between individual rights and criminal law enforcement in a way that keeps the great power of the state and its agencies under check ..." (Emphasis added.)

I admire the "really", and its echo of Sexton and Maher's "lawyers

73

[are seen] as the priests who reveal these principles to laymen ... especially in the case of judges". In fact, as we saw in the last chapter, the priests tend to be cocooned in the bliss of ignorance.

Justice Kirby continued: "Our accusatory criminal procedure has, it is true, weaknesses and faults. But its great strength is that it has defended us from the oppressive state ... The controls imposed by the mode of trial are an ingredient in our liberties. They lie at the very core of our system of criminal justice. That core should not be readily surrendered to **inquisitions**, special tribunals, enforced self-incrimination, the reversed onus, obligatory pre-trial discovery and the many other means that might secure the truth. They may do so at **too high a price**. That is why in criminal law and procedure there must be continuity and respect for fundamentals as well as vigilant attention to reform." (Emphases added.)

Five centuries on from Torquemada, "inquisitions" may seem to be stretching it a bit, but it's nice to learn that dear old Knight-Bruce's Othello Defence still has its adherents. Sadly, however, and with very great respect, I fear His Honour is seriously misinformed. He seems to feel that all nine anti-truth devices are designed to prevent oppression. In fact the only anti-oppression devices are the adversary system and the exclusionary rule and perhaps the right of silence, and they do not defend us from the oppressive state. People who are rightly concerned about oppression should thus surely be examining procedures elsewhere which actually do prevent oppression, and which at the same time seek the truth, but not of course at too high a price.

13

Magic Trick 3

The Adversary System; How Defence Lawyers Captured the Common Law Trial

[The adversary system] operates unfairly in that, both in specific cases and by its general operation, it causes injustice to those who are affected by it.

— Justice Geoffrey Davies, Queensland Court of Appeal, 1996

Ignorance. Legal academics tend not to teach the origins of the adversary system, perhaps because they don't know themselves. In any event, their students know there is money in knowing how to work the system, but none in knowing where it came from. Very few lawyers and judges thus know why, or even when, the system was invented. In the interests of research, in 1996 I unkindly asked a conference of 120 Australian magistrates to raise their hands if they knew. It was reassuring to find that the magistracy are people of integrity: no hand was raised.

European Adversary System. To avoid the pejorative "inquisitorial", some describe the European system as non-adversarial to distinguish it from the English adversarial system. This may be a useful shorthand, but it is not a true dichotomy: all legal systems which set out to be fair and to prevent oppression have some sort of adversary system. In the truth-driven European adversary system, lawyers watch the interests of the accused and the community before the trial and during it; the judge is responsible for gathering **ALL** the facts; he informs himself beforehand and controls the trial. It is accepted that these trials are fair.

English Turnaround. The English accusatorial felony trial has never been fair. Until the 1730s, neither accused nor community had lawyers to watch their interests. A accused B; the judge took the witnesses, including the accused, through their evidence. By the end of the century, defence lawyers had turned the trial round completely: they invented an adversary system so grotesquely extreme that, as Justice Davies observes, it too is unfair and unjust, this time largely to the victim and the community, but sometimes to the accused. Lawyers now control the trial and produce only those facts which will help them win. The system is clearly not truth-driven. Nor does it prevent oppression, and it does not always protect the innocent. But it does make it easy for defence lawyers to get the guilty off.

Swift. In handing over control of trials to lawyers, the judges really had no excuse. In 1726, Dean Swift described them as "a society of men ... bred up from their youth in the art of proving by words multiplied for the purpose that white is black and black is white, according as they are paid". It will be recalled that in 1997 a friend of Sir Garfield Barwick, former Chief Justice of Australia, described him in almost precisely those terms.

The Accused Speaks. In his 1994 piece on the privilege against self-incrimination and the right of silence, Dr John Langbein explains how defence lawyers "captured" the criminal trial. Apologising for the inelegance of the terms, he describes the earlier form of trial as an "accused speaks" procedure and the later form as a "testing the prosecution" procedure. He says: "My theme in this essay is that the privilege against self-incrimination is an artifact of the adversary system of criminal procedure. Only when the modern 'testing the prosecution' theory of the criminal trial displaced the older 'accused speaks' theory did the criminal defendant acquire an effective right to decline to speak to the charges against him. The historical bearer of the new criminal procedure was defense counsel, who crept into the ordinary criminal trial almost unnoticed, and who then worked a drastic procedural revolution with consequences that still reverberate through Anglo-American criminal justice."

Dr Langbein says that from the period of our first knowledge of criminal trials, the middle of the 16th century, until late in the 18th century the fundamental safeguard for the accused "was not the right to remain silent, but rather the opportunity to speak". He had to speak for two reasons:

1. As in the European system, he was regarded as a valuable source of information: whether innocent or guilty, he was close enough to the event to have come under suspicion.

2. He was not allowed to have counsel, although litigants in civil cases were allowed to use lawyers. Without representation, the accused could either speak or, as Langbein puts it, "slit his throat".

Judge As Counsel. The judge was supposed to serve as counsel for the accused, but did not necessarily do it; John Hawkes noted in 1689 that in the 1688 political trials that led to James II's departure, judges "generally have betrayed their poor Client to please, as they apprehended, their better client, the King".

There was usually no prosecution counsel either; the trial judge had to help the accuser establish the prosecution case as well as help the accused on matters of law, but not fact. Langbein quotes John M. Beattie (*Crime and the Courts in England* 1600-1800, 1986) on the process: "The common practice clearly was for the judge to take [the victim and any accusing witnesses] through their testimony line by line, acting as both examiner and cross-examiner, until he was satisfied that the fullest possible case had been presented."

How full is moot; trials were said to be "nasty, brutish and short".

Professor J.H. Baker says "a trial for felony could rarely, in any period have taken more than half an hour". He quotes various sources as estimating the time around 1300 as 10-30 minutes; around 1600 as 15-20 minutes; and 30 minutes at most in the 1750s.

Beattie noted that the judge had the power "to comment on the testimony as it was being given", and so had "immense influence on the way the jury received the evidence and the impression it made on them". The judge thus had total control of the court and the trial, but in the English accusatorial way rather than the European investigative way; he came in without knowledge of the case, and he was not a fact-gatherer in the European sense.

Langbein quotes another work by John M. Beattie, *Scales of Justice: Defense Counsel and the English Criminal Trial in the Eighteenth and Nineteenth Centuries* (1991): "Judges were only occasionally moved to engage in vigorous cross-examination [of suspicious prosecution witnesses] ... For the most part they took the evidence as they found it ... They certainly did not prepare in detail for examination and cross-examination; they were not briefed." The slackness of the judges in not properly cross-examining dubious witnesses no doubt eventually gave defence lawyers the excuse to offer to do it themselves.

Origins. The "epochal" change in criminal trials from the "accused speaks" procedure to the silencing of the accused in the "testing the prosecution" procedure occurred almost unnoticed over a period of a century from 1692. Justice David Ipp quotes Professor Stephan Landsman (*The Rise of the Contentious Spirit: Adversary Procedure in Eighteenth Century England*, Cornell Law Review 1990) on an acorn that, in combination with other factors, grew into the grossly excessive adversary system.

Blood Money. In 1692, Parliament offered rewards of £40 (at least $12,000 of our money) for the arrest of highway robbers and other criminals. Oliver Cyriax says other rates were set at £1 for betraying a deserter and £10 for a horse thief. To get the reward, constables and others concocted evidence. Jonathan Wild, the famous organised criminal mentioned earlier, had it coming and going: he ran a large gang of thieves and accused them for the reward.

Treason Act. Defence lawyers got a toe in the criminal door in 1696 when Whig reformers enacted the Treason Act "to even things up". It allowed lawyers to appear on behalf of accused, but only in rarely-held treason trials. They were allowed in to even the scales: unfair treason trials under the Stuarts used prosecuting counsel who did their job with more than ordinary "skill and zeal". The Treason Act gave the accused the right to make "full defence, by counsel"; Dr Langbein says this meant that "defense counsel would be permitted not only to examine and cross-examine, but also to sum up and to address the jury about the merits of the defendant's case". That is fine, except for cross-examination: as Dr Langbein observes, "cross-

77

examination ... is often an engine of oppression and obfuscation, deliberately employed to defeat the truth".

Langbein says: "There appears to have been a considerable increase in the use of prosecution counsel in the 1710s and 1720s." To again even the scales, judges began to use a judicial discretion in the 1730s to allow defence lawyers into ordinary felony cases.

Cricket. The English were always fond of games; as it happens, the invention of the adversary system and the concept of law as a game came a generation after the formal invention of cricket. The London Cricket Club drew up the first authoritative set of cricket rules in 1744. It is said that in the adversary system the lawyers occasionally shout, "How's that?" and the judge raises his finger or shakes his wig.

The Fox-Hunter's Argument. If the cricket (or baseball) image is accurate for the new and diminished role of the judge, fox-hunting is an accurate image for the new criminal justice system invented by defence lawyers via the adversary system and rules for concealing evidence. In *Miranda* (1966), the US Supreme Court made it obligatory for police to warn suspects to say nothing and get a lawyer, a case of fairness happily coinciding with the interests of lawyers in the cartel. Judge Harold Rothwax said: "*Miranda* has been called, derisively, a 'fox-hunter's argument' – that is, the defendant, like a fox during a hunt, must be given a fair chance to escape. In this way, the criminal justice system becomes a sporting event in which the defendant has a sporting chance to evade society's punishment." Roscoe Pound's sporting theory of justice is noted in chapter 15.

CROSS EXAMINATION

Defence Counsel Appear. Dr Langbein says: "The sources are not good enough to allow us to measure with precision how frequently defense counsel appeared in the eighteenth century. Beattie's cautious account points to the 1780s [i.e. the last years of Lord Mansfield's period (1756-88) as Chief Justice.] His calculations reckon percentages of defense counsel at the Old Bailey as low as 2.1% in the 1770s, increasing to 20.2% in 1786, and to a high of 36.6% in 1795."

Langbein also says: "We do not yet have an adequate historical account of the stages by which this transformation occurred, and the historical sources are sufficiently impoverished that we may never recover the events in adequate detail. Nevertheless, the outline seems tolerably clear. Across these decades, defense counsel broke up the 'accused speaks' trial ... The initial restrictions on the role of defense counsel at trial suggest that his primary responsibility in the eighteenth century was cross-examining prosecution witnesses. Especially in cases involving reward seekers and crown witnesses, those shady figures whom the embattled London authorities sometimes employed to compensate for the English reluctance to institute professional policing, vigorous cross-examination often proved decisive. Thus, as Beattie remarks, defense counsel 'began to shift the focus of the defense in a fundamental way by casting doubt on the validity of the factual case being presented against the defendant, so that the prosecution came increasingly under the necessity of proving its assertions'."

What Judges Accepted. Langbein notes six elements which defence lawyers had persuaded judges to accept by the end of the process:

1. The concept of "cases" for prosecution and defence.

2. The beyond-reasonable-doubt standard of proof and its implied presumption of innocence. Defence lawyers could now insist that the prosecutor prove his case by means other than out of the mouth of the accused. Langbein notes: "We have seen how relentlessly the earlier system of trial pressured the criminal defendant to speak. Within the space of a few decades, the expectation that the accused would defend himself disappeared. Defense counsel made possible that remarkable silence of the accused that has ever since astonished European commentators.

"As early as 1820, an official French observer, Cottu [M. Cottu: *On the Administration of Criminal Justice in England*, 1820], reported back to his government that in English criminal procedure prosecuting counsel was 'forbidden to question the prisoner ... in England the defendant acts no kind of part; his hat stuck on a pole might without inconvenience be his substitute at the trial'."

3. Diminution of the prosecution case by the invention of rules for concealing evidence. Beattie says "defense counsel sought to limit the case their clients would have to answer" by objecting to the

admission of certain kinds of evidence, "and most especially by [their conduct of] cross-examination".

4. An upward spiral of lawyers in courts: the growing use and effectiveness of defence counsel resulted in greater use of prosecuting counsel.

5. The decline in importance of the judge's role as counsel for prosecution and defence took over the job of examining and cross-examining witnesses. Cottu wrote in 1820 that "the judge ... remains almost a stranger to what is going on"; all he did was take notes and summarise them for the jury at the end of the trial.

6. The end of the judge's influence over the jury. Langbein says: "Counsel's increasing control of the conduct of the trial was inconsistent with the older informal system of jury control that presupposed the casual intimacy of judge and jury."

It seems that lawyers did not immediately begin to string criminal trials out. Professor Baker says: "The unseemly hurry of Old Bailey trials even in the early nineteenth century was disgraceful; the average length of a trial was a few minutes, and 'full two-thirds of prisoners, on their return from their trials, cannot tell of any thing which has passed in court, not even, very frequently, whether they have been tried'." (Anon: *Old Bailey Experiences*, 1833)

End of Blood Money. Reward money for highwaymen and other criminals was withdrawn in 1826. By then defence lawyers had contrived to lock the grossly excessive version of the adversary system in to the common law; the nominal reason for it – blood money – was probably forgotten.

* * *

Summary. I pause for a brief summary. The common law has never had independent fact-gatherers in the truth-seeking European sense. From the 13th century the judge was not really a fact-gatherer; he questioned the accused and the witnesses on the basis of the accuser's claims. In the 18th century, judges handed the process over to lawyers, but it remained accusatorial: defence lawyers questioned witnesses on the basis of the accuser's claims. The lawyers also got control of civil trials, but it would be ludicrous to describe them as fact-gatherers in the European sense: they seek to gather only those facts which help their case and to hide those which don't. Judge Marvin Frankel (see chapter 39: Solutions to the Agonies of Civil Litigation) says: "It is the rare case in which either side yearns to have the witnesses, or anyone, give *the whole truth*." (Judge Frankel's emphasis.)

* * *

Adversary System Queried. In October 1996, Australia's first law officer, federal Attorney-General Daryl Williams QC, asked the Australian Law Reform Commission to examine the adversary system to see if there was something better. Fia Cumming reported *(The Sun-Herald* October 13, 1996) that Williams told the commission to virtually wipe the slate clean and come up with a simpler, cheaper, and more accessible system for civil, family and administrative law; the commission would consider "dramatic" changes in the education of lawyers and judges and the "culture" of litigation lawyers. Cumming said it was not expected to recommend changes to criminal trial procedures, and that it would be assisted by an advisory group of leading judges, retired judges and academics.

Does that group sound like elements of the cartel? It would be surprising if they knew much about the origins of the grossly excessive version of the system, and even more surprising if they recommended winding it back to the reasonable European version.

14

Lord Thankerton Knits; Lord Coleridge Sleeps

Lawyers, and the law itself, are more at home making and observing rules than exercising judgment

— Adrian Roden QC, 1989

Legal academics John Beattie and John Langbein, having researched the invention of the grossly excessive version of the adversary system, agree that the impetus came from defence lawyers. That makes sense; along with criminals, they were the major beneficiaries. Short of handing the courts over to the criminals, it would be difficult to imagine a worse solution to a problem of oppression: defence lawyers have to accept instructions from their clients even when they believe they are lying; prosecution lawyers may also feel obliged to believe fabricating police witnesses. The extreme adversary system effectively became a riot of fabrication and perversion of justice by defence and prosecution alike.

A question remains: why did judges give up such huge power to lawyers? Because of the "impoverishment" of the sources, we can only speculate; I note a few possibilities:

The Malady? Discussing Lord Mayors of Sydney with the Town Clerk, Leon Carter, I observed that Mayor Leo Port was a crook. Carter said perhaps he was mad; perhaps he thought he was doing the right thing. Likewise judges: if they could not foresee the consequences of giving lawyers control of trials, they clearly found it hard to think straight.

Sloth? Until the 18th century, common law judges were looking for a result rather than truth, so they never had to do the work that European judges did: they did not have to master the brief or examine and cross-examine so thoroughly. Perhaps the prospect of doing even less was attractive. Some later judges apparently found it so. John Duke, Lord Coleridge (1820-94, Chief Justice of the Court of Common Pleas 1873-80, Chief Justice of the Queen's Bench 1880-94) caught up with his sleep; Lady Coleridge had to sit on the bench and kick him when he dropped off. The once and future financier, Rufus Isaacs, Lord Reading (1860-1935), caught up with his business correspondence. Willie Watson, Lord Thankerton (1873-1948, Lord of Appeal in Ordinary 1929-1948), caught up with his knitting.

Blackmail? As a politician and member of corrupt Cabinets, Lord Chief Justice Mansfield, who presided over the transfer of power from judges to lawyers, may have been susceptible to blackmail by unscrupulous lawyers. His acolyte, Sir William Blackstone, legal academic and judge, was not the sort of lawyer to blow the whistle on Mansfield or the system.

The Bureaucrat. What you lose on the roundabouts, you make up on the razzle dazzles. Former Justice Adrian Roden observes: "[Common] lawyers, and the law itself, are more at home making and observing rules than exercising judgment." John Wareham, a New York management consultant who uses personality tests in his business, says the law attracts a wide range of people, including the bureaucratic type, who tend to become judges. Bureaucrats score highly on rule consciousness, conformity, timidity, avoidance of risk; they must operate in a zero-risk environment or be crucified for making a mistake. The bureaucrat blindly follows rules even when they have no meaning. Defence lawyers, in a way, were offering the judges power of a different sort: the power to rule on a series of shiny new rules (magic tricks) which defence lawyers said the adversary system made necessary.

The Psychopath. Wareham says the law also attracts a few psychopathic types, and they tend to remain lawyers. A psychopath has no conscience, lies easily, conceals information, and is very interested in money. It is tempting to suspect that psychopaths were behind the invention of the adversary system, but that is not necessary; non-psychopathic lawyers are sometimes more sharply intelligent and aggressive than those who have gone up to the bench; the judges may simply have been overborne by such advocates.

15

The Adversary System: Defence and Criticism

There is no difference in principle between a decision based on a contest of procedural skill between two attorneys and a decision based on a contest of strength between two armed champions.

— Professor Sunderland, 1926

"Duty". Justice Byron (Whizzer) White, Rhodes Scholar and professional football player with the Detroit Lions, explicated the "duty" the adversary system imposes on "the most honorable defense counsel" in *United States v Wade* (Supreme Court, 1967). He said: "But defense counsel has no comparable obligation to ascertain or present the truth. Our system assigns him a different mission ... Defense counsel need present nothing, even if he knows what the truth is. He need not furnish any witnesses to the police, or reveal any confidences of his client, or furnish any other information to help the prosecution's case. If he can confuse a witness, even a truthful one, or make him appear at a disadvantage, unsure or indecisive, that will be his normal course. Our interest in not convicting the innocent permits counsel to put the State to its proof, to put the State's case in the worst possible light, regardless of what he thinks or knows to be the truth ... more often than not, defense counsel will cross-examine a prosecution witness and impeach him if he can, even if he thinks the witness is telling the truth ... In this respect, as part of our modified [!] adversary system and as part of the duty imposed on the most honorable defense counsel, we countenance or require conduct which in many instances has little, if any, relation to the truth."

Getting The Guilty Off. Justice White is saying in effect that the importance of not convicting the innocent sometimes requires honourable defence lawyers to deceive the jury, i.e. the community, on behalf of their clients. That is presumably the basis of the response of a Sydney lawyer, Stuart Littlemore QC, to a television interviewer, Andrew Denton, on Channel 7 in October 1995: "It's a classic question," Denton said. "If you're in a situation where you are defending someone who you yourself believe not to be innocent – can you continue to defend them?"

"Well, they're the best cases," Littlemore replied. "I mean, you really feel you've done something when you get the guilty off. Anyone can get an innocent person off; I mean, they shouldn't be on trial. But the guilty – that's the challenge."

"Don't you in some sense share in their guilt?"

"Not at all ..."

Littlemore also anchors a community-funded television programme called Media Watch and is properly scathing when reporters deceive the community. This points up the difference between the common law and journalism: lawyers are allowed to deceive the community but reporters are not.

Goodpaster. Nicholas Cowdery QC quotes remarks by one Goodpaster (*On the Theory of American Adversary Criminal Trial*, 78 Jnl Crim Law & Criminology, 1987, 118): "The major explanations of adversary trial are that its purpose is truth-finding; that it leads to fair decisions; that it protects the people from oppression or potential oppression by government; that, as a stalemate system, it is conducive to bargaining; and that finally [and somewhat by way of contradiction, notes Cowdery] it is a process designed to produce publicly acceptable conclusions which project substantive legal norms, whether or not those conclusions are grounded in true facts."

The Mallory Justification. Professor David Luban, of Georgetown University, says: "There are four standard arguments on behalf of the adversary system. These are:

1 that it is the best way to find the truth;

2 that it is the best way to ensure that all parties' rights are protected;

3 that it is part of our tradition and culture; and

4 that it follows from the notion that a lawyer is an agent whose client is the principal ... the lawyer is giving voice to arguments that the client would make, and is entitled to make ... the adversary system is the way clients participate in the litigation process."

Luban says that all those arguments fail but, "unlike such scholars as John Langbein, I **don't** propose abandoning the adversary system ... a common-law country should retain the adversary system because

1 it needs **some** procedural system;

2 the available alternatives aren't demonstrably better than the adversary system; and

3 the adversary system is the system in place. This is the pragmatic justification for the adversary system. It is logically weak but practically strong".

On my reading Professor Langbein does not advocate abandoning the adversary system; he merely suggests it be used properly. It also appears that the available alternative is fairer and more accurate in verdict, and is not haunted by the miscarriages (both ways) that disfigure the adversary system. In the end, Professor Luban's pragmatic defence sounds like the Mallory Justification. George H. Leigh Mallory (1886-1924) was last seen one afternoon in 1924 "going strong for the top" of Mt Everest. Why? Because it was there.

Dingo Cleared. In response to a piece on the defects of the adversary system (The Australian, 11.2.97), Ian Barker QC (who was elected president of the NSW Bar Association in December 1997), wrote: "One of the sillier books of the decade is by Evan Whitton, called Trial by Voodoo ... In it, Mr Whitton tries to mount an attack on our criminal justice system, urging that it be replaced by some sort of standing inquisition ... People like Evan Whitton assume they will never be arrested ... To me, Mr Whitton's fulminations on the subject of criminal justice are a good argument for retaining our adversarial system, imperfect as it is."

I gently replied that Mr Barker may have been right but perhaps not the right person to say so. Those who saw the 1988 Meryl Streep/Sam Neill film, *A Cry in the Dark* (Australian title: *Evil Angels*), will recall that a dingo (a wild dog) murdered Lindy Chamberlain's baby, Azaria. The adversary system did not help the innocent Mrs Chamberlain: she was arrested, charged with murder, found guilty, and sent to prison. In effect, the prosecutor, Ian Barker QC, got the guilty dingo off.

Judgment of God Reinvented. Justice David Ipp said: "It has been pointed out that we smile when we are told about trial by battle, but in essence trial by battle flourishes under the unadulterated or classical adversarial system." He then quoted Professor Sunderland's observation (in *The English Struggle for Procedural Reform*, Harvard Law Review, 1926) noted in the epigraph to this chapter. Six centuries after European courts opted for truth, common law defence lawyers had contrived to reinvent the Judgment of God.

As Justice Ipp and Professor Sunderland imply, justice is bound to miscarry one way or the other if the lawyers are not evenly matched. In the case of a powerful prosecutor and a weak defence lawyer, the adversary system achieves the very thing it was supposed to stop:

the conviction of the innocent. In the circumstances, the cartel's spin doctors would have to work hard to get the adversary system accepted by the community. They did their best; Justice Ipp notes that "the 19th century opened upon a legal system which inspired the most extravagant eulogies from the Bench and Bar. There was a startling degree of smugness and self-satisfaction".

It did not quite work; Justice Ipp: "The press and the general community did not share this sense of wellbeing. There was considerable tension between the public and the courts". Nor did all the fulminating against the adversary system over the next two centuries come from the Press and the general community.

Lawyer-Infested. The invention of the extreme adversary system presumably caused a sharp increase in the number of lawyers. The US now has one lawyer for every 350 persons; Australia has one for every 660. Japan, which does not have an adversary system, has one for every 9000. Europe does not have an adversary system; as noted in chapter 1, Dr Edward de Bono says if a US company has 50 lawyers, its European equivalent is likely to have one lawyer. The European approach to civil litigation is examined in chapter 39.

Accessories after the Fact. Jeremy Bentham (1748-1832), jurist and would-be law reformer, suggested that where the accused is guilty the defence lawyer is effectively an accomplice after the fact, not to mention a perverter of justice. He said of the cartel and the adversary system: "A man has committed a theft; another man who has assisted him in making his escape is punished as an accomplice. But the law (that is, the judges) ... have contrived to grant to their connexions acting in the character of advocates a licence for this purpose. What the non-advocate is hanged for, the advocate is paid for and admired."

At best, the defence lawyer is proceeding with a reckless disregard for the truth that no respectable trade would tolerate. Prosecution lawyers can also effectively be accessories after the fact of police fabrication.

Roscoe Pound's Sporting Theory. Professor Landsman reports in *Readings on Adversarial Justice* that in 1906 Roscoe Pound (1870-1964) "delivered a speech before the American Bar Association that shocked the organised bar. He challenged lawyers' smug and complacent belief in the excellence of the legal system and suggested that there was much with which to be dissatisfied". Pound's speech might seem an elaboration of the obvious; the cartel was presumably shocked not so much by what Pound said but that a member of the cartel would let the cat out of the bag.

Pound said: "A ... potent source of irritation lies in our American exaggerations of the common law contentious procedure. The sporting theory of justice ... is so rooted in the profession in America that most of us take it for a fundamental legal tenet ... So far from being a fundamental fact of jurisprudence, it is peculiar to Anglo-American law ... Hence in America we take it as a matter of course that a judge should be a mere umpire, to pass upon objections and hold counsel to the rules of the game, and that the parties should fight out their own game in their own way without judicial interference ...

"The idea that procedure must of necessity be wholly contentious disfigures our judicial administration at every point. It leads the most conscientious judge to feel that he is merely to decide the contest as counsel present it according to the rules of the game, not to search independently for truth and justice. It leads counsel to forget that they are officers of the court and to deal with the rules of law and procedure exactly as the professional foot ball coach deals with the rules of the sport ... It turns witnesses, and especially expert witnesses, into partisans pure and simple. It leads to sensational cross-examinations 'to affect credit' which have made the witness stand 'the slaughter house of reputations'. It prevents the trial court from restraining the bullying of witnesses and creates a general dislike, if not fear, of the witness function which impairs the administration of justice ... The inquiry is not, What do substantive law and justice require? Instead, the inquiry is, Have the rules of the game been carried out strictly? If any material infraction is discovered, just as the foot ball rules put back the offending team five or ten or fifteen yards, as the case may be, our sporting theory of justice awards new trials, or reverses judgments, or sustains demurrers in the interest of regular play.

"The effect of our exaggerated contentious procedure is not only to irritate parties, witnesses and jurors in particular cases, but to give to the whole community a false notion of the purpose and end of law. Hence comes, in large measure, the modern American race to beat the law. If the law is a mere game, neither the players who take part in it nor the public who witness it can be expected to yield to its spirit when their interests are served by evading it ... the courts, instituted to administer justice according to law, are made agents or abettors of lawlessness ..."

He concluded with what may now seem a large dose of irony: "With law schools that are rivaling the achievements of Bologna and of Bourges to promote scientific study of the law; with active Bar Associations in every state to revive professional feeling and throw off the yoke of commercialism; with the passing of the doctrine that politics, too, is a mere game to be played for its own sake, we may look forward confidently to deliverance from the sporting theory of justice; we may look forward to a near future when our courts will be swift and certain agents of justice, whose decisions will be acquiesced in and respected by all."

Roscoe Pound was Dean of the Harvard Law School from 1916 to 1936; the sporting theory has long outlived him.

The Price of Justice. Janet Chan and Lynne Barnes observe some effects of the adversary system in *The Price of Justice? – Lengthy Criminal Trials in Australia.* They quote an unidentified judge talking about an unidentified case: "The defence were very suspicious of the Crown and the Crown of the defence. Everyone's sort of paranoia came to the fore ... the committal hearing went on for months ... The Crown was appalled by what had happened at the committal. They took the view that the defence would stop at nothing to 'derail the trial'; [that] was one of the prosecutor's favourite expressions ...

"They made up their mind that the defence would stop at nothing to secure the acquittal of the accused ... So they, I think, became paranoid about the defence tactics and of course that produced even more theory on the defence side and nothing could ever be agreed. They were at loggerheads the whole time. They'll tell you they weren't, but they were." The lawyers would no doubt say they were only doing their job.

The Bar Culture. There was much hand-wringing about the police culture during Justice James Wood's 1994-97 Royal Commission on police corruption, but the Bar culture may be an equally intractable problem. In a way, the two collided in a Victorian case noted by Chan and Barnes; in terms of length and cost to the community, the adversary system reached perhaps its finest flower and logical conclusion: the judge apparently felt obliged in the interests of fairness to let lawyers speak endlessly. *R v Higgins* could not compare with Dickens' *Jarndyce v Jarndyce* in *Bleak House*, but it seemed to be heading in that direction: it proceeded for six years.

Chan and Barnes derive the details from a Victorian Court of Criminal Appeal (CCA) judgment on the case in 1994.

Paul William Higgins, a detective, was charged in 1987 with obstructing the course of justice between 1977 and 1983; it was alleged that he conspired to protect brothel-keepers. The committal hearing began in October 1987 but was "aborted after 10 months when the Director of Public Prosecutions (DPP) withdrew the information against the accused on the basis that the conduct of the defence case was an abuse of the court process".

Oppression. Chan and Barnes note that the trial judge said of the committal hearing: "Issues were canvassed interminably often in an abrasive way and, on occasions, in an offensive way ... It seems to me that the Director [of Public Prosecutions] had good grounds for concluding that what was occurring was inordinately protracted and at times excessively oppressive to the witnesses."

The DPP filed new charges in August 1988. Chan and Barnes state, apparently on the basis of the CCA judgment: "Counsel for the defence went to trial with the view that the Crown was determined to obtain conviction at all costs, while the prosecution saw every defence effort as a tactic to subvert the trial." The CCA judges "suggested that the care with which the trial judge considered all questions at times contributed to the length of the proceedings". The barristers obliged the judge to listen to legal argument, i.e. what relevant evidence would be concealed from the jury, for more than 120 days.

"An Alarming Culture". The trial proper finally began in November 1991 and ran for 298 sitting days. Chan and Barnes note that the trial judge blamed the length of the trial partly on "an alarming culture at the Victorian Bar, which dictates to those afflicted by it that there is no such thing as a case which is too long or too costly, that no issue is too small to be explored at excruciating length, that no number of questions is too many, that no speech is too long, and that concessions or admissions must practically never be made for fear of their unknown consequences".

Higgins was found guilty in March 1993 of four counts of conspiracy to obstruct justice. The CCA judges, who presumably had the melancholy duty of reading the transcript, grumped: "That the trial itself should see two Christmases come and go, extending over a period of 17 months, with the final addresses and summing up spread over three months, is itself a reproach to the legal system." Chan and Barnes say that "at an estimated $20,000 per day ... a trial such as *Higgins* has the potential of taking up a considerable slice of the criminal justice budget". Not to mention the legal aid budget. *Higgins* must have cost the community something like $12 million; at $800 a day, a fact-gathering judge must be a better proposition.

Elliott. Apparently nothing changed. Speaking for the Victorian Court of Appeal in September 1997, Justice Robert Brooking said of *Elliott* (1996, see chapter 29): "This case reinforces my view that criminal proceedings in this State are in some respects out of control ... Nowadays actual or contemplated criminal proceedings spawn civil proceedings, and as a result quasi-criminal cases, civil in form but really concerned with criminal liability, which were unknown not so long ago, now occupy our lists. In the present case we have had four years of legal proceedings. I cannot regard as satisfactory a criminal justice system which can permit what has happened here."

Lord Devlin. Justice Michael Kirby was Chairman of the Australian Law Reform Commission 1975-84, President of the NSW Court of Appeal 1984-96 and a judge of the Australian High Court since 1996. He told a Rotary Club in 1980: "At the end of last year, Lord Devlin, a former judge of the House of Lords, published a scathing criticism of the adversary trial ... he acknowledges that this remnant of the medieval trial by ordeal remains the 'centrepiece' of the English way of doing justice ... Both in the criminal and civil courts, Lord Devlin urged that we should reconsider the cost effectiveness of the adversary trial system. In the criminal area particularly, Devlin asserted that there should be less emphasis on 'winning the case' and a greater stress on dispassionately finding the truth of the matter ... It is when lawyers stop talking of justice and fairness and content themselves with the form of things and the letter of the law that society expresses its disquiet. The Law Reform Commission is one instrument designed to ensure that fundamental questions are asked about our legal system and that assumptions about its fairness are constantly put to public test. In our inquiry into Federal evidence law, there will be no sacrosanct procedures: not even the centrepiece of our legal system: not even the adversary trial itself."

Kennedy. Sir (as he now is) Ludovic Kennedy, the leading authority on miscarriages, said in 1989 that the adversary system "is not only extremely childish, but a most unsatisfactory way of attempting to dispense justice". He said that by the time it was invented in England in the 18th century, "in France they had already established the system of the examining magistrate sifting out prosecution witnesses and preparing a dossier on the case for the trial judge". In England meanwhile, Kennedy said, "the adversary system came about, in the words of Charles Langbein, Professor of Law at Chicago University, 'slowly, incrementally, without plan or theory' until it became the top heavy, wholly artificial creature that it is today ... Is that really the best we can do? If we were devising a system of justice today from scratch, would it ever occur to us to dream up something so patently idiotic and inefficient as this?"

De Bono. Dr Edward de Bono, author of *Teach Your Child to Think*, says: "The adversarial method is the basis for our politics, law and daily life. The method is a very limited and defective system ... would one party be inclined to bring forward a point that favoured the other side?" The technique was demonstrated in October 1993, when John Howard, then leader of the Australian Opposition, asked the then Prime Minister, Paul Keating: "How can you justify opposition to non-union competition on the waterfront in Fremantle which would deliver a 20 per cent reduction in costs to users?"

"I cannot understand," Keating replied, shifting the goalposts, "why the leader of the Opposition hates working people the way he does."

Dobies. John Dobies, an Australian lawyer, said in 1996: "Court procedure has little to do with truth or justice. Once we are in court we play this game called Courtroom. The idea is to win this game using this set of strange – at times impenetrable – rules."

Posner. Judge Posner speaks of " ... the lawyers' mystical faith in the production of truth by contests of liars – contests more likely to produce dizziness than knowledge ..."

Cowdery. Nicholas Cowdery QC is Director of Public Prosecutions in NSW, and so has a first-hand and informed view of the effects of the system. He told Sydney's St James Ethics Centre in August 1997: "The adversarial system ... is another obstacle to the marriage of lawyers and justice. It is not directed to the ascertainment of truth, despite our pretences to the contrary, especially in criminal law. The attainment of justice becomes incidental to the immediate battle ... In war the first casualty is truth. It has become a casualty in the battles of law as well – and with it has gone any commitment to the cause of justice ... As a general proposition in our system a lawyer with a client works hard to avoid justice being done or, even worse, the truth being discovered and orders being made accordingly – unless of course justice or the truth coincides (as it does occasionally) with the selfish interests of the client."

Frank. Cowdery quoted Jerome Frank [*Courts on Trial*, Princeton UP, 1950]: " ... the lawyer aims at ... winning in the fight, not at aiding the court to discover the facts. He does not want the trial court to reach a sound educated guess, if it is likely to be contrary to his client's interests. Our present trial method is thus the equivalent of throwing pepper in the eyes of a surgeon when he is performing an operation."

Parasites. Cowdery continued: "In many quarters of society we are seen as useless and expensive parasites. Those of us in narrow specialities do a necessary job, but so do undertakers and garbage collectors, and they do not cost nearly so much."

A Bulwark of Liberty. Despite persistent criticism of the extreme version of the system over two centuries, the cartel's public relations apparatus has contrived to entrench it as what Justice Lionel Murphy, of the Australian High Court, would probably have called "a fundamental bulwark of liberty", if largely for the guilty, e.g. Justice Murphy.

16

Playing the Saxophone:
The Adversary System in Action

The great defect of much of the fiction written about legal life is that the barrister there discovers what really happened. The reality is that the adversary process of a trial more often leaves the truth mysteriously hidden, covered over by the evasions and half-truths of competing contentions.

– David Pannick QC

Perry Mason. Erle Stanley Gardner (1889-1972), an "ingenious lawyer for the defence" 1922-1938, is, or should be, one of the great heroes of the defence lawyers, along with Procurator Pontius Pilate, Sir James Dyer, Lord Mansfield, Sir William Blackstone, Sir James Lewis Knight-Bruce, Lord Reading, and Justice Tom Clark. Beginning with *The Case of the Velvet Claws* (1933), he wrote 82 courtroom dramas in which defence lawyer Perry Mason often persuaded the guilty person to confess in the witness box. Gardner and most of his spawn thus give citizens the false notion that the common law and its adversary system seeks and finds the truth.

Anatomy of a Murder. Judge John D. Voelker (1903-91) is another hero of the defence lawyers. He wrote *Anatomy of a Murder* in 1958 under the pen name Robert Traver. Otto Preminger made it into a 160-minute film in 1959 with James Stewart as Paul Biegler, a small-town lawyer, Ben Gazzara as the client charged with murdering a bartender who had assaulted his wife, George C. Scott as the prosecutor, and Joe Welch as the judge. As lawyer for the Army, Welch had put Senator Joe McCarthy out of business in 1954. The film (and no doubt the book) is a useful document in that it shows how the common law really works, but in a sense it is more sinister than Gardner's drivel: all-American hero Jimmy Stewart gives viewers the impression that it is proper for a lawyer to help his client fabricate a defence to murder.

The Lecture. Fred D. Shapiro quotes from the book *Anatomy of a Murder*: "The Lecture is an ancient device that lawyers use to coach their clients so that the client won't quite know he has been coached and his lawyer can still preserve the face-saving illusion that he hasn't done any coaching ... 'Who, me? I didn't tell him what to say,' the lawyer can later comfort himself. 'I merely explained the law, see ...'"

"You mean," [the client] said, "that my only possible defense in this case is to find some justification or excuse?"

My lecture was proceeding nicely to schedule. "You're learning rapidly," I said, nodding approvingly. "Merely add *legal* justification or excuse and I'll mark you an A."

"And you say that a man is not justified in killing a man who has just raped and beat up his wife?"

"Morally, perhaps, but not legally."

In the film, Stewart "lectured" Gazzara that the law might find a murderer innocent if he was momentarily mad at the time, and told him to go back to his cell and think about it. Gazzara took the hint and Stewart duly got him off. The film, and presumably Judge Voelker's book, did have a tiny nod in the direction of justice, but not for murderer, victim or community: the murderer decamped without paying his shyster the fee. More than 30 years later, lawyers for Lorena Bobbitt successfully used the same defence in her penis-slicing case.

Corruption. In the common law adversary system, police, not judges, are in charge of the pre-trial fact-gathering process; lawyers, not judges, are in charge of the fact-gathering process at trial. On August 3, 1995 Justice James Wood, inquiring into police corruption in NSW, summed up what may be seen as some of the consequences of the system on prosecution and defence.

Justice Wood said: "I regard the manipulation of the criminal court process as the ultimate and potentially most cynical, arrogant and dangerous face of corruption that can exist. It in fact is a quintessential hallmark or sign of the existence of systematic corruption and it can take a number of forms, including, but without being exhaustive, at least the following:

"One, the watering down of a prosecution case, either in terms of withholding vital evidence or witnesses, or in reducing the quantity of drugs or money involved.

"Secondly, the manufacture of a false brief on the prosecution side by means of 'bricking in' or 'loading' an accused.

"Thirdly, on the defence side, the manufacture and use of untrue or slanted evidence, whether it be of fact or expert opinion.

"Four, the provision and use of fake or untrue character references.

"Five, the withholding or doctoring of criminal antecedents.

"And six, the failure of the prosecution to offer a case for the ostensible reason that witnesses cannot be found or are unwilling to co-operate as a result of fear or pressure exerted upon them, that is, without appropriate investigation of the truth of such an assertion ...

"It is exceedingly bad if it is the Police Service or members of it who are corrupt; it is totally unacceptable and a horrifying situation once it extends to experts, private inquiry agents, the legal profession or others."

In his report in 1997, Justice Wood did not recommend that the system be changed.

O.J. Simpson. The O.J. Simpson criminal trial probably did as much to destroy the adversary system as Erle Stanley Gardner did to preserve it. Professor Luban says: "The O.J. Simpson trial has persuaded most Americans that the adversary system is at best grotesque."

"Legal argument" is a euphemism for discussion between the lawyers and the judge about what evidence will be concealed from the jury. There were some 16,000 objections at the Simpson murder trial. Dickens seems to have been right.

Only Doing His Duty. Soon after Simpson's former wife was murdered, Simpson was sighted in his white Bronco and tracked by television cameras. Robert Shapiro, his lawyer, announced that Simpson had only US$50, but it emerged that he had a passport, a false beard, a loaded gun and US$8000. Shapiro's apparent economy with the truth was accepted on the basis that "he was only doing his duty to his client". The jury at Simpson's criminal trial did not hear about his apparent attempt to flee the country, nor did they hear from Simpson.

Shifting the Goalposts. In February 1995 Gloria Allred, a lawyer for the family of the murdered Nicole Brown Simpson, said during the Simpson criminal trial there had been a "calculated strategy to put the victim and her family on trial and the purpose of this strategy is clear: to cheapen the reputation of Nicole by describing her, for example, as a party girl rather than as a mother of two children, and by portraying her as a slut rather than the devoted daughter of her mum and dad."

Carl Douglas, a lawyer for Simpson, accused Ronald Shipp, a former policeman who described himself as a longtime friend of Simpson, of a list of misdeeds including chronic drinking and using Simpson's spa bath with a woman not his wife. Prosecutor Christopher Darden complained to Judge Lance Ito in chambers about the questioning of Shipp. He said: "We can't destroy the lives of every witness who takes the witness stand, you know, just to suit Simpson's needs. We've hit an all-time low here, I think I don't know if you guys can go any lower."

"That's baloney," Simpson's lawyer, Johnnie Cochran replied.

In Simpson's case, the shift was from murder to race. In the case of Said Morgan, a Sydney policeman who admitted firing six shots into a man, the shift seems to have been to the victim, an alleged paedophile. In the case of Dean Waters, who admitted taking part in a killing on his father's instructions, the shift seems to have been to parental abuse. All were acquitted.

Expert Witnesses. Edward St John QC said: "Everyone knows that certain cases are decided by which side gets to the most expert witness first." Dr Michael Crowley notes the difference between the common law system, where expert witnesses are appointed by the lawyers, and the European system, where they are independently appointed by the court.

The "Saxophone". Defence lawyers often find the civil liberties "violin" a useful instrument to pluck. Professor John Langbein notes another instrument. He said: "At the American trial bar, those of us who serve as expert witnesses are known as 'saxophones'. This is a revealing term, as slang often is. The idea is that the lawyer plays the tune, manipulating the expert as though the expert were a musical instrument on which the lawyer sounds the desired notes. I sometimes serve as an expert in trust and pension cases, and I have experienced the subtle pressures to join the team – to shade one's views, to conceal doubt, to overstate nuance, to downplay weak aspects of the case that one has been hired to bolster. Nobody likes to disappoint a patron; and beyond this psychological pressure is the financial inducement. Money changes hands upon the rendering of expertise, but the expert can run his meter only so long as his patron litigator likes his tune. Opposing counsel undertakes a similar exercise, hiring and schooling another expert to parrot the contrary position.

"The result is our familiar battle of opposing experts. The more measured and impartial an expert is, the less likely he is to be used by either side. At trial the battle of experts tends to baffle the trier, especially in jury courts. If the experts do not cancel each other out, the advantage is likely to be with the expert whose forensic skills are the more enticing. The system invites abusive cross-examination. Since each expert is party-selected and party-paid, he is vulnerable to attack on credibility regardless of the merits of his testimony ...

"The case against adversary domination of fact-gathering is so compelling that we have cause to wonder why our system tolerates it. Because there is nothing to be said in support of coached witnesses, and very little to be said in favour of litigation-biased experts, defenders of the American status quo are left to argue that the advantages of our adversary procedure counterbalance these grievous, truth-defeating distortions. 'You have to take the bad with the good; if you want adversary safeguards, you are stuck with adversary excess'."

"Deeply Corrupting". Dr Crowley quotes J. R. Spencer and R. Flin (*The Evidence of Children*, Blackstone, 1990) as stating that in Britain "courts tend to distrust expert evidence". He says "they suggest this distrust is related to the 'deeply corrupting effect' of the adversarial system which ensures 'that much of the expert evidence the court receives is unreliable through bias'." By contrast, Dr Crowley notes, in France, Germany and Sweden "the potential for bias in the presentation of expert evidence is minimised as the expert gives his/her evidence as a 'neutral servant of the court' within the framework of an inquisitorial system of law".

Justice Geoffrey Davies, chairman of the Queensland Litigation Reform Commission, said in *A Blueprint for Reform* that the adversary system "tends to make advocates of the witnesses. This view, or at least our consequent proposal for court-appointed experts, is one which is strongly and emotionally opposed by many members of the practising profession. But there is little doubt that most witnesses, at least unconsciously, take sides".

Gladiatorial. Nicholas Cowdery QC reports the Former Chief Justice of Western Australia, Sir Francis Burt, as saying in 1997: "The law today is in significant trouble. In many cases a lawyer sees himself as the aggressive gladiatorial fighter for his client's perceived rights and, for his price, will join in and fight the good fight with all his might – in some cases with little regard for morality or ethics."

F. Lee Bailey. Francis Lee Bailey likened the role of criminal defence lawyer to the heroic struggle of a single-combat warrior in his 1971 memoir, *The Defense Never Rests*. In 1993 he was the most admired lawyer in America, according to *The National Law Journal*'s public opinion poll. In 1995 he was on O.J. Simpson's defence team. Ira Silverman and Fredric Dannen (*The New Yorker*, March 11, 1996) noted that Bailey's former colleague, Edward Shohat, said in early 1996: "Lee is a terrific lawyer. Terrific. On his feet. He just dominates a courtroom. But no way could I work with that son-of-a-bitch prick."

Federal prosecutor David McGee told Judge Maurice Paul in February 1996: "What you have is proof that F. Lee Bailey has stolen from the people of the United States in excess of twenty million dollars ... he gives up ethics, he lies and he cheats ... I ask that the court place him in jail." Judge Paul obliged.

Zeal. Sir James Knight-Bruce advised prosecutors against too much zeal in searching for the truth, but the adversary system demands zealotry, not necessarily for the truth, of defence counsel. Nicholas Cowdery says: "Professor Luban of Georgetown University also argues that the adversary system implies a vision of legal ethics combining extreme partisanship with moral nonaccountability. The principle of partisanship requires advocates to advance their clients' partisan interests with the maximum zeal permitted by law. The principle of nonaccountability insists that an advocate is morally responsible for neither the ends pursued by the client nor the means of pursuing those ends (provided that both means and ends are lawful)."

Cowdery then asks: "Is it a breach of professional standards not to go judge-shopping to the fullest extent possible?"

The Habit of Nastiness. Bright young lawyers apparently equip themselves with the habit of nastiness just as rapidly as bright law students pick up the knack of casuistry. Cowdery: "The attitudes that are fostered among practitioners are illustrated in an example given by another American writer in the context of discovery as it occurs in the USA [Yablon: *Stupid Lawyer Tricks: An Essay on Discovery Abuse*, 1996, 96 Columbia Law Rev. 1618): "'Because litigators rarely win or lose cases, they derive job satisfaction by recasting minor discovery disputes as titanic struggles. Younger lawyers, convinced that their future careers may hinge on how tough they seem while conducting discovery, may conclude that it is more important to look and sound ferocious than to act co-operatively, even if all that huffing and puffing does not help (and sometimes harms) their cases. While unpleasant at first, nastiness, like chewing tobacco, becomes a habit ... it is easy for young lawyers not only to stay mired in contumacious, morally immature conduct, but to actually enjoy it'."

Lawyers' Abuse of Privilege. Lawyers complained that a Sydney politician, Franca Arena, had abused parliamentary privilege in October 1996 when she asked in Parliament if a former Supreme Court Justice, David Yeldham, had been given preferential treatment by Justice James Wood's inquiry on paedophilia. Yeldham later committed suicide after he learned that the inquiry had evidence of his activities in lavatories at railway stations. I noted that "lawyers may overlook – or perhaps hope we do not notice – that parliamentarians' 'abuse' of their privilege does not begin to compare with the enormity of lawyers' abuse of THEIR privilege. Lawyers are obliged to follow a client's instructions even when they know he is guilty; a lawyer, one year out of law school and not elected by anyone to anything, has an absolute privilege to make the most monstrously false assertions about the victim".

Fabrication by Prosecution Witnesses. In more than two centuries, the adversary system has not achieved its initial purpose, which was to defeat fabrication by prosecution witnesses. Indeed, it seems that fabrication has increased by way of a circular effect: prosecution fabrication led to fabricated defences, which led to more prosecution fabrication, and so on.

Detective Constable Duncan Demol confirmed at Justice James Wood's NSW police corruption inquiry in July 1995 that police were prepared to fabricate at the "scrumdown" before trial. Demol said the law was "a joke"; that it was "hard to prove"; that "no one believed the coppers", and "you had to do it to get a conviction". Detective Sergeant Neville Scullion told Wood in July 1995: "The hierarchy was more interested in the arrest rate" than in the conviction rate.

An officer of the Australian Federal Police, codenamed JTF 16, told Michael Finnane QC, counsel for the NSW Police Service at the Wood inquiry, in October 1995 that he gave false evidence in perhaps 25 per cent of cases as the only way of convicting people he believed were guilty of major crimes.

Finnane: You felt if you didn't "load" they wouldn't get a sentence?

JTF 16: I would agree with that ...

Finnane: There is concern that the system is loaded against police unless you give it a push?

JTF 16: Yes.

In *Beyond Reasonable Doubt*, David Yallop explores a case in which Arthur Thomas, an innocent New Zealand man, was convicted on evidence fabricated by police.

Kelly. A Sydney Homicide detective, Sergeant Ray Kelly, may have enunciated the essence of the extreme adversary system when he charged John Frederick (Chow) Hayes with murder in 1951. David Hickie, author of *Chow Hayes, Gunman*, reported: "Chow Hayes told me that Kelly told him: 'I will tell as many lies as I can to convict you, and you tell as many lies as you can to beat it. Is that fair enough?' Hayes said it was fair enough. He admitted to me 40 years later that even the paper boys knew he was guilty, but it took the prosecution three trials to prove it."

Winning. As noted, Justice Callinan said: "In ordinary adversarial litigation ... the object of the parties is simple, to win the case." David Pannick notes that Lord Denning said that when he was a young advocate, "I wasn't concerned so much with the rightness of the cause, I was concerned only, as a member of the Bar, to win it if I could." Chrissa Loukas, a Sydney public defender, said in April 1996 that "lawyers only talk about their wins".

Lying. Stan Ross, who teaches legal ethics at the University of NSW Law School, says that lawyers "frequently lie to opposing counsel and/or the court. [They] do things for their clients that they would find immoral if they acted similarly for themselves or non-clients".

Professor Luban quotes a leading member of the cartel, Lord Macaulay (1800-59, legal adviser to the Supreme Council of India 1834-38), as observing that an advocate "with a wig on his head and a band round his neck will do for a guinea what he would otherwise think it wicked and infamous to do for an empire".

The Spectator said in a leading article, *Lesson in Law*, on 26 March 1994 that the behaviour of the British Government's lawyers in the original Matrix-Churchill prosecution "suggests that the principal effect of a legal training is the elimination of any sense of justice".

The Guilty Client. Rule 33 of the rules of the NSW Bar Association states: "A barrister ... whose client confesses guilt to the barrister but maintains a plea of not guilty ... may argue that for some reason of law the client is not guilty of the offence charged." The lawyer must also accept the client's instructions even though he knows or believes he is lying.

A Better Lie. The lawyer may even suggest that the guilty client change his lie. Robert Mannion reports: "A young lawyer recalls how she sat next to two colleagues in the library of Auckland's High Court who were planning a defence case for rape. She discovered that the alleged rapist wanted to say he was somewhere else at the time of the crime. But his lawyer had persuaded him to change to a defence of consent. Now he would say he had had intercourse, but that the woman had agreed. As a strategy, the advice was probably sound. But the young lawyer's unease will be familiar to anyone who has ever worried about how little the truth seems to count in our system."

The Classic Defence. The common law makes it relatively easy to get the guilty off. A jury is only as good as the evidence put before it, and cross-examination is as great an engine for obscuring the truth as for exposing it. The elements of the classic defence of a guilty man are thus: his lawyer persuades the judge to conceal relevant evidence; the guilty man exercises his right to avoid cross-examination; his lawyer uses verbal thuggery to confuse prosecution witnesses sufficiently to create a reasonable doubt; his lawyer shifts the goalposts, e.g. from accused to victim.

The lawyer sets it up at the committal hearing, where he can ask all the questions he would not dare ask at the trial. The complainant, perhaps traumatised, and other witnesses have made statements to the police, and no one says the same thing in the same way twice or three times. Also, there is pressure on police (as well as lawyers) to get a result, and some believe that "the brief can only improve"; they improve the statement by adding phrases or actions. Either way, there is likely to be a conflict between the witnesses' written and oral evidence.

The accused's lawyer begins his cross-examination in this menacing but courteous fashion: "I show you a document. Is that your signature which appears at the bottom of pages 1, 2, 3 ...?

"Yes."

"Please look at paragraph one."

Paragraph one says something like: "This is a true statement .... I make it knowing that if it is deliberately false I am subject to prosecution." At this stage the witness generally looks worried, and we are back to trial by ordeal, but not of the suspect.

Rapists. The common law sportingly gives rapists 99 chances in 100 of getting off. *The Guardian Weekly* of April 25, 1993 said an English Home Office study found that only between a tenth and a quarter of raped women report it to police; only 15 of 114 cases reported to two London police stations between 1988 and 1990 got to trial; only five suspects were convicted, a conviction rate of between 0.438 per cent and 1.096 per cent.

Getting Off Rape. Julia Griffith, a psychologist, noted in *The Sydney Morning Herald* in 1996 a case in which a man, who had already been imprisoned for child sexual assault, got off two charges of rape against a girl neighbour when she was 13 and 15. Griffith said the girl, now 17, was subjected to "a week-long assault" in the witness box, and "had nightmares afterwards". His lawyer "called her character into question", but the jury was not allowed to hear character evidence in her favour, or evidence of his character as revealed by the pattern of his previous behaviour.

"The adversarial system does not elicit the truth in these cases," Griffith said.

Sex victims fear going in the witness box; the European procedure of a judge questioning the woman or child in a neutral way would be a better alternative.

The Holocaust. A man who denied the Holocaust was charged with violating a Canadian prohibition on ethnic hate-speech. Professor Luban notes the technique: "The defense lawyer cross-examined witnesses who had survived concentration camps where their parents had perished. He challenged them with the utmost brutality, asking whether they had actually watched their parents be gassed to death (of course they hadn't since they were survivors), and when they admitted that they had not, went on to suggest that for all they knew their parents were alive but simply didn't want to see them again."

Woolf. Lord Woolf was perhaps elaborating the obvious when he reported in 1996 that the adversary system is too expensive, too slow, too unequal, too uncertain, and incomprehensible to many.

* * *

Summary. Recalling that the adversary system was invented to counter state oppression via fabricated evidence **BY** prosecution witnesses, we may summarise the system's defects as follows (12 and counting):

1   It has achieved oppression **OF** prosecution witnesses.

2   It has increased fabrication by defence witnesses.

3   It obscures the truth from the community, i.e. from its representatives on the jury.

4   It took control of trials away from judges.

5   It gave control of trials to lawyers whose object is not to deliver justice but to win.

6   It causes paranoia in prosecution and defence lawyers.

7   It encourages defence lawyers to deceive the community, i.e. the jury.

8   It has a "deeply corrupting" effect on expert witnesses.

9   It increases the cost of trials.

10 It prevents the legal aid budget from being fairly distributed.

11 Imbalance in the skills of the lawyers tends to make a trial unfair to either the community or the accused.

12 It allows defence lawyers to engage in legal thuggery on victims of crime, particularly women and children who are victims of sex crimes.

17

Prophylaxis Substitutes for Cure:
How Defence Lawyers Invented Rules
for Concealing Evidence

*... the judges' evaluation of the mental calibre of the jury [was]
to some extent ... excessively low.*

– Stone and Wells, 1991

The Domino Effect. Pernicious in itself, the extreme form of the
adversary system was the cause of further pernicious developments
in the common law: it gave defence lawyers the excuse to persuade
judges to accept six barriers to truth and justice.

"If O.J. is so innocent, why are they trying to suppress all the
evidence?" asked Nicole Brown Simpson's sister, Denise Brown, as
reported by Dominick Dunne in the February 1995 issue of *Vanity
Fair*. Dunne said Simpson's lawyer, Robert Shapiro, responded that
"that is what lawyers are supposed to do".

Simpson's former wife, Nicole, was thought to have been
murdered between 10.15 pm and 10.30 pm on Sunday, June 12 1994.
It might thus be thought that evidence of Simpson's precise
movements between 9.30 pm and 11 pm would be crucial. But
Simpson claimed the right of silence, and his lawyers managed to
avoid providing the jury with that information and his alibi, if he had
one. The trial, in which Simpson was found not guilty on October 3,
1995, cost Los Angeles County US$12 million.

Professor John Langbein says in his article on the origin of the
privilege against self-incrimination: "In the later eighteenth and
especially in the nineteenth century ... under the influence of
defense counsel, the criminal trial came to be seen as an opportunity
for the defendant's lawyer to test the prosecution case. The privilege
against self-incrimination entered common law procedure (together
with the beyond-reasonable-doubt standard of proof and the
exclusionary apparatus of the modern law of criminal evidence) as
part of the profound reordering of the trial. It was the capture of the
criminal trial by lawyers for prosecution and defense that made it
possible for the criminal defendant to decline to be a witness against
himself."

The barriers to truth and justice were: a privilege against self-
incrimination (including a right of silence), a rule against patterns
of criminal behaviour (similar facts), a rule against secondhand
evidence (hearsay), a confusing formula for the test for guilt, and
a power (the *Christie* discretion) to conceal virtually all evidence.

A late barrier to truth, the exclusionary rule invented in 1961 by a possible Mafia appointee to the US Supreme Court, Justice Tom Clark, purports to prevent oppression, but does not.

The rationale for the other barriers was fairness to the accused; defence lawyers successfully argued that he/she had to be protected from jury error now that the adversary system isolated jurors from the judge. Stone and Wells put it this way: "(The rules for concealing relevant evidence) sprang from the exigencies of protecting lay jurymen from dangers of confusion and prejudice. They represented the judges' evaluation of the mental calibre of the jury. To some extent this evaluation was excessively low, and presented unnecessary obstacles for the free exercise of their common sense [but] the rules are today applied to all trials, whether before a jury or before a judge alone."

Judges' Self-Contempt. In effect, this means that the lawyers persuaded judges to accept that no-one, including judges, has sufficient intelligence and sense of fairness to hear all the relevant evidence without being unfairly prejudiced against the suspect. It is surprising that judges could admit to being so deeply contemptuous of themselves. The fact that the common law elsewhere says that judges cannot be prejudiced merely means that it simultaneously holds two irreconcilable propositions: judges can and cannot be prejudiced.

"Fair" Trials. The cartel is never happier than when talking about "fair" trials through its outlets in the media, law associations, lawyerised civil liberties groups, and on the bench. But a fair trial does not exist at common law: either the rules for concealing evidence weights it so much in favour of the suspect that it is unfair to victim and community, or the adversarial prosecutor is stronger than the defence lawyer and it is unfair to the suspect.

Contempt. There was still another domino. To stop the jury hearing evidence that would be concealed from them, a law of criminal contempt was invented.

First Amendment. In the US, however, the First Amendment to the Constitution has guaranteed free speech since 1791; this tends to ensure that in major cases the concealed evidence gets into the public domain, and it appears that this does not prejudice jurors. Susan Wyndham, an Australian reporter stationed in New York, reported in 1995 in the context of blanket coverage of the O.J. Simpson case: "A recent study found that Press-induced bias is a serious problem in only one in 10,000 cases."

Gotti. The 1970 RICO legislation meant that the previously-concealed pattern of gangster's criminal behaviour could now be put into evidence, but a 1990 case against John Gotti, boss of the New York Gambino family, suggests that jurors are capable of adhering to their oaths to be fair, that such material does not unfairly prejudice them, and that they still have to be convinced that the prosecution has proved the particular charge.

Hours of surveilled conversations on wiretaps convinced the jurors that Gotti was the head of an organised crime family and that he was a thug and a mobster, but they found him not guilty. The foreman, William Buchanan said: "I have to admit that voting not guilty was a very unpleasant result for me. I felt truly that he was guilty as hell, but I have to admit that the evidence just didn't hold up."

All that may seem to make rather a nonsense of defence lawyers' invention of the rules for concealing evidence and the law of criminal contempt, but removing the jury from its isolation would make assurance doubly sure.

Prophylaxis. In his article on the Ryder sources, Professor Langbein writes: "The exclusionary system of the modern Anglo-American law of evidence, exemplified in the hearsay rule, has an essentially prophylactic purpose. In modern practice it is quite difficult for the trial judge to correct error in a jury verdict once error has occurred. Accordingly, our law of evidence strives to prevent error by excluding from jurors information that might mislead them. The judge-operated calculus of admission and exclusion is designed to prevent error from infecting adjudication. Prophylaxis substitutes for cure."

Penicillin. Dr Langbein's startling image suggests, to me at any rate, a poxed jury system and the use of prophylactics rather than penicillin to protect accused. But the prophylactics were, and are, faulty, as confirmed in chapter 32: How the Innocent Go to the Electric Chair, etc.

Cure. The cure was always at hand: to formalise the jurors' previous informal arrangement with the judge; i.e. by putting them up on the bench.

18

Magic Trick 4

The Right of Silence Protects the Guilty Only

The crux of the matter is that immunity from being questioned is a rule which by its nature can protect the guilty only. It is not a rule that may operate to acquit some guilty for fear of convicting some innocent.

– Professor Glanville Williams, *The Proof of Guilt* 3rd edn 1963

The right of silence is part of a privilege against self-incrimination. It was, Dr John Langbein says, "the creature of defense counsel", and it followed another of their creatures, the extreme adversary system, only some two centuries ago, but Lord Parker (1900-72, Lord Chief Justice – in succession to the sexually depraved Lord Goddard – 1958-71) claimed in *Rice v Connolly* (1966) that it is "the whole basis of the common law".

Inventing a rule that protects the guilty only may seem rather extreme, even for self-interested defence lawyers; if we didn't know better, we might think it the work of shysters. The Macquarie dictionary suggests that "shyster" may derive from *Scheuster*, an unscrupulous 19th century New York lawyer, and the German *scheisser*: a shitter.

Peril of Conviction as a Criminal. Sir Harry Gibbs, who succeeded Sir Garfield Barwick as Chief Justice of the High Court of Australia in 1981, defined the privilege against self-incrimination in *Sorby v The Commonwealth* (1983). Quoting *Lamb v Munster* (Queen's Bench Division, 1882), he said it operates so that a person cannot be compelled "to answer any question, or to produce any document or thing, if to do so 'may tend to bring him into the peril and possibility of being convicted as a criminal'." The right of silence allows a suspect to refuse to answer at a police interrogation; at his own trial; and as a witness at someone else's criminal or civil trial.

Alun Jones QC, an English lawyer, says: "I am told that over half of all defendants in America decline to give evidence." Professor David Dixon, of the University of NSW, said in August 1997 that about half of those who exercised the right to remain silent were convicted. This may suggest that the mere fact of using Magic Trick 4 immediately gives a guilty person a 50 per cent chance of getting off, and he still had the other eight magic tricks at his command.

Confusion on Origin. There has been some confusion about the origin of the privilege. It was formerly thought that it was a reaction to torture in the Star Chamber in the 16th and 17th centuries and

Trial by Voodoo accepted those views. But good advice must give way to better, which is that the privilege followed the invention of the adversary system in the late 18th century.

The confusion arose because the privilege really had two origins, both dubious. The mantra, "no man shall be forced to produce evidence against himself", was first fraudulently uttered by a leading member of the cartel in 1568. It was thereafter endlessly and mindlessly repeated, but trial procedure made it impossible for it to become operational until defence lawyers invented the adversary system more than two centuries later. They then used the mantra to give doubtful authority to their implementation of the privilege.

Or as Dr John Langbein puts it: "The privilege against self-incrimination became functional only as a consequence of the revolutionary reconstruction of the criminal trial worked by the advent of defense counsel and adversary criminal procedure. The error has been to expect to find the privilege in operation before the adversary system was in place." Thus:

Cartel v Monarch. In the 16th and 17th centuries there were ostensibly three power blocs in England: Parliament, the law and the monarch. In practice there were only two: the cartel and the monarch. The lawyer-controlled Parliament sought supremacy over the monarch; common law courts sought supremacy over the royal courts, the Star Chamber and High Commission, which used the investigative techniques of European courts.

For the common law judges, money as well as power was at stake; Justice Ken Marks said in 1984: "It is to be remembered that the common law judges shared in the fines collected by their courts, and thus had a personal interest in resort to them." The common law judges thus had a pecuniary interest in the abolition of the royal courts: they were competitors for business.

Dyer. Both common law and royal courts used torture, but the royal and ecclesiastic courts could force a suspect to take an oath and give evidence, whereas, as noted above, the common law courts could not proceed if the suspect refused to plead. The first shot in the cartel's campaign seems to have been fired by Sir James Dyer (1512-82). Like Lord Mansfield two centuries later, Dyer straddled the law and politics: barrister c. 1537, MP 1547, Serjeant 1552, Speaker of the House of Commons 1553, judge and president of the court of common pleas 1559.

Fraudulent Origin of the Mantra. Gregory O'Reilly, a Chicago public defender, says that in 1568 Dyer "granted a writ of *habeas corpus* freeing a prisoner who was being forced to take the oath. In granting the writ, Dyer was the first to justify objecting to the oath in what became a famous maxim [or mantra]: *nemo tenetur seipsum prodere*, or, no man shall be forced to produce evidence against himself".

Dyer was being economical with the truth. Justice Marks said: "The common lawyers took the words *nemo tenetur seipsum prodere* out of context to mean something quite different – rather the opposite of its modern meaning ... The *nemo tenetur* maxim was part of an old and established ecclesiastical one. The full Canonist rule was: "*Licet nemo tenetur seipsum prodere, tamen proditus per famam tenetur seipsum ostendere utrum possit suam innocentiam ostendere et seipsum purgare.*" One translation is: "*Although* no one is compelled to accuse himself (i.e. to come forward voluntarily to tell of his misdeed), *yet one accused by rumour is compelled to present himself to show his innocence if he can and to clear himself.*" In other words, you don't have to voluntarily confess, but when found out you have to give an account of yourself. Chief Justice Dyer's fraud lay in omitting the italicised words.

Dr Langbein remarks: "Across the centuries the privilege against self-incrimination has changed character profoundly, from the original privilege not to accuse oneself to the modern privilege not to respond or to testify." The *nemo tenetur seipsum prodere* mantra thus has some parallels in libel law: to prevent disclosure of corruption, judges changed the function of libel law from protecting the peace of the realm to protecting reputation.

Cartel Victorious. The cartel, led by Sir Edward Coke, won its two contests in the 17th century: Parliament abolished the royal courts in 1641, cut off the head of King Charles I in 1649, and got rid of King James II in 1688. But the right of silence was not mentioned in the Bill of Rights of 1689 or in the reforming Whigs' Treason Act of 1696. The privilege was still not available for the simple reason that accused were not allowed to have counsel. (The malady seems to ensure that the common law is one of extremes: grossly unfair to accused for six centuries, and grossly favouring accused for the last two.)

Right to Commit Suicide. Dr John Langbein notes: "Without defense counsel, a criminal defendant's right to remain silent was the right to forfeit any defense; indeed, in a system that emphasised capital punishment, the right to remain silent was literally the right to commit suicide."

Privilege not Asserted. Langbein says: "Fifteen years ago I pointed out [*The Criminal Trial Before the Lawyers*, 1978] that, in the pamphlet reports of London trials "from the 1670s through the mid-1730s [where my study lapsed] I have not noticed a single case in which an accused refused to speak on asserted grounds of privilege, or in which he makes the least allusion to a privilege against self-incrimination. I have subsequently followed this set of pamphlet reports into the 1770s without finding any articulated claim of the privilege.

"[John M.] Beattie, concentrating on Surrey sources for the years between 1660 and 1800, makes a similar observation [in 1986]: 'There was no thought that the prisoner had a right to remain silent on the grounds that he would otherwise be liable to incriminate himself ... the assumption was clear that if the case against him was false the prisoner ought to say so and suggest why, and that if he did not speak that could be because he was unable to deny the truth of the evidence'."

Hawkins. In 1721, William Hawkins (1682-1750, Serjeant-at-Law 1724) accurately stated the case for having an accused give evidence in his *Treatise of Pleas of the Crown* (two vols, 1716 and 1721). If he is guilty, "the very Speech, Gesture and Countenance and Manner of Defence of those who are Guilty, when they speak for themselves, may often help to disclose the Truth, which probably would not so well be discovered from the artificial Defence of others speaking for them."

Wood. Hawkins' view was confirmed, if such were needed, nearly three centuries later at the Wood Royal Commission of Inquiry on Police Corruption in NSW (1994-97). Suspects had to give evidence on the basis that they would go to prison for contempt if they refused, and that if they made a formal objection to answering, their evidence would not be used against them if they were later charged at common law. Police are trained to give evidence, and some become adept at giving fabricated evidence in a sincere and plausible way, but at times it was apparently obvious to spectators that they were lying; Justice James Wood had to make plaintive appeals: "Please do not laugh; this is a serious matter." This may indicate the magnitude of defence lawyers' coup in securing a right of silence for their clients late in the 18th century.

A Testimonial Resource. Dr Langbein says the previous "aspiration to capture the defendant as a testimonial resource is perfectly understandable. He is, after all, the most efficient possible witness. Guilty or innocent, he had been close enough to the events to get prosecuted for the offense. Modern continental systems continue to emphasise the advantages of treating the accused as the central testimonial resource."

As noted, Ludovic Kennedy said that when Hawkins wrote (in 1721) "in France they had already established the system of the examining magistrate [*juge d'instruction*] sifting out prosecution cases and preparing a dossier on the case for the judge". The *juge*, not a right of silence, is the key to preventing oppression.

Accused Must Speak. Dr Langbein says that even after judges allowed accused to have counsel towards the middle of the 18th century, they still pressured the accused to speak. John Beattie reported a 1752 Surrey case in which the accused tried to leave his defence to his counsel, but counsel declined, and the judge said: "Your counsel knows his duty very well, they may indeed speak for you in any matter of law that may arise at your trial, but cannot as to matter of fact, for you must manage your defence in the best manner you can yourself."

A few years later, at the end of the prosecution evidence the trial judge called on the defendant to make his case.

"My counsel will speak for me," the defendant said.

"I can't speak for you," his counsel said; "you must speak for yourself."

In 1777, a judge at the Old Bailey told a defendant: "Your counsel are not at liberty to state any matter of fact. They are permitted to examine your witnesses, and they are here to speak to any matters of law that may arise, but if your defence arises out of a matter of fact, you must yourself state it to me and the jury."

Dr Langbein comments: "Thus even with defense counsel on the scene, the English legal system of the mid-eighteenth century was telling the criminal defendant that 'you must speak for yourself'." It was only after the adversary system was accepted in the last quarter of the 18th century that defence lawyers could persuade judges to accept the privilege.

Fifth Amendment. The right of silence was set in concrete in the US Constitution in 1791; the Fifth Amendment states: "... nor shall he be compelled in any criminal case to be a witness against himself." The Fifth appears to derive from the mantra rather than from English practice; until 1848 English pre-trial procedure was inquisitorial vaguely in the manner of the French *juge*, and the evidence gained could be used against the accused at the trial.

English Examining Magistrate. Quoting E.M. Morgan's *The Privilege Against Self-incrimination* (1949), Dr Langbein says "the accused was 'expected to answer' the inquiries of the examining magistrate, 'and, indeed, any refusal to answer, whether of his own initiative or on advice of another, was reported and stated by the magistrate in his testimony at the trial'."

Sir John Jervis (1802-56) was Attorney-General 1846-50 and Lord Chief Justice 1850-56. In 1848 he introduced the measures relating to justices of the peace known by his name. Dr Langbein says: "Not until Sir John Jervis' Act of 1848 – that is, well into the age of modern lawyer-dominated criminal procedure – was provision made to advise the accused that he might decline to answer questions put to him in the pretrial inquiry and to caution him that his answers to pretrial interrogation might be used as evidence against him at trial."

Ludovic Kennedy notes a succession of steps: "... first to the accused earning the right not to speak, then his being forbidden to speak, and finally, under the Criminal Evidence Act at the turn of the last century, to him being permitted to speak if he wanted to."

Bonus. The Criminal Evidence Act (1898) gave defence lawyers and their clients another giant bonus. A.A.S. Zuckerman says the Act: " ... forbids the prosecution from commenting on the accused's failure to testify in his own defence." Nor can the judge "suggest that failure to testify amounts to an admission of guilt". Dr Langbein says "the modern American rule forbidding adverse comment on the accused's silence [is] a rule so recent [*Griffin v California*, 1965], historically, that the ink is still wet." .

Miranda. In 1966, the US Supreme Court gave Ernest Miranda, a convicted rapist, a new trial because police did not warn him he could remain silent and consult a lawyer. Since then US police have been obliged to read the Miranda warning. It sounds like a benefit for defence lawyers as well as suspects: "You are under arrest. You have the right to remain silent. Anything you say can be used against you in court. You have the right to consult a lawyer before we question you. If you cannot afford a lawyer and want one, a lawyer will be provided for you."

Exceptions. Athol Moffitt QC, President of the NSW Court of Appeal 1974-84, notes that there is "no such thing as an absolute right to silence in the criminal law", e.g. a person caught in possession of narcotics deemed to be of sufficient quantity to peddle; "the accused [has] to prove he was not involved in peddling".

Goods in Custody. Moffitt continues: "Another example is a criminal offence under the law of every State in Australia and England since the last century. This is the criminal offence popularly known as 'goods in custody'. The accused is found in possession of goods, for example, a dozen transistor radios, in circumstances where there is reasonable suspicion that he stole them, or came by them unlawfully, for example, as a receiver. He is liable to be convicted and sent to gaol unless he accounts for his possession, which usually means proof that he came by them legally. One might say that he is convicted on suspicion unless he proves his innocence." In short, there is no such thing as an absolute presumption of innocence either.

Alcohol/Blood Exceptions. Legislators have made other exceptions to the privilege. Breathalyser tests allow drunk drivers to incriminate themselves; in 1995 the Victorian Parliament made further exceptions, including making it obligatory for suspects to allow a blood sample to be taken, thus anticipating NSW legislation brought down because of the Fernando case (see chapter 18, The Right of Silence in Action).

Exception for Companies. The common law world is split on whether companies should have a privilege against self-incrimination. In December 1993, the Australian High Court noted that the privilege against self-incrimination was available to corporations in England, Canada and New Zealand, according to decisions by those countries' highest courts, but the US Supreme Court had removed the privilege from US corporations. By a 4-3 majority, the court removed the privilege from Australian corporations.

In a joint judgment, Chief Justice Sir Anthony Mason and Justice Peter Toohey said: "If it ever was the common law in Australia that corporations could claim the privilege against self-incrimination in relation to the production of documents, it is no longer the common law." The issue arose in 1990 when a forerunner of the NSW Environment Protection Authority sought documents from an oil company, Caltex Refining Company Pty Ltd, in connection with an allegation that it polluted the Pacific Ocean by discharging grease and oils in contravention of the NSW Clean Waters Act of 1970. Caltex claimed the privilege and was upheld by the NSW Court of Appeal, but that court was narrowly overturned by the High Court.

The privilege against self-incrimination enjoyed by companies in England may be a factor in the difficulty the Serious Fraud Squad seems to have in securing convictions.

19

The Fox-Hunter's Reason
For and Against the Right of Silence

... one of the most pernicious and most irrational notions that ever found its way into the human mind.

– Jeremy Bentham, 1827

Frank Hollis Rivers Vincent QC, chairman of the Victorian Criminal Bar Association, gave evidence before an Australian Senate committee examining legislation for a National Crime Authority on February 6, 1984. The NCA came into being later that year, and was charged with investigating organised crime, white collar and blue. It had the power to oblige suspects to give evidence, but they could bring lawyers to the in camera hearings, and could decline to answer questions which might incriminate them. Vincent said: "The power to compulsorily interrogate ... was a matter that I could say that I regarded as being as subversive of the values of this country as the activities of people who just want to steal off it."

The committee chairman, Senator Michael Tate, former Dean of the Faculty of Law at the University of Tasmania, asked Vincent: " ... if the interrogation is undertaken in a situation which does not have any element of physical abuse or intimidation about it, what is the underlying principle that causes lawyers such as yourself to require that this principle be observed for the good of society?"

Vincent replied: "One of the earliest uses I know of the right to remain silent was that of Jesus Christ, who refused to answer questions on the ground that he might incriminate himself, because he knew the kinds of ways in which the answers that he gave could be used against him. We have a system which starts off on the assumption that I am innocent. He who makes an allegation against me has to prove it. I am not to have my own words, thoughts, perceptions or anything else used to assist in that. I do not have to have my words thrown back at me, whether I am skilful or inarticulate or intelligent or otherwise. The right to silence is frequently abused by some of the more clever people, the people who know how to cope with complicated situations. Many of the people for whom I act are black, poor and ignorant, inarticulate and uneducated. One of the few protections they have that stops situations being distorted against them and gives reality to that presumption of innocence – and the burden of proof – is that right of silence."

Marks. Justice Kenneth Marks said in his 25,000-word treatise on the privilege in April 1984: "The irrationality of the rule has been long recognised by intelligent legal commentators but change is resisted. Change always meets opposition."

Vincent. Justice (as he now was) Frank Hollis Rivers Vincent, gave evidence to a joint parliamentary committee on the NCA on Monday, November 5, 1990. Neil O'Keefe sought his comment on a submission by a Melbourne legal academic who said "that the traditional right against self-incrimination developed over a particular historical period within which particular social and legal values prevailed and that there is no immutable rule that these values cannot change or that sacred cows such as the right to silence are fixed in stone forever."

Like most of us, Justice Vincent was apparently unaware that the right of silence was invented by defence lawyers in the late 18th century. He replied: "The general proposition about the abolition of the right to silence is one I will not have a bar of. I am conscious of that kind of argument; it has in fact been enunciated in relatively recent times by one of my brother judges on the Supreme Court. I think it is ridiculously naive. It was not all that very long ago when we were on the verge of banning a political party in this country and it may well have been an offence not to reveal your knowledge of who was a member of that political party. Now that is within my lifetime. I regard the right to silence, which emanated historicially to some extent out of the kind of civil and religious turmoil of the seventeenth century, as not having been retained as a value of our society because we have been just so conservative that we would not change it. All manner of things have changed in the law, and values have changed in the law, but not that one. That one has not changed because, as I said, it seems to be that there is a recognition that there is a point beyond which the executive powers should not reach."

Richter. Robert Richter QC, President of the Victorian Council of Civil Liberties, told a conference on victims in 1995: "There are those who argue for the removal of the right to silence because it will make it easier, so it is said, to convict the guilty. The rationale seems to be that if the victim must give evidence and be subjected to cross-examination, so too should be the accused. That argument is fallacious. At the trial phase, it is only the accused who stands in peril. Not the victim of the crime." As a magistrate drily noted, Richter is seriously misinformed: the community and the victim (if still alive) are in peril every time a guilty person gets off by way of the right of silence or the other magic tricks.

In 1996, Justice Vincent and Richter QC were involved in an important NCA case, *R v John Dorman Elliott and Ors.* (See chapter 29, Ninian Stephen's Middle of the Road Exclusionary Rule – Australia.)

The Old Woman's Reason. A.A.S. Zuckerman says Jeremy Bentham said [*Rationale of Judicial Evidence*, 1827] that one supposed justification for the privilege against self-incrimination was the "old woman's reason: 'tis hard upon a man to be obliged to criminate himself". Bentham said what was hard was not making the incriminating statement, but the likelihood of punishment created by the statement, and "since we are prepared to inflict punishment it is pusillanimous to recoil from the lesser hardship of questioning the accused".

The Fox-Hunter's Reason. Zuckerman quotes Bentham as giving "the fox-hunter's reason" as another supposed justification: "This consists in introducing upon the carpet of legal procedure the idea of *fairness*, in the sense in which the word is used by sportsmen. The fox is to have a fair chance for his life: he must have (so close is the analogy) what is called *law*: leave to run a certain length of the way, for the express purpose of giving him a chance for escape."

Wigmore. The American jurist, John Henry Wigmore (1863-1943) said in 1891: "... the privilege is not needed by the innocent ... the only question can be how far are the guilty entitled to it?"

Kilbrandon. Justice Donald Stewart noted remarks by Lord Kilbrandon, a lord of appeal in ordinary 1971-76: "It is said that a man ought not to be called upon to incriminate himself. One may ask, why not? It is hard to see how an innocent man can incriminate himself, and if a guilty man does, so much the better. The reported cases are full of expressions such as 'fair play' [but they] tend to mislead. The procedure we are considering is not a game. The prevention of crime and the prosecution of criminals are war. In this war rules are necessary to prevent, even at the cost of letting crime go unpunished, the smallest chance of an innocent person being convicted or even, if possible, charged. But any weapon which, harmless to the innocent, is deadly to the guilty should be legitimate. I have great difficulty in seeing how an innocent man could ever be harmed by being questioned **before a judge** [emphasis added]; on the other hand the guilty man's answers, or more especially his refusal to answer, might have a devastating effect when reported at this trial."

Deane. *Reid* (Australian High Court, 1995) is mentioned in chapter 20, The Right of Silence in Action. In his judgment in *Reid*, Justice Sir William Deane, who became Governor-General of Australia in 1996, said: "If the privilege against self-incrimination were susceptible of being overridden by the courts **in the interests of justice** in the circumstances of a particular case, it would be arguable that the orders made by the Court of Appeal were justified ... As has been seen, however, the privilege is not subject to judge-made exceptions ..." (Emphasis added.) Justice Deane appeared to be saying that the privilege can cause injustice and that judges are powerless to prevent it.

20

The Right of Silence in Action

It is better that some innocent men remain in jail than that the integrity of the English judicial system be impugned.

– Lord Denning, 1988

If protecting us from oppression by agents of the state was an excuse offered for the invention of the right of silence at the end of the 18th century, it never worked. And what can be done about oppression by untrained, amateur judges?

Lord Denning and the Birmingham Six. Detectives tortured the Birmingham Six to obtain false confessions to murder in 1974. The Six mounted a civil action alleging assault against the police. Lord Denning (b. 1899) heard their case in 1980. The noble lord had risen high in the cartel: barrister 1923, KC 1938, judge 1944, lord justice of appeal 1948, lord of appeal in ordinary (Law Lord) 1957-62. In 1962 he accepted demotion to the court of appeal because, he said, he was too often in the minority, and "in the Lords it is no good to dissent". And in any event the appeal court made more law: it heard some 800 cases a year, against the House of Lords' 50 or 60. He was Master of the Rolls (head of the appeal court) 1962-82.

Dismissing the Six's civil action for assault, Lord Denning said: "If the six men win it will mean that the police were guilty of perjury, that they were guilty of violence and threats, that the confessions were involuntary and were improperly admitted in evidence and that the convictions were erroneous... This is such an appalling vista that every sensible person in the land would say it cannot be right that these actions should go any further."

The Six continued to seek justice. As noted, Lord Denning offered the leviathan state this advice in 1988: "Hanging ought to be retained for murder most foul. We shouldn't have all these campaigns to get the Birmingham Six released if they'd been hanged. They'd have been forgotten, and the whole community would be satisfied ... It is better that some innocent men remain in jail than that the integrity of the English judicial system be impugned."

What does the cartel say about that? Is that the mask dropping? Is it proper for judges to oppress the innocent to protect the reputation of the cartel, the judges, the courts and the common law? Appeal Court Lord Justices Lloyd, Mustill and Farquuharson apparently did not think so; they acquitted and freed them in 1991. The Six had been in prison for 16 years.

Garvey. Agents of the state also use torture to get information:

Justice James Wood's NSW inquiry on police corruption was told in June 1996 that Superintendent John Garvey, then in charge of security for Sydney's Olympic Games in 2000, had sprayed mace in the face of a handcuffed burglary suspect to make him talk.

McKinney and Judge. It was not until 1992, in *McKinney and Judge*, that the Australian High Court ruled that a charge should not proceed if the only evidence against a suspect was a challenged confession obtained by agents of the state.

Cornish. Superintendent Philip Cornish says the law allows your fingerprints to incriminate you but not your tongue. Or your hair; a Sydney woman was found stabbed to death with hairs still clutched in her fists. There was a suspect; his hair would show whether or not he was the murderer. He claimed the privilege and that was the end of it.

The Fernando Cousins. Vester and Brendan Fernando abducted, raped and almost beheaded a nurse, Sandra Hoare, at Walgett, NSW, in 1994. Charged with murder by machete, they refused to give samples of their blood on the ground that the common law allowed them to refuse to answer any questions and to refuse to produce any document "or thing" that might tend to bring them "into the peril" of being convicted as criminals. Judges of the NSW Court of Appeal and the High Court said the Fernandos were right. The NSW Parliament then legislated to overturn the common law to allow blood to be taken from suspects. In the event, their blood did not prove anything but they were convicted in 1997.

A Jekyll and Hyde Judge. Justice Lionel Murphy, of the Australian High Court, claimed in *Pyneboard Pty Ltd v Trade Practices Commission* [1983], that the privilege against self-incrimination is a "fundamental bulwark of liberty which protects the innocent as well as the guilty". It is perhaps churlish to note that it was certainly a bulwark of liberty for Justice Murphy himself three years later. Charged with attempting to pervert justice on behalf of a lawyer, Morgan Ryan, Murphy went in the witness box and claimed his character was unsullied. He was shifty and evasive; the jury did not believe him; he was sent down for 18 months.

Shortly after, Justice James McClelland told finance reporter Maximilian Walsh and the present writer: "Lionel is a Jekyll and Hyde figure. And who among us would want to be judged on the Hyde part of our character?" Who indeed? This is not a handbook for the criminally-minded, but Watson & Purnell's *Indictable Offences in New South Wales* is more than three inches thick; if a High Court judge can find himself in the dock, perhaps anyone can.

In the end Murphy knew how to get off. Chief Justice Sir Larry Street and four other judges of the NSW Court of Appeal gave him a re-trial. For the second trial, the prosecutors, Ian Callinan QC and Nick Cowdery, were armed with new material about Murphy's character from various sources, including a secret judicial inquiry on telephone tapping: Morgan Ryan had been a subject of the taps and Murphy's voice had been picked up on the tapes. Callinan suspected Murphy would not give evidence and make his character an issue, and that the prosecution would thus not be able to use the material. (See also, Magic Trick 5, The Rule Against Patterns, in chapter 23.) To Cowdery, it was unthinkable that a High Court judge would hide behind the right of silence.

"I couldn't accept that," Cowdery told me in 1997; "Perhaps I was naive. I bet Callinan a dollar that Murphy would give evidence. I lost. I had a dollar mounted as a trophy and presented it to him."

Having thus manipulated the law to prevent the jury hearing the evidence about his character, Murphy duly got off and went back to the High Court.

Simpson. Orenthal J. Simpson, did it the opposite way round. He refused to answer questions at his first (criminal) trial and was found not guilty. His next (civil) trial, for damages relating to the alleged murders, was a quasi-inquisitorial proceeding: evidence concealed at the murder trial was admitted and he had to answer questions. He was apparently shifty and evasive; the jury found him liable for the murders and ordered him to pay $A43.5 million in damages. After the second trial, Anise Aschenbach, a juror at the first trial, said: "I'm convinced now beyond a reasonable doubt that O.J. Simpson is guilty. They finally came up with all the evidence. It's depressing; he basically got away with murder, in the legal sense."

Reid. *Reid* (Australian High Court 1995) should remove any lingering belief that the common law is concerned with truth and justice. According to the judgment, the case concerned an accountant who admitted to police he stole from his clients, but apparently not in sufficient particularity for charges to be laid. In an attempt to get some of their money back, his clients brought a civil action to examine his financial records. He claimed the privilege. The NSW Supreme Court and Appeal Court said he should hand over the documents, but the High Court said there could be no exception – except by the legislature – to the privilege against self-incrimination; he could therefore destroy them.

The Case of the Tattooed Buttock. A Victorian woman claimed that the leader of a motor cycle club and his wife held her at gunpoint and raped her at club parties. She said the wife "supervised and assisted", and had engaged in oral and digital rape, and that in the process a rose tattoo on her buttock had become visible. A magistrate said this did not come within the ambit of new legislation, and ruled that police could not examine the allegedly offending buttock. He was overruled by Justice Howard Tomaz Nathan in the Victorian Supreme Court in February 1996, and Justice Nathan was upheld by the Victorian Appeal Court. By then, however, the complainant appeared to be having second thoughts about subjecting herself to the oppression of the adversary system, and it seemed unlikely that the case would proceed.

21

Diminishing the Right of Silence

A long overdue victory for common sense.

– Richard Stern 1996

Importance of Right of Silence Overstated. Justice Donald Stewart notes that Professor Michael Zander "has argued impressively that the theoretical and practical importance of the right to silence has been overstated. In his essay in *Re-shaping the Criminal Law* [Stevens & Sons, London, 1978] he gives nine reasons for this view". Stewart quotes the first three:

"1. Most defendants plead guilty. For the defendant who pleads guilty the right of silence is irrelevant ... This is what happens in the great majority of cases dealt with by the criminal justice system. The guilty plea is the norm; the not guilty plea the exception.

"2. The common law system accepts a guilty plea without proof [and proceeds straight to sentence]. The inquisitorial system of continental countries is often said to be less fair than the common law system in imposing on the defendant the duty to explain himself. Yet in the inquisitorial system, no matter what the defendant says, the prosecution must to some extent at least prove its case by producing the evidence of guilt ...

"3. The system creates strong pressure to induce guilty pleas ... The essence of the rhetoric is that it is objectionable to permit the defendant to participate in proving himself guilty and that the burden of this is supposed to be shouldered by the State. Yet in fact the opposite is the case. There are a variety of pressures that lead defendants to plead guilty. Thus the defendant who agrees to plead guilty will often do so in order to get bail from the police station or the court. He may be told (or may gather) that it will result in some of the more serious potential charges not being laid, or if laid, not being proceeded with. If he decides to plead guilty, the police will often say they will 'put in a good word for him' on sentencing. The case will be dealt with more quickly, commonly with less publicity and with less expense.

"Above all, the courts have ruled that a guilty plea normally entitles the defendant to a lower sentence than if he pleads not guilty. However this concept is rationalised or dressed-up, it amounts to the clearest possible inducement to plead guilty...

"There is something hypocritical about a system that makes a great fuss over the importance of the defendant's right to silence and of the prosecution's duty to prove its case and at the same time induces guilty pleas by offering a lower sentence."

German Courts. In Germany, an accused may admit to the crime but the judge and jury must still hear the case in the ordinary way to make sure he/she actually did it. Admission, *Vollgestandigkeit*, is taken into account in sentencing.

Poisoning Justice. Lord Chief Justice Taylor, the judge at the apex of the English criminal justice system, admitted to *The Guardian*'s Hugo Young (*The Guardian Weekly* 2 August 1992) that the right of silence and the rules of evidence poison justice in two ways: they tilt the system in favour of criminals and they thus encourage police fabrication. Young reported: "[Lord Taylor's] keenest eye addresses ... the trial process itself, one which Lord Runciman's Royal Commission is now deliberating." (I note what happened to the Runciman inquiry in chapter 41: How the Cartel Obstructs Reform.)

"The biggest inducement, he reckons, to bent police procedures is the tilting of the rules in the defendant's favour." Lord Taylor, to whom everyone seems to be a "chap", said: "The chap has to be cautioned. If he says nothing, no comment can be passed. He doesn't have to give evidence. Meanwhile, the police, who are not always intelligent chaps, are cross-examined all over the place. They're easily bamboozled and they resent it, and they try and make up for it by other means."

Young said: "This points straight at the right to silence, which at present means that no comment can be passed on a silent accused, even if he produces a florid uncheckable defence at the last minute."

Taylor went on: "If the police felt a shift in the total balance could be made, they wouldn't be so bothered about a chap saying No comment as he was found leaving the warehouse. They'd think: 'Jolly good, he's not going to give us an explanation, now he's stitched up because the jury can take account of it'."

Howard. In August 1994, 426 years after Chief Justice Dyer began the right of silence frolic, Michael Howard QC, Minister for Home Affairs in England, diminished it via the *Criminal Justice and Public Order Act*. It is necessary to emphasise that the Act does not abolish the right of silence; the suspect/accused can still refuse to answer questions from police or a court. However, the prosecution and the judge can now do what they could not do previously. That is, they can draw to the jury's attention "proper inferences" from the fact that the accused did not explain his actions to police or the jury.

When Howard first mentioned his plans, James Lewis noted in *The Guardian Weekly* (December 26, 1993): "The main objection raised by the Bar Council, the Law Society and legal reform groups is against abolishing the right of silence, which is seen as breaching the fundamental principle of British law that defendants are innocent until proven guilty."

The old police caution to suspects was: "You do not have to say anything unless you wish to, but what you say may be given in evidence." The proposed new caution was: "You do not have to say anything. But if you do not mention now something which you may later use in your defence, the court may decide that your failure to mention it now strengthens the case against you. A record will be made of anything you say and it may be given in evidence if you are brought to trial."

Richard Ferguson QC, chairman of the Criminal Bar Association, responded: "To me it is unintelligible and contradictory … The right of silence has effectively been abolished." Andrew Puddenphatt, secretary of Liberty, said: "What the new caution is saying is that if you don't say anything you've had it. It undermines the presumption of innocence which is a cornerstone of our criminal justice system."

The Act came into force in April 1995, but elements of the cartel apparently see it in the same light as tax law, a challenge to their ingenuity in getting round it. In 1996 Sir Paul Condon, Commissioner of the Metropolitan Police, said "lawyers are deliberately undermining last year's Criminal Justice Act in respect of the right of the prosecution to comment on a suspect's refusal to speak to police".

Stern. Reviewing David Rose's book on the collapse of criminal justice, Richard Stern wrote in *The Spectator* (February 10, 1996): "Rose seems uneasy about the abolition – more accurately the diminution – of the time-honoured 'right to silence' in the 1994 Criminal Justice and Public Order Act. Since April last year, failure to answer questions put by the police and failure to give evidence in court allows the Bench to draw a 'proper inference'. This is simply a long overdue victory for common sense over the special (and specious) pleading of lawyers.

"It may bring us to call into question the entire adversarial game prevailing in this country, and to re-examine the merits of the Continental 'inquisitorial' system, whereby a key role is played by an examining magistrate. As Rose says, the vested interests against change remain powerful. 'For most barristers, the structures of English justice have become a fetishistic totem which preserves their own privileges.' More than 100 MPs in the current Parliament are barristers. That's one in six! What hope?"

Goldring. In August 1997, the NSW Attorney General, the Hon Jeffrey Shaw QC, referred the right of silence to the NSW Law Reform Commission to inquire as to whether it should similarly be diminished. Professor Jack Goldring, who believes the common law does have truth as a goal, was given the task of inquiring.

22

Error Entombed in the US Constitution

We, the people of the United States, in order to ... establish justice, insure domestic tranquillity ... promote the general welfare, and secure the blessings of liberty ... do ordain and establish this Constitution for the United States of America.

– Preamble, US Constitution, 1787

An unfortunate confluence of events trapped the United States in the English legal system. A panegyric to the common law by Sir William Blackstone appeared in 1765. The revolution broke out in 1775; the US Constitution, largely the work of a lawyer, Thomas Jefferson, was signed in 1787. The first nine Amendments, constituting the Bill of Rights, were made in 1791. They are largely credited to a non-lawyer, James Madison, but he must have had a common lawyer at his elbow.

Overriders. It is difficult to change the Constitution; an amendment requires a vote of two-thirds of Congress and the Senate and has to be ratified by three-fourths of the States. However, it seems to me that overriders in the Preamble to the Constitution would allow the Supreme Court to get rid of anything, including the common law, that defeats justice. However, Supreme Court Justices are members of the cartel and are subject to the malady.

Preamble. The Preamble states: "We, the people of the United States, in order to form a more perfect union, establish justice, insure domestic tranquillity, provide for the common defense, promote the general welfare, and secure the blessings of liberty to ourselves and our posterity, do ordain and establish this Constitution for the United States of America." It can hardly be claimed that "justice" and "the general welfare" are promoted by the common law and its various rules and procedures, including the right of silence and the adversary system. The Amendments were designed to guarantee individual liberties, to prevent oppression by the state, and to confirm that the framers were determined to persevere with English common law. Judge Rothwax's preference for truth suggests he believes that the last was a grave mistake. I collate them here for ease of reference.

Fourth. The Fourth Amendment provided the nominal basis for Justice Tom Clark's famous exclusionary rule. It is designed to prevent unreasonable search and seizure. It states: "The right of the people to be secure in their persons, houses, papers, and effects against unreasonable searches and seizures shall not be violated, and no warrants shall issue but upon probable cause supported by oath or affirmation and particularly describing the place to be searched and the persons or things to be seized." Probable cause means a reasonable belief that a crime has been committed or is about to happen.

Fifth. The Fifth provides a privilege against self-incrimination and a right of silence. It repeats Justice Dyer's 1568 fraudulent use of canon law. It states: "No person shall be ... compelled in any criminal case to be a witness against himself, nor be deprived of life, liberty or property without due process of law ..."

Oliver Cyriax says that, according to the FBI, "taking the Fifth" was invented by Murray (The Camel) Humphreys (1899-1965). If so, this Mafia identity may have had roles in the development of both the Fourth and Fifth Amendments in ways that assist criminals of his stripe.

Sixth. The Sixth confirmed the use of the adversary system. It states: "In all criminal prosecutions, the accused shall enjoy the right to a speedy and public trial by an impartial jury ... and to be informed of the nature and cause of the accusation; to be confronted with witnesses against him; to have compulsory process for obtaining witnesses in his favor; and to have the assistance of counsel for his defense."

Seventh. The Seventh confirmed the retention of the common law. It states: "In suits at common law where the value in controversy shall exceed twenty dollars, the right of trial by jury shall be preserved, and no fact tried by a jury shall be otherwise re-examined in any court of the United States than according to the rules of the common law."

Fourteenth. The 14th Amendment (1868) arose out of the Civil War; it guaranteed civil rights to former slaves. It stated: "No State shall make or enforce any law which shall abridge the privileges or immunities of citizens of the United States, nor shall any State deprive any person of life, liberty or property without due process of law, nor deny to any person within its jurisdiction the equal protection of the laws."

If judges could ignore the 14th amendment for at least a century, there seems no reason why they should not ignore the more damaging amendments.

23

Magic Trick 5

The Rule Against Patterns (Similar Facts)

... stripping away legality and coming back to common sense and reality, how can the committee determine whether someone is sick or not without looking at the entire picture?

– Justice James Wood, February 1995

The rule against similar facts says jurors cannot hear relevant evidence showing that the accused had a propensity to commit the crime with which he is charged. They thus cannot hear evidence of a pattern of dubious behaviour, including his criminal record, if any.

Menendez. Lyle and Erik Menendez murdered their parents, Jose and Kitty, for US$15 million in 1989. The jurors were not allowed to hear that Erik earlier wrote a screenplay in which an heir kills his parents for their money. Police believed a motive was that Jose had learned that Erik was homosexual and was about to cut the sons off financially. Their lawyer, Leslie Abramson, "fought tigerishly" to keep this out of court. It took six and a half years and two trials to find them guilty of murder.

Sex Offenders. The pattern rule is convenient for sex offenders. In March 1994, a man appeared in the Sydney District Court charged with sexual assault. Unknown to the jury, he was serving a prison sentence on another charge. They found him not guilty, and were surprised when Judge Thomas Ducker ordered him to be taken back to prison. Judge Ducker explained that the law had obliged him to keep certain evidence from them, and said the truth "is being hidden from juries at times in circumstances which are productive of injustice and unfairness".

The Mafia. It is also convenient for organised criminals who insulate themselves from the crimes they order. In the US, senior members of the Mafia were virtually untouched for 60 years, partly because of the similar facts rule. (It also helped that J. Edgar Hoover, head of the FBI from 1924 until his death in 1972, made no attempt to investigate the Mafia. There are suggestions that his sexual proclivities made him subject to blackmail and to small bribes via fixed horse races.)

RICO. President Richard Nixon and his first law officer, John Mitchell, are not usually the subjects of unbridled admiration, but they were responsible for the Organised Crime Control Act of 1970 and its RICO (Racketeer-influenced and Corrupt Organisations) provisions. RICO tends to eliminate the rule against similar facts for organised criminals. Oliver Cyriax says RICO was largely unappreciated until June 1980, when one of its architects, Professor G. Robert Blakey, held a seminar at Cornell University to explain to FBI agents how the law could be used against the Mafia's entire organisational structure.

Fat Tony et al. An indication of the number of miscarriages of justice in favour of organised criminals caused by the rule against similar facts in the US from 1800 to 1981, and the number of similar miscarriages still occurring in other common law countries, is available. James B. Jacobs *et al* note that between 1981 and 1992, 23 previously untouchable heads of Mafia families throughout the US were convicted on RICO charges. The New York families are Genovese, Lucchese, Colombo, Bonnano and Gambino. The family heads put off the streets were:

Frank (Funzi) Tieri, Genovese.
Anthony (Fat Tony) Salerno, Genovese.
Anthony (Tony Ducks) Corallo, Lucchese.
Carmine (The Snake) Persico, Colombo.
Philip (Rusty) Rastelli, Bonnano.
Carlos Marcello, New Orleans.
Eugene Smaldone, Denver.
Joseph Aiuppa, Chicago.
Nick Civella, Kansas City.
Carl Civella, Kansas City.
Dominick Brooklier, Los Angeles
Frank Balistrieri, Boston.
Gennaro Anguilo, Boston.
Russell Buffalino, Pittston, Philadelphia.
Nicodemo Scarfo, Philadelphia.
James Licavoli, Cleveland.
Michael Trupiano, St. Louis.
Sam Russotti, Buffalo.
John Gotti, Gambino.
Raymond Patriarca, Providence, Rhode Island.
Vittorio Amuso, Lucchese.
Vicorio Orena, Colombo.
John Riggi, DeCavalcante family, New Jersey.
Vincent (Chin) Gigante, Genovese family, was sent down in 1997.

Frank Costigan QC and other experts on organised crime have been recommending RICO-type legislation in Australia since 1984. A recent recommendation for RICO was made in 1994 by the judge mentioned in chapter 6 who spoke about how juries work. Nothing has been done: the community's non-lawyer representatives in Parliament have not forced the issue; the cartel usually resists change and Attorneys-General departments necessarily consist of members of the cartel. In 1993 Justice Sir William Kearney, of the NT Supreme Court, said: "Our laws are deficient in contemplating how to deal with the menace presented by organised criminal activity."

Leonard. On October 13, 1997, Richard Leonard, a Sydney abattoir worker, pleaded guilty in closed court to murdering a taxi driver, Ezzedine Bahmad, by stabbing him on November 18, 1994. Later that day he pleaded not guilty to murdering landscape gardener Stephen Dempsey with a bow and arrow on August 2, 1994. The jury was not informed of the first murder. After four days of deliberation, they found Leonard guilty. Justice Jeremy Badgery-Parker then told them that he had pleaded guilty to the other murder.

Character. The character rule is related to the rule against similar facts; relevant evidence of the accused's general bad character must be concealed.

Exceptions. Stone and Wells refer to "the heavy bias of this rule against the prosecution" and note that the English Parliament made three exceptions that "seem to indicate ... an abandonment ... of a basic principle of the whole common law system of evidence, and a corresponding adoption of continental principles ... Modification was not by abandonment *en bloc* of old principles, but by the creation of exceptions to them, wherever the minimum of efficiency in the administration of justice seemed to require it".

The first exception is that evidence of a person's bad character can be introduced if he claims his character is good. Stone and Wells say this came in via the Larceny Act of 1861 which provided: "... if upon the trial of any person ... such person shall give evidence of his good character, it shall be lawful for the prosecutor in answer thereto, to give evidence of the conviction of such person for the previous offence or offences."

The second exception was inspired by "the great difficulties of proving guilty knowledge in prosecutions for receiving stolen property". Section 19 of the Prevention of Crimes Act of 1971 provided that in cases of receiving stolen property evidence might be given "that there was found in the possession of [the accused] other property stolen within the preceding period of twelve months" or that he has "within five years immediately preceding been convicted of any offence involving fraud or dishonesty".

"The third and most radical" exception was via Section 1(f) of the Criminal Evidence Act of 1898. In contrast to the first two exceptions, this applied to all criminal trials, but the terms of the provision caused "considerable difficulties of interpretation ... it subjected the accused, in certain contingencies, to searching cross-examination tending to show that he has committed or been charged with or convicted of some other offence, as well as to show his bad character".

Domestic Violence. Queensland Premier Wayne Goss said in January 1996 that the Evidence Act would be changed to allow juries to hear the whole story in cases where women were charged with killing their partner. The jury could now hear evidence of the history of the partners' violence towards them.

Albert. Marv Albert, 56, television sportscaster, was charged with forcing a receptionist to engage in oral sex in an Arlington, Virginia, motel room in February 1997. At the trial in September 1997, Judge Benjamin Kendrick allowed in evidence from another woman who said Albert assaulted her, but she escaped by pulling his wig off. Albert then agreed to plea bargain the charge down to assault.

Murphy. It was noted in the section on the right of silence how Justice Lionel Murphy, of the Australian High Court, manipulated the law to keep evidence of his bad character and 14 other possible crimes out of his perversion trial.

Germany. At a trial in Germany, the first thing the judge does is examine the accused about his past and general character.

24

Magic Trick 6

The Rule against Hearsay

The nonsense that the rule against hearsay can perpetrate was acknowledged by Lord Diplock in a rare piece of judicial candour about its artificiality in Jones v Metcalf.

— Adrian Roden QC, 1989

Like all evidence concealed by the common law rules, hearsay evidence should be weighed rather than subtracted. Stone and Wells note that "hearsay was constantly admitted" prior to the end of the 18th century, presumably on the ground that the judge could informally advise the jurors to give it less weight than direct evidence. The rule to conceal hearsay thus derives from the adversary system, and like that system, it can get the guilty off and imprison the innocent.

The theoretical basis of the rule is that the person who made the original statement is not available for cross-examination which might show he/she was wrong, confused or had a secret agenda, but that is not a reasonable argument for suppressing it altogether. The artificiality noted by Roden QC is easily demonstrated: as Ambrose Bierce notes (see below) it wipes out all history prior to, say, 1910; the people who could give evidence about it are not available for cross-examination. If in the real world we took the slightest notice of the rule, we could take no account, for example, of the amendments to the US Constitution.

Precedent. As noted in chapter 8, the rule against hearsay is at odds with the rule of precedent. Judges are obliged to accept the decisions of dead judges who are not available for cross-examination which would probably show they were wrong, confused or had a secret agenda, or perhaps all three, as in the case of Lord Mansfield's assertion about the greater the truth the greater the libel.

O.J. Simpson. At the O.J. Simpson criminal trial in January 1996, Judge Lance Ito felt obliged to conceal evidence that Simpson's murdered former wife, Nicole, rang a refuge five days before she was murdered and said Simpson was stalking her and that she was afraid. He also concealed diary entries in which she wrote that she was afraid Simpson might kill her.

Judge Ito said: "To the man or woman on the street, the relevance and probative [tending to prove guilt] value of such evidence is both obvious and compelling ... it seems only just and right that a crime victim's own words be heard". But, he said, legal precedents "clearly held that it is reversible error" to admit them.

Riley. There is an exception to the rule against hearsay for statements made by people who know they are dying. Nicole Brown Simpson may have feared she was going to be killed, but she did not "know" she was going to die; therefore her (in effect) dying statements could not be admitted.

Likewise statements by Stoker J.J. Riley, said to have been stabbed 14 times by Acting Leading Stoker A.R. Gordon in company with Stoker E.J. Elias at about 7.50 pm on Tuesday, March 12, 1942. on board the battle cruiser HMAS *Australia*. Commander James Goldrick reports that the ship was on its way to Noumea, New Caledonia after acting as support for American air attacks on Japanese units in New Guinea waters.

Riley's wounds included "general peritonitis following a penetrating wound of the abdominal cavity, a perforating wound of the small intestine, penetrating wounds of the right pleural cavity, laceration of the right lung, a penetrating wound of the liver and perforation of the diaphragm, as well as severe blood loss and shock."

Surgeon Lieutenant M.J.L. Stening questioned Riley in the sick bay at 8 pm.

"What has happened to you?"

"I have been stabbed."

"Who stabbed you?"

"Leading Stoker Gordon."

"Why did he stab you?"

"Because I found out he was a poufter." (So spelled in a report of an interview with Stening eight days later.)

The second-in-command of the *Australia*, Commander J.M. Armstrong, and Surgeon Lieutenant N. Larkins interviewed Riley when he became conscious early next evening, Wednesday, March 13. He again named Gordon and Elias as being responsible.

"Can you tell me exactly what happened?" Armstrong asked.

"We were standing up on deck talking and the [call] went for the First Watch. I turned to walk away and copped it in the back ..."

"Did you accuse them of being bugger-boys?"

"Yes."

"Have you ever seen them at it?" Dr Larkins asked.

"No, but I have certain proof."

Armstrong asked: "Did you try and get money from them at any time?"

"No."

Riley could answer no more questions; he became unconscious and died at 9.55 pm on March 13.

Goldrick explains the legal position: "At no time had Riley been informed of the seriousness of his condition; thus, his statements would be inadmissible to a court. The unsworn statement of a deceased person is not valid in law unless the deceased was formally aware when making such a statement that he was dying, or if he, having made allegations, was subsequently warned of his state and given adequate opportunity to withdraw or modify them. In consequence, since Gordon and Elias had not been positively identified as striking a blow, and as no weapon was ever found, the evidence would be entirely circumstantial in nature. Furthermore, no motive could be imputed in court."

The Navy was not unhappy with this drivel; rum, sodomy and the lash may have been a tradition in the English Navy, but in 1942 the Australian Navy took the view that it might not play in, say, Brisbane. As it happened, there was little chance of a miscarriage; the circumstantial evidence was overwhelming. A court-martial found Gordon and Elias guilty, a verdict later confirmed by a Royal Commission.

West. The evidence of a dead man was heard for the first time in an English court in November 1995. Rosemary West was charged with murdering 10 girls and young women between 1972 and 1987. The jury heard tapes of four of 145 conversations between Rosemary West's late husband, Fred, and police in January 1994. He hanged himself in prison on January 1, 1995. On the tapes, Fred West described strangling his daughter, 16 and others and cutting them up. He insisted his wife knew nothing of his activities. She was found guilty.

Connell. In a case mentioned in chapter 29 below, in which Perth financier Laurie Connell was charged with fixing a horse race at Bunbury in 1983, his counsel, Alec Shand QC, called a brothel madam, Lidia Coyle, to give evidence that a Connell associate, Sam Franchina, told her that he and another man were involved in rigging horse races in early 1983, and that Connell was set up as a fall guy to protect the identity of the other man. Justice Desmond Heenan ruled it was hearsay and not admissible. The jury found Connell not guilty on that charge.

Bierce: Ambrose Gwinett Bierce (1842-1914?) had a clear notion of the stupefying unreality of the common law. In *The Devil's Dictionary* (1906, 1911) he noted that "hearsay evidence is inadmissible because the person quoted was unsworn and is not before the court for cross-examination, yet most momentous actions ... are daily undertaken on hearsay evidence. There is no religion in the world that has any other basis than hearsay evidence ... It cannot be proved that the Battle of Blenheim ever was fought, that there was such a person as Julius Caesar."

Keeping the Meter Running. In ambiguity lies power. Frank Bates, Reader in Law at the University of Tasmania, says that "the rule against hearsay is both highly technical and cumbersome in its operation". It thus gives advocates opportunity for legal argument about whether or not particular evidence can be admitted.

Jones v Metcalf. As noted in the epigraph to this chapter, Adrian Roden QC, former Justice of the NSW Supreme Court, said: "The nonsense that the rule against hearsay can perpetrate was acknowledged by Lord Diplock [in 1967] in a rare piece of judicial candour about its artificiality in *Jones v Metcalf*."

In that case, a man saw a truck cause a minor accident and remembered the number long enough to inform the police. Police interviewed a man; he admitted he was the driver of the truck, but denied causing the accident. The driver was charged, but when the case came before justices of the peace the witness no longer remembered the truck's number, nor could he swear he saw the policeman write it down. The justices found the offence proved.

The man appealed. The Court of Appeal found that the justices should not have admitted the policeman's note because it was hearsay; the accused thus had no case to answer. Lord Diplock said: "I have every sympathy for the justices because the inference of fact that the appellant was the driver ... is irresistible as a matter of common sense. But this [the rule against hearsay] is a branch of the law that has little to do with common sense."

Sparks v The Queen. *Sparks* worked the other way; it caused a miscarriage against a man charged with a sexual offence against a very young girl. Roden says: "It is true that as a general rule hearsay is less reliable than direct evidence. But much that is strictly hearsay can be of value, while much that is direct and admissible is not. *Sparks v R* [1964] AC 964 provides a commonly cited illustration of potentially relevant and valuable evidence being 'properly' rejected as hearsay."

The girl told her mother shortly after the incident that a "coloured boy" was responsible, but a white man was charged. The child did not give evidence, and the trial judge concealed from the jurors, as hearsay, the mother's evidence about the girl's identification of a "coloured boy" as the offender. The man was found guilty. The Judicial Committee of the Privy Council, which hears appeals from certain parts of the British Commonwealth, ruled that the child's statement had been rightly excluded as hearsay, but allowed the man's appeal on other grounds.

Stygian Waters. Stygian is defined as dark, gloomy, infernal, hellish, pertaining to the lower world river Styx, over which the souls of the dead were ferried. Stone and Wells say it is important to grasp the distinction between facts to be proved and the way they can be proved. They say: "... the student must grasp this distinction or remain forever lost on the Stygian waters of hearsay".

Subramanian. *Subramanian v Public Prosecutor* (1956) is a famous case in which a Malayan judge sank in the Stygian waters and the innocent accused sank with him. During the "Emergency"

(1948-60), when Communist guerillas were trying to take power, the accused was found in possession of ammunition and was presumed to be guilty of terrorism. His defence was that he had been captured by guerillas and was acting under duress. He tried to give evidence of being taken to the Communists' leader, but the judge stopped him with the words: " ... hearsay evidence is not admissible and all the conversations with bandits are not admissible unless they are called."

The judge did not understand that, while what the absent leader said was hearsay, it was not hearsay for the accused to give direct evidence that a conversation took place, and that fact of itself might point to his mental state. The accused was found guilty; the judge sentenced him to death, but the Privy Council found the judge was wrong and quashed the conviction.

Exceptions. Some think hearsay can never be admitted, but Stone and Wells note a number of exceptions to the rule. They say the exceptions "represent situations in which experience has shown that hearsay is not as unreliable as it usually is ..."

The Verbal. That is arguable; the best-known exceptions are alleged verbal admissions and confessions to police. A false accusation that a suspect has made a verbal admission is thus known as a "verbal". Police routinely "verbal" suspects, according to evidence before Justice Wood's inquiry on police corruption in NSW.

Some believe police only "verbal" those they know are guilty because the rules for concealing evidence will otherwise get them off. That is not true, particularly in cases where the crime involved an ethnic minority: police are not above verballing the nearest available person of a different colour. It is thus remarkable that the law, so tender in its anxious care for the "low" intellectual calibre of judges and jurors and for fair trials for suspects, had contrived to find an exception to the hearsay rule which practically guaranteed miscarriages of justice.

McKinney & Judge. As noted in chapter 16 (Playing the Saxophone: The Adversary System in Action), Detective Sergeant Neville Scullion told Justice Wood in July 1995: "The [NSW police] hierarchy was more interested in the arrest rate" than in the conviction rate. The "verbal" became so notorious that, as noted in chapter 20 The Right of Silence in Action, the High Court of Australia ruled in *McKinney and Judge* (1992) that a charge should not proceed if the only evidence against a suspect was a challenged confession.

Emasculation. Mark Weinberg says: "The rule against hearsay is unquestionably the most important exclusionary rule in our law of evidence. Whether it should be retained, and if so in what from, have been questions of great moment in recent years. Opinions range across a broad spectrum. Wigmore describes the rule as a 'most characteristic rule of the Anglo-American rule of evidence – a rule which may be esteemed, next to jury trial, the greatest contribution of that eminently practical legal system to the world's methods of procedure'."

So much for Wigmore. Weinberg continues: "More recently far less laudatory views have been expressed about the rule, including calls for its total abolition, or at least its partial emasculation."

To repeat, common sense indicates that hearsay should be weighed, as in Europe, rather than subtracted. Australia is moving towards emasculation, i.e. the acceptance of certain types of hearsay.

25

Magic Trick 7

A Confusing Formula for the Standard of Proof

Milat. Serial killers like to keep trophies. The case against Ivan Milat, charged in May 1994 with murdering seven backpackers in the Belanglo State Forest in the NSW Southern Highlands, looked open and shut: his Sydney home had several identified articles belonging to murdered German, English, Welsh and Australian backpackers, and an Englishman, Paul Onions, gave evidence that Milat had tried to abduct him.

A Reasonable Doubt. Milat was found guilty in 1996, but some reporters covering the case thought he might get off, or that there might be a hung jury. This was because the criminal standard of proof is formulated in a negative and confusing way: the jury have to find him guilty "beyond a reasonable doubt". No one knows what "reasonable" means, and judges are not allowed to try to explain it to jurors for fear of further muddying the waters.

Unreasonable Doubt. If a juror works at it, he can doubt anything. The thought process may be: I am a reasonable person. I have a doubt, therefore it must be reasonable. Therefore I must find him innocent, although I think he is guilty." Where unanimous verdicts are required, the defence lawyer needs only one such juror to provide a hung jury and the chance that the Crown will decide not to have a retrial. His basic strategy is thus to try to create even a tiny doubt.

Professor Langbein notes: "Adversary procedure pressured the judge towards passivity and broke up the older working relationship of judge and jury. In a system of 'trial that was coming to be more commonly conducted by lawyers,' Beattie [J.M. Beattie, *Crime and the Courts in England: 1660-1800 (1986)*] observes, 'the judge came to play a much less active role in producing the evidence'. In the 17th and 18th centuries [here Langbein quotes himself], 'it was the trial judge who examined the witnesses and the accused, and ... like the modern Continental presiding judge, dominated the proceedings'.

"By the early 19th century a visiting French observer [Cottu] reported that the judge 'remains almost a stranger to what is going on', while counsel for prosecution and defense examined and cross-examined the witnesses. Other hallmarks of lawyer-driven criminal procedure fell into place in these years, including the privilege against self-incrimination, and the articulation of the beyond-a-reasonable-doubt standard of proof".

Professor Langbein says he explains in a 1994 article "why it is appropriate to see the recognition of the privilege "as a consequence of the revolutionary reconstruction of the criminal trial worked by the advent of defense counsel and adversary criminal procedure" in these years.

He says: "The concept that the application of horrific criminal sanction merited special caution was centuries old ... However, the precise doctrinal formulation of the beyond-a-reasonable-doubt standard of proof in Anglo-American criminal procedure occurred at the end of the 18th century as part of the elaboration of the adversary system of criminal procedure. Beattie points to formulations of the standard of proof used in jury instructions of the 1780s that were still well short of beyond-reasonable-doubt."

The reasonable doubt formula is thus the third product of the adversary system. The French formula is similar, but is expressed in a way jurors can understand: they and the judge have to be "intimately [thoroughly] convinced". And, unlike common law jurors, they have to give reasons.

26

Magic Trick 8

The Christie Discretion:
How to Conceal Virtually All Evidence

If there ever was such a thing as judicial corruption it might well reside in the expanding and almost inscrutable discretions which can alter the whole course of a criminal inquiry.

– Professor John Forbes, University of Queensland, 1992

To repeat: in ambiguity lies power. If the hearsay rule is "dark, gloomy, infernal", the *Christie* discretion (from a 1914 case in the English Court of Appeal) belongs perhaps to some even more "hellish" section of the common law's Stygian waters.

Probative means tending to prove (the charge). The *Christie* discretion gives a judge power to conceal evidence if, **in his opinion**, it is factually only slightly probative, but it may cause great prejudice against the accused in the minds of jurors of allegedly feeble intelligence and sense of fairness. (How judges cope when sitting without a jury is a matter for speculation).

The Last Nail. The *Christie* discretion is the last nail in the truth coffin. The judge's opinion concerns fact, not law, and so cannot be the subject of appeal. It thus effectively gives judges a non-appealable power to conceal almost any relevant and probative evidence at all. As Dr Forbes suggests, this gives extraordinary power to corrupt judges, if such exist. Murray (The Camel) Humphreys would know how to use the discretion.

Stone and Wells say the "relevant facts" to be concealed by the discretion "must be of comparatively little probative weight [and] this slight relevance must be accompanied by a great potentiality for prejudice, such that 'the effect on the minds of the jury ... might seriously prejudice the fairness of the trial'," (as Lord Moulton said in *R v Christie* [1914]).

The Chaos Theory. "Slight" is the problem. How slight is slight? Can a person be slightly pregnant? Can evidence be slightly probative? Judge John Helman, chairman of the Queensland District Court, said there might be "chaos" if different judges used the discretion on the same probative evidence. Judge Boulton disclosed the "chaos" theory when he again appeared as judge in a case, *R v Rooklyn*, (1992) which he had aborted eight months earlier because a media report had allegedly prejudiced its fair hearing. He said that

Judge Helman had taken the view "that once a judge had matters, particularly dealing with questions of admissibility of evidence, that there be some consistency rather than putting matters to different judges who, on discretionary matters and so forth, might presumably bring the whole system into chaos".

The Lottery Effect. This confirms the common law's lottery effect and the cost to the community of bringing charges that may have had no chance of succeeding: the Director of Public Prosecutions cannot know what relevant and admissible evidence a judge may conceal via the discretion.

Working the Wrong Way Round. As Stone and Wells note, judges are not supposed to even consider the possible prejudicial effect of a fact unless it is only slightly probative, but there is room for speculation that some judges, pressed by anxious care to be fair to the accused, may subconsciously work the other way round: they see that the fact is highly damaging, and decide it is more prejudicial than probative and wrongly conceal it that way.

Defence Lawyers. The *Christie* discretion is thus fertile ground for defence lawyers: they can claim that almost any relevant fact is only slightly probative but highly prejudicial. And, depending on the judge, they might get lucky with some of the evidence. At the least, they can keep the meter ticking over.

A Case Study. Sir Terence Lewis (b. 1928) was Police Commissioner of Queensland (pop. 1986: 2,675,300) from 1976 to 1987. He was corrupt at least from 1978, when a former Detective Sergeant, Jack Herbert, became Lewis's bagman (collector and distributor of bribes/extortion moneys from prostitution and illegal gambling). Herbert had been the force's bagman in the same lucrative areas from 1960 to 1974.

In 1987, the Hon Gerald Fitzgerald QC (he is now President of the Court of Appeal) began a commission of inquiry into police and political corruption in tropical and sub-tropical Queensland. His inquiry appeared to confirm the late Robert Haupt's theory that corruption increases as the square of the distance from the North or South Pole. The inquiry and Lewis's subsequent trial offer an informative case study of the difference between the evidence heard at an inquisitorial proceeding and a common law criminal trial, and of evidence that can be concealed via the *Christie* discretion.

Jack Herbert "rolled over" (as the police phrase had it) in return for immunity and gave evidence of the corruption of himself, Lewis and others. The inquiry thus exposed a mountain of evidence indicating that Lewis had reached level 5 (the highest) on Professor Alfred McCoy's scale of police corruption, i.e. organised crime being franchised by a small group of senior police, as it was in Hong Kong before an Independent Commission Against Corruption was set up there in the early 1970s.

Sir Terence was obliged to give evidence at the inquiry but he appeared to be troubled by a form of amnesia. It is said that an ounce of evidence is worth a pound of demeanour, but spectators can see when a witness is being evasive, probably because he cannot afford to tell the truth.

The Queen v Lewis (I). Herbert's evidence included assertions that he and Lewis extorted monthly bribes from an organised criminal, Jack Rooklyn, from 1978 to 1987. In July 1989, Lewis was charged on 15 counts of corruption, including that he corruptly agreed to accept bribes from Herbert from 1978 to 1987, and that between 25 May and 31 December 1980 he corruptly agreed to accept a bribe of $25,000 from Rooklyn for a particular purpose.

The Crown retained the leader of the criminal bar, Bob Mulholland QC, to prosecute; John Jerrard appeared for Lewis; Judge Anthony Healy presided in the District Court. Herbert was to be the major witness. It is accepted that witnesses like Herbert may have a motive to lie; the law says jurors can convict on the evidence of an accomplice alone, if they believe him, but it would clearly be better if he was corroborated (supported) by independent evidence.

Lewis began on May 14, 1990 with legal argument without a jury being empanelled. There had been a lot of publicity about Lewis; Judge Healy seemed determined to make sure no one could say he did not get a fair trial. After a fortnight of legal argument, Judge Healy detailed the material he would not allow the jury to hear. Without the full background it may be largely unintelligible, but a sample is included to indicate the volume of evidence a jury does not hear at a common law trial. It can first be noted that:

- The material does not include relevant evidence already concealed by the prosecution because it would be ruled inadmissible on the ground that it was hearsay, similar fact evidence, or character evidence.

- If Judge Healy were sitting without a jury he would have to hear the evidence before concealing it on the ground that it might prejudice him. This either means that such evidence cannot prejudice a judge, in which case he should admit it, or that it can prejudice him, in which case, having concealed the evidence, he should hand the trial over to another judge. The process may thus seem another product of the malady.

- Sir Terence did not propose to give the trial jury an opportunity to see him attempting to answer Mulholland's questions; he intended to utilise Magic Trick Number 4, the right of silence. He instructed Jerrard to tell the jury that Herbert was an informant, not an accomplice.

- A legal system that conceals this much evidence may be trying to be fair, but it is not trying to find the truth; as Judge Rothwax says: suppressing evidence is suppressing truth.

Evidence Generally Excluded. Listed below is some of the evidence excluded on the ground of Judge Healy's opinion that it was not relevant, not probative, or that it contravened the rules for concealing evidence. If the assertion was that Sir Terence Lewis was an organised criminal, and if Australia had RICO legislation, some of it would have been admitted as showing a pattern. The excluded material included:

- Conversations in which Herbert told another person that Lewis was corrupt.

- A list of numbers and names [of illegal bookmakers] in Herbert's handwriting found among the possessions of an admittedly corrupt Assistant Commissioner, Graeme Parker (irrelevant).

- Noel Kelly, an admittedly corrupt officer, gave Herbert a message from Parker that Herbert should go overseas when the Fitzgerald inquiry was announced (irrelevant).

- Herbert's evidence that Parker told him Lewis wanted him to go overseas.

- Illegal bookmakers' belief that Lewis was corrupt.

- Herbert's dealings with Bulger (an admittedly corrupt officer).

- Taped evidence concerning a conversation between Kelly and Herbert's son, John.

- A letter Herbert's daughter wrote to Lady Lewis and her reply.

- A code Herbert gave his son John and Bulger.

- A code shared with Bulger.

- The way Herbert contacted Geraldo Bellino (an illegal casino operator) from England because he wanted to learn Bulger's version of events, and the document containing answers to questions from Herbert to Bulger.

- The evidence of Herbert's wife, Peggy, except about money paid directly to her by Lady Lewis.

- The entire evidence of Herbert's son and daughter.

Herbert asserted that back in the 1960s he gave Lewis small sums at the request of another policeman. Judge Healy's reason for excluding some of that evidence was: "The evidence does not appear to be probative of corrupt conduct on the part of the accused at that time as it is not even alleged by Herbert that the accused was doing anything which could be called corrupt in exchange for the money that he was allegedly receiving from Herbert."

On the other hand, a juror might think that Lewis would know the money came from bribes/extortions; that by accepting it he was compromised in Herbert's eyes; and that this gave Herbert the confidence to approach him with an extortion scheme after Lewis became Commissioner. In fact, when Lewis's trial finally got under way more than a year later, it inadvertently emerged, as a result of a question from Jerrard, that Herbert's motive for paying him the small sums in the 1960s was that he knew Lewis was close to the corrupt Commissioner, Frank Bischof.

Evidence Excluded via the Christie Discretion. Judge Healy said: "I turn now to the evidence which is said to be corroborative of Jack Herbert's evidence. Much of that evidence is capable of corroborating Jack Herbert and is therefore probative. However, some of the evidence identified by Mr Mulholland as corroborative appears to me to be of little probative value but of the kind that would be highly prejudicial to the accused if I admit it."

It was Judge Healy's opinion that the evidence he excluded only slightly tended to prove Lewis's guilt, but, as Judge Boulton said, different judges might have different views. So might jurors, who are supposed to bring their common sense to bear on the evidence. Some of the evidence excluded on the basis that Judge Healy thought it was only slightly probative was:

- Lewis's diary entries, which Mulholland said he could prove were false, purporting to show that he was a successful punter in a period, 1979 to 1987, when it was alleged that he was corrupt.

- Analysis of his financial records from 1982 to 1987 showing that he had unexplained cash of more than $30,000 plus what he would have paid over six years for living expenses, including food and clothing for himself, Lady Lewis, and one son.

- His false sworn denial in 1980 that he had ever had anything to do with Jack Rooklyn.

- His transfer to Lady Lewis of his half interest in their mansion immediately after he became aware that Parker was confessing his corruption.

- His false sworn explanation for putting his house entirely in Lady Lewis's name, i.e. to protect the house from his creditors, but he had no difficulties with creditors at the time.

Court of Criminal Appeal. Mulholland had the proceedings stopped in order to test in the Court of Criminal Appeal (CCA) whether Judge Healy was right to exclude the evidence. He told the CCA that Judge Healy had excluded "almost all" the evidence from Lewis's own actions that would corroborate Herbert, and that some of it was "incapable of being categorised as of slight or trifling weight".

In August 1990, the CCA, consisting of Chief Justice John Murtagh Macrossan and Justices Jack Kelly and Peter Connolly were persuaded by David Jackson QC, for Lewis, that even if Judge Healy was wrong, there was nothing they could do about it: his errors, if any, were errors of fact, not of law, and they could only deal with questions of law.

The implication is that a common law trial judge can never be wrong on a question of fact. This is clearly unreasonable; European courts of appeal accept that the trial judge can be wrong on fact.

The Queen v Lewis (II). The Lewis matter started again on 18 March 1991. Judge Healy again presided. Technically, it was the first Lewis trial because a jury had not been empanelled the last time, and Jerrard and Mulholland went round the legal argument all over again. Dickens was not wrong.

Judge Healy said he was not going to depart from his previous rulings to exclude evidence via the *Christie* discretion. In addition, he now ruled out a 1980 tape of Herbert's phone calls to Barry MacNamara, an accomplice of Herbert and Lewis in their extortions from Rooklyn. On the tape, which was contemporaneous with the event, Herbert and McNamara discuss Lewis's vile behaviour in giving them only $9000 instead of the agreed $10,000 of Rooklyn's $25,000 bribe. Apart from bitter denunciation of Lewis for trousering $1000 of their end of the bribe, Herbert says: "Terry loves this stuff".

In the real world inhabited by jurors, the tape might seem to corroborate Herbert's contention that Lewis was a crook, that Herbert negotiated the bribe with Rooklyn, that Lewis gave him the $9000 at the Mayfair Crest Hotel at a certain time. It might also seem to corroborate the evidence of waiter, Serge Pregliasco, who placed Lewis and Rooklyn in a room in the hotel about that time.

But the common law can be some place other than the real world; the jurors never heard the tape. After lengthy argument, the Judge decided to exclude it on two grounds. He told Jerrard on April 4: " ... I have come to the conclusion that this tape is not capable of corroborating Herbert because it is not independent of him. I do not think that the taped conversation between Herbert and MacNamara involves acts which could be said to be in furtherance of any corrupt agreement between them and I do not think it is part of the *res gestae* [the material facts of a case as opposed to hearsay]. Therefore I exclude it.

"But if I am wrong about that, the conversation tends to suggest, and this is Herbert's evidence, that your client is a person who is capable of ratting on his friends. That's not part of the indictment either. It would be very prejudicial to him to let it in, so I am excluding it."

Judge Healy had admitted items from Lewis's notebooks which were codes for people, including Rooklyn, that Lewis and Herbert discussed on the telephone, and also for places where, Herbert said, they met for Lewis to receive his share of the bribe money from prostitution and illegal gambling. At the earlier inquiry Fitzgerald QC seemed to think that, along with Herbert's evidence, the codes were the smoking gun that proved Lewis was corrupt. So did Mulholland; he said the codes were "like a fingerprint on a gun in a homicide case".

Jerrard, addressing the jury after Mulholland, suggested that Lewis made the codes in response to an offer from Herbert to inform on the people in the list. Had Lewis given evidence, Mulholland could have asked him what action he took on the information; the answer would have had to be, none. Jerrard said Lewis's only crime was to be a loyal friend to Herbert, who betrayed him and used his name to build an empire of corruption.

Summing up on Wednesday 31 July 1991, Judge Healy told the jury that Herbert's evidence was worthless: "the character of the accused has not been tarnished by it". The same applied to Peggy Herbert: "She has every reason to lie in order to save her husband and herself." And, he said, there was no evidence to support Herbert's evidence. He said it was "not fanciful" to consider that he was no more than an informer for Lewis. He said the lists were "not evidence from which you can draw an inference that the accused and Herbert were in a corrupt association ... I direct you as a matter of law that there is no evidence which is capable of corroborating ... Jack Herbert's evidence that the accused entered into the corrupt agreements in the indictment ..."

Judge Healy was wrong about that; the Appeal Court later found that the codes did corroborate Herbert. He concluded: "You may convict on the uncorroborated evidence of the Herberts, but it would be dangerous to do so."

Rogerson. Jurors can go either way on that instruction; for example, a case concerning Roger Rogerson, the Sydney detective who shot Warren Lanfranchi dead in 1981. A heroin dealer, Alan David Williams, later claimed that in 1983 he procured Rogerson to bribe detective Michael Drury to get Williams off a heroin charge. The attempt failed; Williams claimed that in 1984 he procured Rogerson and a professional assassin, Christopher Dale Flannery, to murder Drury. That failed also, if barely. Flannery was murdered on or about May 9, 1985. Rogerson was tried in May and June 1985 on charges of attempting to bribe Drury on behalf of Williams. He was found not guilty.

Williams pleaded guilty in 1988 to conspiring with Rogerson and Flannery to murder Drury, and was sentenced to 14 years with a minimum of six. Rogerson was tried in 1989 on the same charges. Williams gave evidence against Rogerson but he could not speak of the earlier attempt to bribe Drury because Rogerson was officially innocent of that charge. This left motive and perhaps internal corroboration rather up in the air. Justice Colin Allen told the jury it would be "dangerous in the extreme" to find Rogerson guilty on the basis of Williams's evidence. They found him not guilty.

A couple of points can be made. Rogerson's activities had been heavily reported over the years so they were in the air if not in evidence. This suggests that jurors do focus on the evidence at the trial, and are not unfairly prejudiced by media reports of events that do not get into evidence.

Second, would the jury have convicted if all the available pattern evidence about Rogerson had been before them? As in the case of the acquittal of the Gambino family boss, John Gotti, it may have made no difference: in the end, jurors rightly insist that the prosecution has to prove the particular case regardless of what the pattern might suggest about the accused.

What the Jury Did Not Hear. After the Lewis jury retired, Mulholland said the judge had "usurped the role and function of the jury", and asked him to change his ruling that there was no evidence capable of corroborating Herbert. He declined to do so. The jury was out for five days. On Monday August 5, 1991, they found Lewis guilty on all 15 counts. Judge Healy said: "The verdicts speak for themselves", and sentenced Lewis to the maximum of 14 years on each charge.

Doney's Case. It has been said that the jury's verdict in the Lewis case shows that the system works. I'm not sure that's so. I suspect that Lewis would have been found not guilty if the trial had proceeded normally when it started in May 1990. At that time, Australian trial judges had the power to direct jurors to enter a verdict of not guilty if, in the judge's view, a verdict of guilty would be unsafe and unsatisfactory. On what Judge Healy later said, it seems possible that he might have directed the jury to find Lewis not guilty. But in December 1990, the High Court ruled in *Doney* that the judge should warn the jurors but generally the jurors should make the verdict. Judge Healy took the view that after Doney he could not direct an acquittal even if, as he said, "I felt that the corroborative evidence was very slight indeed and really not of much weight".

Gagliardi. The day after the verdict, the Brisbane *Courier-Mail* ran J.J. Gagliardi's account of some of the evidence excluded in May 1990 and again in March 1991. The editor, Desmond Houghton, instructed his court reporters that in future they were to make a note of evidence excluded from major trials and to report it when the trial was over.

Strippage. The Appeal Court confirmed Sir Terence Lewis's conviction and sentence in August 1992; the High Court refused leave to appeal; Her Majesty stripped him of his knighthood. The Governor-General, Bill Hayden, a former Queensland detective, had graciously acceded to my request to ask Her Majesty how often she and previous monarchs had been obliged to perform this melancholy duty. I was thus able to report that Sir Terence was the 14th person since the 14th century to be subjected to strippage, and that he had the consolation of knowing that anyone can get a knighthood, but that he had now joined an exclusive club consisting of the Earl of Carlisle, Sir Ralph Grey, Lord Scrope, the Duke of Buckingham, Lord D'Arcy, Sir Francis Mitchell, Lord Cochrane, Sir Roger Casement, Sir Joseph Jonas, Lord Kylsant, Sir Anthony Blunt, Sir Joe Kagan, and Sir Jack Lyons.

27

Magic Trick 9

Tom Clark's Exclusionary Rule
Or Was it the Mafia's?

Did I become a judge for this? Is this the system I am proud to be part of? The Coolidge reversal makes me ashamed. Stories like this are an insult to common sense and fair play. There is certainly little feeling for the victim, who was brutally tortured and murdered. There is also little feeling for the truth.

— Judge Harold Rothwax, 1996

Muddle. Truth, as we have noted, is more than a goal; it is a brake on spurious argument, intellectual dishonesty, sophistry, injustice, self-delusion, folly, muddle, madness. The versions of the exclusionary rule in the United States and Australia seem the product at least of muddle.

The rule is concerned with concealing evidence said to have been unlawfully gained by the authorities. It is supposed to relate to two public interests: the law's duty to protect the community from criminals and its duty to protect the community from police oppression. It might be thought that the balance would be achieved by using the evidence if it was reliable and by severely punishing the offending authorities.

The US version of the rule does not punish the guilty authorities; it punishes the innocent community. Some judges think that concealing the evidence will deter police misbehaviour, but Justice Geoffrey Davies, of the Queensland Court of Appeal, says "there is not the slightest evidence that excluding evidence illegally or improperly obtained does discourage such conduct. Statistical studies in the United States indicate rather that it does not. On the other hand exclusion can often result in a plainly guilty person going free".

The solution put forward by Justice Davies and others is to admit the offending evidence and put police who deliberately offend before a special tribunal with the power to fine or imprison.

Fourth Amendment. There is nothing wrong with the Fourth Amendment which James Madison and others made to the US Constitution in 1791. It was presumably a reaction to oppression by agents of the corrupt English oligarchy which had previously ruled their American colonies. It states: "The right of the people to be secure in their persons, houses, papers, and effects against unreasonabale searches and seizures shall not be violated, and no warrants shall issue but upon probable cause supported by oath or affirmation and particularly describing the place to be searched and the persons or things to be seized."

Probable Cause. "Probable cause" means a reasonable belief that a crime has been committed or is about to be committed. The amendment says nothing about concealing evidence gained from unreasonable and improper search and seizure, but the US Supreme Court says judges must **always** suppress improperly gained evidence.

Reagan. Judge Rothwax had been "a card-carrying member of ACLU" (the American Civil Liberties Union), and hence would be seen as being on the liberal side of politics. From the other side of the spectrum, President Ronald Wilson Reagan (b. 1911), or his speechwriter, agreed with Rothwax. Peter Irons quotes Reagan as telling a police convention in 1981 that the exclusionary rule "rests on the absurd proposition that a law enforcement error, no matter how technical, can be used to justify throwing an entire case out of court, no matter how guilty the defendant or how heinous the crime". He said "the criminal goes free, the officer receives no effective reprimand, and the only ones who really suffer are the people of the community".

How did this "absurd proposition" happen? As noted, precedent means that judges must adhere to decisions by previous judges who are not available for cross-examination which might show they were wrong, confused or had a secret agenda.

Justice Clark. There can be no doubt that the inventor of the exclusionary rule, Justice Tom Campbell Clark, was at least wrong and confused; it is open to speculation that he had a secret agenda. As noted in chapter 8 on precedent, Lord Eldon said in 1803 that "it is better the law should be certain than that every judge should speculate upon improvements in it". David Pannick QC says Lord Eldon's attitude "retains few adherents and deserves even fewer", but in nearly 40 years no-one has found a way to effect improvements to the exclusionary rule.

The Camel. It appears that Justice Clark may effectively have been appointed to the Supreme Court by Murray (The Camel) Humphreys (1899-1965), the only Welshman to reach the higher echelons of the US Mafia. Humphreys was a major fixer in Chicago. Carl Sifakis reports the view of Alphonse Capone (1899-1947): "Anybody can use a gun. The Hump uses his head. He can shoot if he has to, but he likes to negotiate with cash when he can. I like that in a man."

Sifakis records The Camel's aphorisms, presumably deriving from his experience in Chicago in the 1920s and 30s: "The difference between guilt and innocence in any court is who gets to the judge first with the most." And: "No good citizen will ever testify to anything if he is absolutely convinced that to do so will result in his quick and certain death."

Oliver Cyriax notes claims that in 1947 Humphreys organised a deal in which President Harry Truman got "a US$5 million backhander"; Attorney-General Clark was to release Chicago Mafia boss Paul (The Waiter) Ricca (1897-1972, b. Felice De Lucia, Naples) from prison; and Clark was to get the next vacant seat on the Supreme Court. Clark released Ricca in August 1947, three years into a 10-year sentence. Sifakis says this "enraged the Chicago press, which published Ricca's claims that his influence extended into the White House. Printed accounts had Ricca instructing his lawyers to find out who had the final say in granting him a speedy release, saying: "That man must want something: money, favours, a seat in the Supreme Court. Find out what he wants and get it for him." The next vacancy on the court was in 1949; Truman appointed Clark to fill it. In 1961 he manipulated the court into inventing the exclusionary rule.

Dollree Mapp. In 1957, Ohio police looking for a bombing suspect used a false warrant to search the premises of Dollree Mapp. They did not find the suspect but they did find some pornography, and Ms Mapp was convicted of possessing obscene materials. She appealed to the Supreme Court.

Mapp v Ohio. Judge Rothwax says *Mapp v Ohio* (1961) was basically a First Amendment (free speech) case. The Fourth Amendment was not raised by the parties at the hearing, nor by the nine members of the Supreme Court when they conferred on the case. They voted 9-0 to reverse the conviction on First Amendment grounds. Justice Clark was assigned to write the opinion, but he did it on Fourth Amendment grounds. Judge Rothwax says Justice Potter Stewart later speculated that Clark and three other judges met in a "rump caucus" to discuss a different basis for the decision. Why? "These were willful men with an agenda and they seized the day."

Clark constructed a new rule stating that, regardless of the circumstances, evidence improperly obtained must invariably be concealed. His main argument was "the exclusionary rule is necessary because nothing else works". That was true only in the sense that the authorities had not (and have not) set up a tribunal with the power to fine or imprison agents of the state who knowingly and deliberately procure evidence improperly.

Judge Rothwax says Stewart immediately wrote to Clark to question "the wisdom of overruling an important doctrine in a case in which the issue was not even raised. It seemed to him rash, if not arrogant, to craft a decision of such magnitude without due discussion". But Clark's opinion in "the most important search-and-seizure decision in American history" stood. Rothwax says: "Although the majority, including Stewart, agreed that Mapp's conviction should be reversed, only four of the judges (a minority) agreed on Fourth Amendment grounds."

To change the law by a minority may seem an example of the malady. A minority of this sort is called a "plurality", which sounds better. The problem, as Rothwax notes, is that "in more than 90 per cent of cases, the police don't know what the law is", i.e. what is reasonable or lawful in that particular case. He says: "A chief judge riding in the back seat of a police car wouldn't know what the law is!"

Judge Rothwax says even the US Supreme Court now realises that "rejection of evidence does nothing to punish the wrong-doing official, while it may, and likely will, release the wrong-doing defendant".

Coolidge. Judge Rothwax is particularly unhappy when he thinks of the Coolidge case. Edward Coolidge cut the throat of Pamela Mason, 14, and left her body in snow outside Manchester, New Hampshire. The Attorney-General used his power under New Hampshire law to issue warrants to search Coolidge's car. It was found to contain particles of Pamela's clothing. Coolidge was found guilty, but the US Supreme Court overturned the verdict. It said the Attorney had no power to issue the warrants; they were therefore invalid; therefore the evidence was unlawfully gained; therefore it must be excluded.

As noted in the epigraph to this chapter, Judge Rothwax says: "Did I become a judge for this? Is this the system I am proud to be part of? The Coolidge reversal makes me ashamed. Stories like this are an insult to common sense and fair play. There is certainly little feeling for the victim, who was brutally tortured and murdered. There is also little feeling for the *truth*."

Dershowitz. US defence lawyers are naturally fond of the exclusionary rule; if you can get the police evidence concealed, it can be game, set and match. In an article in *The New Yorker* of March 27, 1995 at the beginning of O.J. Simpson's first trial, Jeffrey Toobin reported; "In the months leading up to the trial, Simpson's defense team attempted an extremely ambitious use of the exclusionary rule. This was no surprise; the law professors who are the architects of Simpson's legal strategy – Alan Dershowitz, of Harvard Law School, and Gerald Uelmen, who until recently was the dean of Santa Clara University School of Law – are leading proponents of the exclusionary rule."

Simpson was found not guilty of the murders at his criminal trial in 1995 and responsible for the murders at a second (civil) trial in 1997. After the second trial, Professor Dershowitz said: "I think justice was done in both trials."

Corrupt Judges. The Clark rule corrupted some US judges in the same way that otherwise honest police are corrupted, i.e. they engage in so-called noble causes corruption. To put criminals they know are guilty off the street, the judges rule that evidence is lawfully gained when they know it is tainted.

Preamble. The circle is vicious, but the cartel cannot seem to find a way out, although, as noted in chapter 22: Error Entombed in the Constitution, overriders in the Preamble to the Constitution should provide enough ammunition to overturn any bad law, as *Mapp v Ohio* clearly is, so long as the legislature could be persuaded to set up a tribunal to punish police who deliberately offend.

Rehnquist. Peter Irons wrote in 1994 that Chief Justice William Rehnquist has tried to overrule *Mapp* but had not yet put together a majority to do so. Rehnquist, b. 1924, was Attorney-General John Mitchell's director of the Justice Department's Office of Legal Counsel from 1969 to 1971 and was appointed to the Supreme Court by President Richard Nixon in 1972. President Ronald Reagan appointed him Chief Justice in 1986.

The "Truth" School. Justice Michael Kirby notes in *Crime In Australia* the existence in the US of a "truth school" of judges and academic lawyers who are trying to secure the abolition, by legislation, of the exclusionary rule on the ground that it prevents the truth being found. They include Justice Stephen Breyer, who was appointed by President William Clinton to the Supreme Court, and presumably Chief Justice Rehnquist.

The truth school encouraged Senator Orrin Hatch, of Utah, to sponsor a Bill to abolish the exclusionary rule for examination by the Senate's Judiciary Committee shortly before June 1995. The cartel was no doubt alert to the danger of having truth as a legal criterion: it would entail the abolition of its other barriers to truth, and hence the end of the common law as they knew it.

28

The Sexually Depraved Lord Goddard's Rule – England

... the court is not concerned with how the evidence was obtained.

– Lord Goddard, 1955

English judges rarely conceal improperly gained evidence, but their rule was largely invented by the sexually depraved Rayner Goddard (1877-1971). Goddard was a criminal court (King's Bench) judge 1932-38, on the Court of Appeal 1938-44, a Lord of Appeal in Ordinary (law lord) 1944-46, and Lord Chief Justice 1946-58. He resigned aged 81 because he was going blind. The *Concise Dictionary of National Biography* notes that he "tried a number of notable murder cases including the Craig-Bentley trial", and that he was a "strong supporter of corporal and capital punishment".

Kuruma. In *Kuruma v R (1955)*, Lord Goddard wrote: "... the test to be applied in considering whether evidence is admissible is whether it is relevant to the matters in issue. If it is, it is admissible and the court is not concerned with how the evidence was obtained."

If the Clark rule tends to corrupt judges, the Goddard rule tends to corrupt police: it virtually encourages them to gain evidence improperly; elements of the West Midlands Serious Crime Squad lived up to their name in the 1970s; their crimes included torture to obtain false confessions from the Birmingham Six. The squad was disbanded in 1989 and outside police were called in to review 97 of their cases.

A Secret Agenda? There is also the question of whether Lord Goddard had a secret agenda. Oliver Cyriax notes that his clerk, Arthur Harris, had "to take a spare pair of the standard striped trousers to court on sentencing days. When condemning a youth to be flogged or hanged, Goddard always ejaculated". This leads to frightening speculation as to whether the Lord Chief Justice may have become a sort of judicial serial killer.

Bentley. The Bentley miscarriage makes a powerful case for using an investigating judge, e.g. the French *juge d'instruction*, to supervise police inquiries. Derek Bentley, 19, was an illiterate, epileptic road-sweeper with a mental age of 10 or 11. He and Christopher Craig, 16, were seen climbing a fence to break into a confectionary warehouse at Croydon, London, on Sunday, November 2, 1952. Police, including marksmen from Scotland Yard, were called. Police soon caught Bentley, but Craig fired several shots. A policeman claimed that Bentley said: "Let him have it, Chris." A policeman was shot dead.

The *juge* re-enacts the crime. In this case, the *juge* may have come to the same conclusion as John Parris (*Scapegoat*, Duckworth, 1991). Oliver Cyriax says Parris believes that Bentley had tried to stop Craig firing, that Craig's gun was empty when the policeman was killed, and that the words ascribed to Bentley were a routine "verbal" to cover up the fact that the fatal shot was actually fired by a police marksman, and to make sure that Bentley was hanged.

The *juge* takes enough time to get the facts right. The Craig-Bentley murder case came before Lord Goddard within a month, on December 4, 1952. Common law judges are supposed to be passive but Cyriax says Goddard "steam-rollered through" the trial and "in effect acted for the prosecution. Puzzling discrepancies in the evidence were dismissed as irrelevant". Craig and Bentley were found guilty. Craig was too young to be hanged, but Bentley was not; Goddard, 75, sentenced him to death and advised against clemency. Bentley was hanged on January 28, 1953. Craig was released in 1963.

Magic Trick No. 12? A *juge* would also have prevented the police oppression of the Birmingham Six, and there would have been no trial. There was a rare upshot of the miscarriage: three retired detectives who had been on the West Midland Serious Crime Squad were actually charged with having gained evidence improperly, by fabricating it, but in October 1993 Justice Garland stopped their Old Bailey trial and ordered a permanent stay of proceedings against them.

In what might be termed Magic Trick Number 12, Justice Garland claimed that the volume and intensity of media comment about the Birmingham Six case made a fair trial impossible. Fair to whom? The Six might echo Judge Rothwax: "Stories like this are an insult to common sense and fair play. There is certainly little feeling for the victims, who were wrongly in prison for 16 years. There is also little feeling for the *truth*." A European trial of the detectives could not have ended that way; since no evidence is concealed, material in the media is not going to tell the jurors something they won't hear at the trial.

The Malady? Part of Justice Garland's reason for letting the detectives off was that the media had identified them as perpetrators of the crimes with which they were charged. This sounds, with very great respect, like the malady at work: it would seem to follow that judges should issue permanent stays against everyone whom the prosecution identifies as being guilty of the charges brought against them.

The Garland Defence. Constantin Karageorge was a lawyer for Leonard Arthur McPherson (1921-96), a Sydney organised criminal with connections in the Chicago Mafia and the Philippines. Arthur Stanley (Neddy) Smith, said in 1995 that by 1957 McPherson was running NSW. Like his criminal colleagues in the US (at least until the authorities began to use the RICO legislation in the 1980s), McPherson was not in the habit of going to prison: his last prison term was in 1949. There was thus some surprise when a national body charged with investigating organised criminals, the National Crime Authority (NCA), charged McPherson with organising an assault on a business rival.

With McPherson's trial approaching, the NCA intercepted a telephone call from Karageorge to reporter Kevin Perkins on December 8, 1993. Karageorge said: "We want utmost exposure given to Lennie McPherson. Then his barrister can argue in court for him that there has been too much publicity in the bloody matter and get a stay of proceedings." A court later heard there was no evidence that Perkins intended to act or did act on the matter.

Karageorge was charged with attempting to pervert the course of justice. McPherson was found guilty; he got 2 1/2 years and died in prison in August 1996. The NCA apparently kept an eye on Karageorge; he was arrested in July 1997, charged with attempting to procure a false passport, and refused bail. In October 1997 he was found guilty on the perversion and got a longer sentence than McPherson: three years and four months.

29

Ninian Stephen's Middle of the Road Exclusionary Rule – Australia

Bunning v Cross. In Australia, the exclusionary rule is known as the *Bunning v Cross* discretion. The community was rarely punished by the exclusion of improperly-gained evidence until the late 1970s. Justice Michael Kirby, as chairman of the Australian Law Reform Commission, recommended legislation "occupying the middle ground between the *Kuruma* decision and the United States 'extremes'." The legislation was not enacted but in 1978 the High Court's *Bunning v Cross* discretion "largely" adopted the ALRC's position.

The court found in *Bunning v Cross* that evidence in a breathalyser case, although wrongly gained, should have been admitted. The judgment was written by Justices Sir Ninian Stephen and Sir Keith Aickin; Chief Justice Sir Garfield Barwick and Justice Ken Jacobs agreed; Justice Lionel Murphy dissented. The judgment gave guidelines for using a discretion to admit or exclude such evidence.

Two steps are involved in the *Bunning v Cross* discretion. The judge has first to decide whether the evidence was unlawfully gained. As Judge Rothwax noted, it is not easy, even for judges, to know what is unlawful in the circumstances. If he decides it is unlawful, he then has to use *Bunning v Cross* to guide his attempt to balance the public interest in putting criminals off the streets with the public interest in making investigators behave properly.

Dr John Forbes summarised the *Bunning v Cross* guidelines in *Evidence in Queensland* in this fashion:

1. Did the investigators deliberately or inadvertently gain the evidence improperly?

2. Is it likely that the impropriety affected the quality or reliability of the evidence? Improper forms of interrogation or the more active forms of entrapment may well affect the quality. On the other hand, blood or breath tests are not intrinsically affected even if the means used to gain it are improper.

3. How serious is the offence charged? The more serious the offence, the greater the public interest in identifying and punishing the offender and the more cautious the court will be about excluding the evidence.

4. How serious is the misconduct of the investigator? In *Irving v Heferen* the Queensland Court of Appeal held that the trial judge was entitled to admit evidence of a drug offence obtained by a motel

manager when, perhaps wrongly, he searched the accused's room because he feared he might leave without paying his bill.

5. Was there a deliberate intent in the relevant legislation to restrict police power?

In *Bunning v Cross*, Justices Stephen and Aickin said: "The magistrate does not appear to have considered some of the above criteria. He seems to have much relied upon what he regarded, we think erroneously, as the 'inherent unfairness' of what occurred ... He also does not seem directly to have accorded any weight to the public interest in bringing to conviction those who commit criminal offences. In the end we believe that the balance of considerations must come down in favour of the admission of the evidence."

Elliott. *R v John Dorman Elliott and Ors* (1996) partly turned on the discretion. It followed a long investigation by National Crime Authority lawyers (not police) of Melbourne businessman John Dorman Elliott and others. The lawyers believed their inquiries were covered by notices of references from the Australian and Victorian Governments. The NCA has the power to oblige witnesses to give evidence, but witnesses still have a right of silence: they can refuse to answer any questions that might put them in "peril" of being convicted as criminals. Elliott and the others did not avail themselves of the privilege. The crimes eventually alleged against them were perjury, conspiracy and theft of $66.5 million from shareholders of a brewing group.

An Elliott associate, Ken Jarrett, pleaded guilty to related charges and spent six months in prison. Jarrett was scheduled to give evidence for the Crown in the Elliott case.

As noted, a major task of defence lawyers is to persuade the judge to conceal as much relevant evidence as possible from the jury or from himself if sitting alone. "Legal argument" on what evidence would be concealed in the Elliott case ran intermittently from January 29, 1996 to August 22, 1996. It was estimated to cost $250,000 per week. A fact-gathering judge working for $4000 a week in an inquisitorial system would necessarily be more cost-effective. And in any event there would have been nothing to argue about: the fact-gathering judge does not conceal evidence.

Vincent. Defence lawyers Robert Richter QC and Jack D. Hammond and John Walker QC and James Judd brilliantly achieved a spectacular result without a jury even being empanelled: they persuaded Justice Frank Hollis Rivers Vincent, 58, to suppress the evidence obtained by the NCA lawyers when they questioned Elliott and the others.

Justice Vincent found the NCA lawyers had inadvertently gone beyond the notices, and hence that some of the evidence was improperly gained. He then had to consider the *Bunning v Cross* guidelines. In the end, he said he "felt constrained" to take the view that "as a matter of public policy the fruits of [the NCA lawyers'] unlawful activities should not be used as evidence". A possible inference is that he took the view that a lawyer's inadvertent offence is a more serious offence than an alleged theft of $66.5 million.

The prosecution said it would enter no other evidence, e.g. the evidence of Ken Jarrett. This meant that it would not be necessary to empanel a jury. Justice Vincent then declared the accused not guilty, and that was the end of it; the common law holds that a judge or jury can be wrong when they find the accused guilty, but, unlike European law, are infallible when they find them innocent.

They are clearly not infallible, as the Victorian Court of Appeal appeared to confirm in September 1997 in its labyrinthine judgment on a point of law raised by the Director of Public Prosecutions (DPP) concerning Justice Vincent's ruling. Justice Robert Brooking, with whom the President of the court, Justice John Winneke, and Justice Robert Tadgell agreed, found that Justice Vincent was wrong to exclude the evidence. Justice Brooking said: "I have concluded that his Honour thought it inappropriate to have regard to the wording of the notices ... This may seem, with respect, a somewhat surprising view ..."

That could make no difference to the acquittal, but it does raise the question as to whether, as in Europe, all cases should automatically be reviewed by a higher court consisting of judges and lay assessors of fact.

30

Miscarriages I

Using the Magic Tricks to Get Off

American criminal procedure is a sporting event at this point. If we are going to allow [O.J. Simpson lawyers] Barry Sheck and Johnnie Cochrane and Alan Dershowitz to run through their truth-defeating bag of tricks, it is a blessing to have a second trial.

– Professor John Langbein, February 1997 (after the second Simpson trial)

We should now be in a position to draw the magic tricks together and see how they are used to procure Type A miscarriages of justice, i.e. by getting the guilty off. Theoretically, lawyers for organised criminals and habitual rapists could utilise the entire bag of nine tricks to get them off a particular charge. (In the US, lawyers for organised criminals cannot use MT5, the rules against similar facts.)

Magic Trick 1. Truth Not Important. The police and the court are not allowed to try to find the truth; they will be trying to find if, after much of the evidence has been concealed, there is enough left: a) to lay charges; b) to persuade the jury to convict.

Magic Trick 2. The Inscrutable Jury. The common law jury system has been defective since the 12th century: the jurors do not have to give reasons. This makes it easier: a) to get away with suborning a juror; b) to persuade a jury to give a verdict against the weight of the evidence. And it makes it impossible for an appeal court to know what was in the jurors' minds.

Tension. Commenting on acquittals in three cases of admitted killing, George Zdenkowski, Associate Professor of Law at the University of NSW, advised readers of *The Sydney Morning Herald* (August 8, 1997): "Inevitably, there is a tension between formal legal principles and the broad-brush approach of a jury. This is part of a legal structure with a long and distinguished history."

Rape-in-Marriage. In a famous rape-in-marriage case in 1993, Justice Derek Bollen, of the South Australian Supreme Court, told the jury of seven women and five men that persuading a wife who was refusing to engage in carnal congress might involve "a measure of rougher than usual handling". The jury found the husband not guilty of five counts of rape and one of attempted rape. The wife said she believed the judge gave the jury the message that it was "OK to bash the wife". The foreman of the jury said it was "absolute rubbish" to say their decision was affected by the summing up, and in any event they were too tired after the four-day trial to take in much of what the judge was saying.

Joh's Jury. The jury in the perjury trial of the former Premier of Queensland, Sir Johannes Bjelke-Petersen, was dismissed when the foreman said they were irreconcilably hung. There was some controversy when it emerged that the foreman had been a member of an organisation that supported Bjelke-Petersen and that he and a woman were the only ones who said he was not guilty. The other ten were quite agitated about what had happened in the jury room and Ian David reconstructed their deliberations in a television docu-drama called *Joh's Jury*. Michael Quinn, president of the Queensland Criminal Law Association, said this was "irresponsible in the extreme" and "a fundamental attack on the jury system ... it seems to suggest that jurors' deliberations in the jury room should be made public ..."

Jury "Perverse and Inconsistent". Laurie Connell, a West Australian financier, was charged with conspiring in 1983 to have a jockey, Danny Hobby, jump off his horse so Connell's beast would win at a provincial race meeting, and with conspiring to pervert the course of justice by paying Hobby $1 million to stay out of the reach of police, i.e. out of Australia, for six years. The trial ran for six months in 1993-94. It cost the state more than $2 million and Connell was reported to have faced a $2.5 million legal bill, including $7000 a day for Alec Shand QC, of Sydney.

The jury found Connell not guilty of conspiring to have Hobby fix the race, but guilty of conspiring to keep Hobby out of the country. He got five years. At the appeal, Roger Gyles QC (also of Sydney), for Connell said the jury verdicts were "perverse and inconsistent". The Director of Public Prosecutions, John McKechnie QC, said there was no inconsistency in the verdicts, and that "it shows better than anything the jury system properly at work".

Convictions Dropping. Dr Lucy Sullivan, of the Centre for Independent Studies in Sydney, released figures in November 1997 showing that in homicide cases in 1964 juries convicted 48.5 per cent of accused in Australia but only 26.5 per cent in NSW in 1993. They convicted 39.5 per cent for rape in 1964 but only 11.5 per cent in 1993. Does this mean that lawyers are becoming ever more efficient in using the magic tricks to allow murderers and rapists to continue as threats to the community?

Magic Trick 3. The Adversary System. The lawyer for the rapist or other accused has an absolute privilege to put forward (on instructions) a concocted defence; to utter lies about the victim and other witnesses; to use verbal thuggery to intimidate and confuse witnesses; to shift the goalposts; and to insert a doubt into the minds of the jury.

Lawyers' Dominance. Defence lawyers' dominance of judges which enabled them to concoct the adversary system 200 years ago apparently continues. In March 1996, Christopher Darden, prosecutor at the O.J. Simpson criminal trial, accused Judge Lance Ito of being weak. He said Judge Ito "gave the defence the keys to the courthouse and surrendered his gavel. Johnnie Cochran ran that courtroom, not Judge Ito."

Janet Fife-Yeomans noted (*The Australian* May 9, 1995) that rape law was changed in NSW in 1981 so that the complainant could only be questioned about her sexual history in exceptional circumstances and only with the prior approval of the judge, but sexual experience was still raised in 40 per cent of cases, sometimes without explanation or challenge. In Victoria, where similar legislation had been enacted, complainants were still being questioned about their sexual history without prior approval of the trial judge.

Privilege: The rapist has an absolute privilege against disclosure of discussions with his lawyer, but his victim has no privilege against disclosure of her confidential discussions with rape counsellors.

Temporary Insanity. Lorena Bobbitt's lawyer persuaded jurors that she was suffering from "temporary insanity" when she sliced off the penis of her sleeping husband, John Wayne Bobbitt, later a star in pornographic films.

The Abuse Excuse. The "abuse excuse" persuaded a number of jurors at the first trials in 1993 of Erik and Lyle Menendez that they should be convicted only of manslaughter, not of murder of their parents Jose and Kitty. Their lawyer, Leslie Abramson, produced a number of psychological experts to support their claims of sexual and emotional abuse as children. One psychiatric researcher said Erik could not know what he was doing because fear had re-wired his brain. To support this contention, she produced research she had done on snails.

Prosecutors at the first trial barely challenged the expert witnesses because they did not want to draw attention to the abuse excuse. Harvard Professor Alan Dershowitz said the result was "one of the great judicial mockeries of modern times".

At the second trial in 1996, prosecutor David Conn got much of the abuse excuse evidence excluded on the ground of irrelevance. Abuse evidence admitted included a claim that Erik suffered from Post Traumatic Stress Disorder (PTSD) and this prevented him from formulating the thoughts necessary for premeditated murder.

Conn ridiculed the expert psychiatric evidence. "Where's the defense in this case?" he asked the jury, offering them a choice of 11. "Battered person's syndrome? PTSD? Fight or flight? Panic state? Panic mode? Automatic pilot? Learned helplessness? Ordinary fear? Hypervigilance? Hyperarousal? Dissociative state? ... Which one is it? Take your pick. That's what the defense wants you to do."

The jury found the Menendez brothers guilty of murder. Professor Dershowitz said: "The good news is that this verdict may well sound the death knell to the abuse excuse."

The Self-Abuse Excuse. It was alleged in October 1997 that a Canberra, Australia, football player, Noa Nadruku, assaulted his wife and "king hit" (without warning) two young women who were strangers to him. Nadruku told the magistrate that prior to the assaults he had consumed 16 pints of beer and half a bottle of wine over 11 hours. Dr Bill Knox, giving expert evidence for Nadruku, said he had consumed so much alcohol he would have suffered an alcoholic blackout and could not have acted with intent. Magistrate Shane Madden said what Nadruku did was an act of drunken thuggery, but his degree of intoxication was such that he did not know what he was doing and could not have formed any intent [*mens rea*] to commit the offences. He found Nadruku not guilty.

This suggests that intending murderers, rapists and armed robbers in common law countries should take the precaution of getting drunk beforehand. However, it will be of no use to reporters and editors charged with criminal contempt in common law countries other than the US. Even if so permanently drunk that they could not possibly form any criminal intent, the law, as noted above, will insist that they are guilty.

Magic Trick 4. The Right of Silence. The habitual rapist does not have to subject himself to cross-examination. This prevents the jury from assessing whether he is shifty and evasive, and whether his explanation is credible.

Magic Trick 5. The Rule Against Similar Facts. The rapist will not make his character an issue. He is secure in the knowledge that the court will not admit evidence showing his pattern of previous rapes, his convictions for them, or other dubious aspects of his character.

Magic Trick 6. The Rule Against Hearsay. Evidence will not be admitted that the rapist boasted of this rape to third persons not available for cross-examination.

Magic Trick 7. The Standard of Proof. The rapist's lawyer will constantly keep the confusing "beyond a reasonable doubt" standard of proof in front of the jurors' minds. It seems to be working; Reginald Blanch, chief judge of the NSW District Court, disclosed in May 1997 that "in relation to criminal trials almost 25 per cent in 1996 resulted in either a discharge of the jury or a disagreement". Law Society President Patrick Fair said: "What the statistics show is that the cases being brought before the courts are not strong enough."

Magic Trick 8. The Christie Discretion. The rapist's lawyer will seek to persuade the judge to suppress evidence tending to prove his client's guilt on the ground that it is only slightly probative and is highly prejudicial. e.g. that he was seen observing the victim's residence.

Magic Trick 9. The Exclusionary Rule. This may be used to suppress all the evidence gained by the police. If that fails to secure an acquittal, it may be used to get a result in an appeal court.

31

How Many Guilty Get Off?

Researchers for David Hare's 1991 play, *Murmuring Judges*, found that three per cent of all reported crimes lead to a conviction. Crimes in which there is a known suspect are something else. The following is an attempt to roughly quantify the percentages of those who get off in common law countries and in countries which use European inquisitorial procedures. That is, countries which have an extreme adversary system and rules for concealing evidence as opposed to countries which have a modified adversary system and no rules for concealing evidence. The figures are no more than an approximation and would not impress a statistician, but they do tend to confirm the view that the common law is a fraud on the community.

Conviction Rates. The "fair and generally accurate" French courts convict some 90 per cent of those charged. That is, the judge and jury are not "thoroughly convinced" in 10 per cent of cases and give the accused the benefit of the doubt. This more or less squares with Blackstone's notion that 10 guilty should get off to prevent the risk of one innocent going to prison.

Ludovic Kennedy says that in English contested trials about 50 per cent are found guilty. A lawyer likewise has the impression that in the Sydney District Court, which hears moderately serious crimes, results go about 50-50 in contested cases. In 100 cases, we might suppose that perhaps 10 are entitled to the benefit of the doubt, but not 50. But that is not the whole story. Many of the known guilty are not even charged because police and prosecutors know there is little point in further burdening the community with the cost of the trial: the rules for concealing evidence make it likely they will get off. Figures from the NSW Independent Commission Against Corruption may give a clearer picture.

ICAC uses French techniques, i.e. truth-seeking lawyers supervise the initial investigation and a truth-seeking judge or lawyer conducts the hearing and does not conceal evidence. But those charged as a result of ICAC inquiries are then tried according to the common law. This means that ICAC lawyers must try to calculate how much of their evidence, if any, will remain after a judge has applied the rules for concealing evidence. They will necessarily recommend charges against fewer people than they know are guilty.

From 1989 to October 1995, the ICAC recommended corruption charges against 208 people; 63, or 30.2 per cent, were found guilty. How many more they would have charged except for the magic tricks is a matter for speculation. Perhaps they believed about half as many again, i.e. 104, were guilty. This may seem high, but Sir Terence Lewis's corruption trial shows how much apparently rock-solid evidence can be kept out. The higher figure would mean a conviction rate of only 20 per cent, or that 80 per cent of the known guilty can expect to get off at a major common law trial as against 10 per cent at a civil law criminal trial.

The US Grand Jury. US grand juries (see chapter 36) use inquisitorial methods; figures for the results of the subsequent common law trials presumably also tell us something, but they may be skewed by ever greater use of the fox-hunting approach to criminal law. In the plea-bargaining process, accused are invited to gamble on their chances of getting off or pleading guilty to a lesser charge. As Professor Langbein notes, this tends to do away with trials, but at least some guilty get some punishment. The result may be rather like the German system, in which more guilty are convicted but sentences are lighter, presumably on the basis that the process seeks to understand as well as punish.

32

Miscarriages 2

How the Innocent Go to the Chair, etc

*Justice — I don't think them people in there have got the intelligence nor
the honesty to spell the word, never mind dispense it.*

— Patrick Hill, Birmingham Six, March 1991

Type B miscarriages, i.e. those in which the innocent are found
guilty, are a grave problem in any country, but particularly so in
countries which have the death penalty: it appears that some
detectives will fabricate even in cases where that penalty applies
and that prosecuting lawyers feel obliged to accept their evidence.
And some judges persist in asserting that no miscarriage occurred
when it clearly did.

Numerous instances of Type B miscarriages demonstrate the
falsity of claims that the adversary system and the rules for
concealing evidence protect citizens from oppression by the
leviathan state. However, members of the cartel are inclined to claim
that miscarriages are merely unfortunate exceptions in an otherwise
splendid system. To Bron McKillop, a comparative lawyer of Sydney
University, this sounds like the famous "rotten apple theory". The
theory that there was unfortunately one rotten apple in every barrel
was popular with spokesmen for the endemically corrupt NSW police
force until 1981, when Justice Edwin Lusher's inquiry into police
administration put an end to the theory.

Innocent in Prison. Ludovic Kennedy said in 1989: " ... the late
Secretary of Justice, Tom Sargant, estimated that at any one time
between 200 and 300 of the prison population [in the United
Kingdom] had been wrongly convicted, and from the
correspondence I have received from prisoners or their families over
the years, I would think that a fair figure." The prison population
was 40,000; 200-300 innocent is .5 and .75 of one per cent. In 1993,
Michael Mansfield QC said probation officers "maintain that on the
basis of studies carried out by them, the number of people wrongly
convicted could total 500 or more. No one will ever know the true
picture and in reality the total is almost certainly higher. Once
sentenced, there is no incentive for a prisoner to contest his or her
conviction because parole is rarely given to those who insist on
protesting their innocence. Keep quiet and you get out earlier —
considerably earlier because the granting of parole effectively
halves the length of a sentence".

The figure for 1993 could thus conservatively be estimated at 500 innocent in a prison population of 50,000, or one per cent. Putting the figures for innocent and guilty together, we can roughly estimate that in 100 contested common law trials, one innocent person will go to prison and 80 known guilty will get off. We cannot say how many innocent people go to prison in European trials, but we do know it is well below the common law's one in 100; a 1992 English study of pre-trial procedures in France and Germany "found that in neither country was it likely that miscarriages of justice such as the Guildford or Birmingham cases would occur". (See chapter 41: How the Cartel Obstructs Reform.)

* * *

Sir Ludovic Kennedy, the leading authority on miscarriages where the innocent are convicted, is the source of some of the examples below. It should be noted that those who sought to right the wrongs thus committed included lawyers as well as journalists and politicians.

Hauptmann. Charles Lindbergh Jnr, 19 months, was kidnapped from the home of a famous aviator, Colonel Charles Lindbergh, near Hopewell, New Jersey in March 1932, and later murdered. A ramshackle ladder was used to gain access to the child's upstairs bedroom. The execution in April 1936 of an innocent man, Richard Bruno Hauptmann, for the murder was the sort of miscarriage the adversary system makes inevitable. It involved evidence fabricated wholesale by New York and New Jersey police, a strong prosecution lawyer and a weak defence lawyer.

Hauptmann was a skilled carpenter who lived and worked in the Bronx district of New York. The identifiable US$50,000 ransom money was discounted in the New York criminal *milieu* at 40 cents in the dollar. A criminal, Isidor Fisch, who owed Hauptmann money, gave him a package containing US$14,000 of the ransom money to mind while he went to Germany, where he died. Suspicion fell on Hauptmann when he used some of the money.

Head of the New Jersey State Police was Colonel Norman Schwarzkopf, father of General Norman (Stormin' Norman) Schwarzkopf, US commander in the 1991 Gulf War. The prosecution was led by David Wilentz, the New Jersey Attorney-General. Hauptmann's lead defence lawyer, paid for by the Hearst Press, was Edward (Death House) Reilly, an alcoholic who achieved his nickname via his habit of losing capital cases. Some of the fabricated evidence noted by Ludovic Kennedy in *The Airman and the Carpenter* (1985) and repeated in *Truth to Tell* (1991) was:

When Hauptmann was arrested, two leading handwriting experts, Albert D. Osborn and Albert S. Osborn, at first said there was no resemblance between his writing and the ransom notes. New York detectives asked him to write out the words in the ransom notes from dictation. He spelled the words correctly. They then made him write the words with the ransom notes' curious misspellings: ouer for our, bee for be, note for not, gut for good, singature for signature. Wilentz offered the second document as proof that it was inconceivable that anyone other than Hauptmann had written the ransom notes.

Before Hauptmann was arrested, Millard Whited said he saw nothing unusual at Hopewell about the time of the kidnapping. New Jersey police paid him to say he saw Hauptmann twice near Hopewell at that time. They also bribed Amandus Hochmuth, 87, to say he saw Hauptmann driving a car with a ladder on the back on the day of the kidnap. Two detectives fabricated evidence that part of the ladder came from a floorboard in the attic of the house Hauptmann rented in the Bronx. They did this after Hauptmann's wife, Anna, left their home. Work time sheets showing Hauptmann could not have had time to kidnap the child were given to New York police and never seen again, like the pages from the passport of Peter James's Sri Lankan who went down for murders committed by Justice Squander. (See Epilogue: How to Get A Frottist off Murder and Other Jokes: Warm Afternoons in Boston.)

Dr John F. Condon, a septuagenarian schoolteacher, was the go-between between Lindbergh and the kidnappers for the US$50,000 ransom. As a joke, a reporter, Tom Cassidy, scrawled Condon's telephone number on Hauptmann's lavatory door. At a police lineup, Condon failed to pick out Hauptmann as the man he gave the money to in a cemetery. Told he would be arrested if he did not change his mind at the trial, Condon then perjured himself, as did Colonel Lindbergh himself. Lindbergh could not recognise Hauptmann's as the voice he heard shout "Hey, Doc" 100 yards away in the dark in the cemetery, but Colonel (Storming Norming?) Schwarzkopf told him there was no doubt Hauptmann was the killer. Lindbergh then swore he recognised the voice as Hauptmann's. Oliver Cyriax notes that, 60 years after the event, Hauptmann's descendants are petitioning for a posthumous pardon.

Byrd. In Texas in January 1985, a woman, 25 and eight months' pregnant, was sleeping in bed with her two-year-old daughter. A door slammed; she was raped by a man who held a knife at her daughter's neck. She said he was "a white male". Four months later she saw Kevin Byrd, a black carpenter, 22, in a grocery store and claimed he was the man. She later told a court the rapist had really been black. Byrd was found guilty and sent down for life.

DNA testing was introduced into Texas in 1989, but it was not until January 1997 that Byrd's family and friends could raise the money to pay a lawyer, Randy Schaffer, to arrange DNA tests. District Attorney John Holmes said the test "shows that Byrd is not the one who committed the assault". Judge Doug Shaver agreed and released Byrd on bail in mid-1997. A new trial might take years. In August, the Texas Board of Pardons unanimously recommended that the Governor of Texas, George Bush Jnr, 51, son of former President

George Herbert Walker Bush, exercise his prerogative and issue Byrd with a pardon. This would enable Byrd to sue for wrongful imprisonment for 12 years. Bush refused, according to a *Sunday Times* report of September 21, 1997.

The Nanny Case. The Nanny Case encapsulates much that is wrong with the common law: its lack of interest in the truth, the adversary system, the fox-hunting approach to justice, the malady, expert witnesses ("saxophones"), the judge's isolation from jurors; jurors who do not give reasons and do not participate in the sentence.

Louise Woodward, 18, of England, was on a working holiday in the US in 1996. In November she got a job in the Cambridge, Massachusetts home of Dr Sunnil Eappen and Dr Deborah Eappen as nanny for their children, Brendan, then two and a half, and Matthew, then five months. Woodward telephoned Dr Deborah Eappen on Tuesday, February 4, 1997 to say Matthew was unconscious. He was taken to hospital with a skull fracture and died after five days in a coma.

We can contrast what actually happened with what might have happened in France. A French investigating magistrate (*juge d'instruction*) would get expert medical advice, independent of Woodward's lawyers and the police. Woodward's lawyers could ask the *juge* to get other medical opinions, but they would still have to be independent. If the experts agreed, as Woodward's experts later suggested, that the skull fracture had been caused a few weeks before, there would have been no argument and the case may have gone no further. Nor would there have been any argument if they found, as the state's experts found, that the fracture had been caused on February 4 by the baby's head being slammed against a hard object.

The *juge* would question Woodward in the presence of her lawyers. As noted in chapter 35 (The Pre-Trial Investigation I), Michael Mansfield QC says the task is truth, not guilt. He quotes a *juge*, Catherine Samet: "Despite my title, my role is not to judge them, but to understand them." Realistically speaking, as the jury later found, something happened on February 4 and a baby died. It also seems probable that Woodward did not murder the baby with premeditation. Depending on the medical evidence and what Woodward said, the *juge* may have recommended a charge of something like negligence occasioning actual bodily harm.

Professor John Langbein notes in his article on the privilege against self-incrimination: " ... when our criminal procedural system crumbled in the twentieth century under caseload pressures, our response was to dispense with trial altogether, transforming the pretrial process into our nontrial plea bargaining system." A negligence charge might have been plea-bargained down and Woodward may have spent a few months in prison.

However, Woodward was charged with murder and was held in prison pending trial. She insisted she would make no admission of guilt whatsoever. Her counsel included Barry Scheck, of New York, a forensic specialist who had been on the O.J. Simpson defence team. It appears that Woodward's refusal to admit to any culpability obliged the defence team to resort to the fox-hunter's defence. Over prosecution objections, Judge Hiller Zobel agreed with Scheck's request for manslaughter to be excluded. The jury thus had only two options: to find her guilty of murder or innocent.

Scheck was confident his expert medical witnesses would negate the state's witnesses, and the jury would thus not be able to find Woodward guilty of murder beyond a reasonable doubt; therefore she would go free. This perhaps overlooked the fact that his witnesses might be vulnerable to a particular strategy noted by Professor Langbein: "A defense lawyer recently bragged [Ryan, *Making the Plaintiff's Expert Yours*, 1982] about his technique of cross-examining plaintiffs' experts in tort cases. Notice that nothing in his strategy varies with the truthfulness of the expert testimony he tries to discredit: 'A mode of attack ripe with potential is to pursue a line of questions which, by their form and the jury's studied observation of the witness in response, will tend to cast the expert as a "professional witness". By proceeding in this way, the cross-examiner will reap the benefit of a community attitude, certain to be present among several of the jurors, that bias can be purchased, almost like a commodity.' Thus, the systematic incentive in our procedure to distort expertise leads to a systematic distrust and devaluation of expertise. Short of forbidding the use of experts altogether, we probably could not have designed a procedure better suited to minimise the influence of expertise."

The trial ran for three weeks at Cambridge, home of Harvard University and the Massachusetts Institute of Technology, in October 1997. Most of the nine women and three men on the jury were highly educated. Prosecutor Gerard Leone's expert witnesses were local scientists. Police claimed that Woodward said she had been "a little rough" with the baby. Woodward gave evidence. We don't know if she got The Lecture referred to by Judge Voelker in *Anatomy of a Murder*. (See chapter 16: Playing the Saxophone: The Adversary System in Action.) She denied saying she had been a little rough with the child; all she did was shake him in a panic when she thought he was having a convulsion and she tried to revive him.

Scheck's expert witnesses were from outside the state. They suggested that the fracture was an earlier injury that might have been reopened by minor jarring. Prosecution lawyers played the saxophone card; they dwelt at length on the fees being paid to Scheck's expert witnesses. Dr Ronald Uscinski, of the George Washington University Medical School, said he got US$300 and hour for preparing his evidence and US$900 an hour while he was in the witness box. In his final address Leone suggested that Woodward's performance was that of an aspiring actor and her lawyers and medical experts were overpaid hired guns. The verdict suggests that the jurors discounted the defence medical evidence.

It was reported that jurors would have preferred to be able to give a manslaughter verdict. They were said to have been initially split 6-6, then 8-4 for conviction on second degree murder, then 10-2. They were finally unanimous, after 27 hours, on October 31. The guilty of second degree murder verdict automatically meant that Woodward would spend a minimum of 15 years in prison. Their lack of reasons would not help an appeal court.

Professor Alan Dershowitz, of Harvard Law School, said Judge Zobel should "act as the 13th juror and the conscience of the community" and move to avert a miscarriage of justice. District Attorney Thomas F. Reilly described what happened next as "surreal". I take "surreal" to be code for the malady. Having originally agreed with Scheck to eliminate manslaughter, Judge Zobel now restored it. He declared Woodward guilty of manslaughter, not murder. Where does that leave the sporting theory of justice? If the jury had found her innocent, would he have overruled them and declared her guilty of manslaughter?

Zobel said: "I am firmly convinced that the interests of justice mandate my reducing the verdict to manslaughter. I do this in accordance with my discretion and my duty. I believe that the circumstances in which the defendant acted were characterised by confusion, inexperience, frustration, immaturity and some anger, but not malice. Frustrated by her inability to quiet the crying child, she was a little rough with him. The roughness was sufficient to start – or re-start – a bleeding that escalated. This sad scenario is most fairly characterised as manslaughter, not murder. I view the evidence as confusion, fright and bad judgment rather than rage or malice. I am morally certain that allowing this defendant on this evidence to remain convicted of second-degree murder would be a miscarriage of justice."

At the sentencing hearing two hours later, Woodward continued to insist she had done nothing wrong. She said: "I said in my last sentencing: I am innocent." Leone said she had shown no remorse and asked Judge Zobel to impose a sentence of 15 or 20 years. Judge Zobel said the nine months she had already spent in prison was sufficient penalty. He ordered her release pending appeals from prosecution and defence.

Earlier, when the fox-hunter's defence misfired and Woodward was going to get 15 years, English tabloid newspapers got into rather a tizzy about the faults of the American legal system. This overlooked the fact that miscarriages are built into the common law, and England, home of the common law, is also the home of the miscarriage. Some English cases:

Evans. Timothy John Evans, hanged in 1950 on a charge of murdering his baby at 10 Rillington Place (now Wesley Square),

Notting Hill, London, was given a posthumous free pardon in 1966. Also living at 10 Rillington Place was John Reginald Halliday Christie. He was hanged in 1953 after confessing to murdering seven women, including Evans's wife.

Bentley. See chapter 28: Lord Goddard's Non-Exclusionary Rule.

Hanratty. James Hanratty, a feeble-minded petty criminal, was hanged in 1962 for the murder of Michael Gregsten in his car on a layby on the English A6 in August 1961. Oliver Cyriax says the real killer was apparently a Peter Louis Alphon, and that Scotland Yard continues to withhold exhibits which might settle the issue by the method of DNA fingerprinting developed in 1985. He says the Crown wants to keep 16 boxes of papers concerning the case secret until the year 2071.

Ward. Judith Minah Ward would have been eliminated from the investigation of the 1974 M62 bombing which killed 12 British soldiers in a day or so if a *juge* was in charge and Ward's lawyer had access to the dossier.

Oliver Cyriax says: "Ward's confession went beyond the familiar domain of extorted admissions into the realms of incontrovertible mental derangement". She said she was not Judith Ward, 24, but Teresa O'Connell, 14. She said she was married to Provisional IRA chief Michael McVerry, but had never met him. Her stories of bombings and accomplices did not match the facts. Police withheld 34 of her 44 interviews. Cyriax says some "contained retractions, others preposterous admissions, all were contradictory and highly suggestive of a suspect with a psychiatric disorder, a diagnosis confirmed by medical reports while she awaited trial. But defence lawyers were never informed, and Ward was presented to the court as a formidable terrorist". She spent 18 years in prison for the murders.

Meehan. Patrick Meehan was alleged to have broken into a house and murdered a Mrs Ross. Ludovic Kennedy says police gave false evidence that they had found incriminating evidence in a friend's coat pocket. Meehan was found guilty and given a life sentence. He was pardoned after seven years in prison and given £50,000 compensation.

Drury. Kennedy says that the late Commander Drury knew that the two men he charged over the Luton Post Office murder were innocent. They were found guilty and given life. The Appeal Court turned down their appeals five times and they served 10 years before being quietly released. The Home Secretary, Sir William Whitelaw, told Lord Chief Justice Lane he proposed to recommend free pardons and compensation, but Lane urged him not to.

Guildford Four. Hotel bombings in Guildford ascribed to the Irish Republican Army killed seven people in 1974. The West Midlands Serious Crime Squad investigated. Ludovic Kennedy says the convictions of four men for murder rested solely on "confessions". In 1976, two other men, members of the IRA, gave the Appeal Court details, confirmed by police files, of the bombings which only participants could have known. They said the Guildford Four were not involved. Lord Roskill concluded that the IRA men and the Guildford Four had bombed the hotels together. The IRA men, who had admitted to the Guildford murders and virtually proved their guilt, were never prosecuted for the murders. In 1989, the Appeal Court ruled that the Guildford Four's "confessions" were extracted by coercion; they were released and their convictions quashed.

Birmingham Six. In November 1974, 21 people were killed in two hotel bombings in Birmingham. The West Midland Serious Crime Squad shortly obtained confessions from six people by torture. Prison officers also tortured them; their injuries were photographed. In 1975 Justice Bridge told the Six they had been convicted on "the clearest and most overwhelming evidence I have ever heard".

Dismissing their appeal in 1976, Lord Chief Justice Widgery (1911-1981, Chief Justice 1971-80, said to have been senile in his last years on the bench) asserted: "There is no evidence to suggest the six had received any knocking about while in custody beyond the ordinary." The Director of Public Prosecutions charged several prison officers with beating the Six; all were acquitted.

In January 1980, the Six sought to take legal action against police and the Home Office for their injuries. Refusing them, Lord Denning, then 81, said, as noted above, that if their story was right the police were guilty of perjury and violence, and that was such an "appalling vista" that it could not be.

Home Secretary Douglas Hurd sent the case back to the Appeal Court in 1987. In 1988, forensic specialists denigrated the scientific tests used against the Six. Lord Chief Justice Lane said the experts were either lying or mistaken and "the longer this hearing has gone on, the more convinced this court has become that the verdict ... was correct". He dismissed the appeal and criticised Hurd for sending the case to the court.

The West Midland Serious Crime Squad was disbanded in 1989 amid inquiries into 97 of their cases, but in 1990 the Appeal Court again found the Six were properly convicted. However, in the same year Home Secretary David Waddington again sent the case back to the Appeal Court. It was following this that Lord Denning produced the rationale noted earlier for bringing back the rope: "We shouldn't have all these campaigns to get the Birmingham Six released if they'd been hanged. They'd have been forgotten, and the whole community would be satisfied."

Michael Mansfield QC, for five of the Six, told the Appeal Court in March 1991 that documents showed that police wove "an intricate web of deceit"; new scientific tests on thousands of West Midland police documents indicated that police may have fabricated or rewritten notes, forged a custody sheet, altered the times of alleged interrogations, and given false evidence. Lord Justices Lloyd, Mustill and Farquharson acquitted and freed the Six.

Complaints Against Lawyers. Sir Paul Condon, Commissioner of London's Metropolitan Police (Scotland Yard), observed in September 1994 that police were the subject of four or five thousand complaints a year but lawyers were the subject of 16,000.

Prime Minister Margaret Thatcher had been forced to resign in November 1990, and was succeeded by John Major. Home Secretary Kenneth Baker, who was not a lawyer, ruled out an inquiry into the case of the Birmingham Six, but announced something that should have been better: a Royal Commission into the criminal justice system, including the "possibility of an investigative role for the courts before and during a case". This was clearly an instruction to the inquiry chairman, Lord Runciman, 57, a sociologist and businessman, to consider a change to the European method of judges investigating the truth before and during the trial. David Rose notes how the cartel frustrated any such change. (See chapter 41.)

Bridgewater Four. Carl Bridgewater, 13, was a newspaper boy who had three newspapers left in his bag when he interrupted a burglary at Yew Tree Farm, Stourbridge, West Midlands, in September 1978. He was shot dead. On evidence fabricated by elements of the West Midlands Serious Crime Squad, prosecutors achieved convictions of James Robinson, Michael Hickey, Vincent Hickey and Patrick Molloy in 1979. Molloy died in prison in 1981.

Oliver Cyriax, a lawyer, notes that the Appeal Court rejected the appeal of the remaining three in 1988, but that was before the Guildford Four "first showed that the unjustly condemned could be released. To air the prosecution case (now unsustainable and virtually non-existent) again would be too humiliating ... The Court of Appeal's primary function is to uphold British justice. This could explain the February 1993 decision of the Home Secretary, himself a member of the Bar, to uphold the Bar's reputation by refusing leave to appeal in the Carl Bridgewater case. As with other miscarriages of justice, it has been patently obvious for years to anyone who studied the facts that the accused are innocent of Carl's murder, with the additional twist that this particular crime was committed by someone else who is identifiable."

However, Home Secretary Michael Howard QC, decided in 1996 that there was enough new evidence to provide a fresh review. In February 1997, Lord Justice Roch, presiding with two other judges in the Appeal Court, released Robinson and the two Hickeys, pending a full appeal. In August 1997, Lord Justice Roch and the other judges formally quashed the convictions. Justice Roch said: " ... this is another case of a miscarriage of justice which is a matter of regret to this court".

Some Australian miscarriages:

McDermott. Frederick McDermott was convicted in 1947 in NSW of a 1936 murder. He was released after a Sydney *Telegraph* reporter, Tom Farrell, demonstrated in 1951 that wheel tracks at the scene could not have been made by McDermott's car.

Bailey. In *The Sundown Murders*, Dr Peter James notes that Raymond John Bailey, was hanged in Adelaide in 1958 after Queensland detectives, Glen Hallahan and a future Commissioner, Norwin Bauer, fabricated evidence against Bailey, according to Shirley Brifman's account of an admission by a distraught Hallahan.

Stuart. An Australian Aborigine, Rupert Max Stuart, framed for the murder of a nine year old girl on the beach at Ceduna, South Australia, got to within nine hours of the Adelaide gallows in 1959 before Father Tom Dixon, financed by Rupert Murdoch's Adelaide *News*, demonstrated that the trial jury heard only half the evidence, and that half did not include a perfect alibi for Stuart.

Chamberlain. A dingo killed Azaria Chamberlain, baby daughter of Lindy Chamberlain, at Ayers Rock, Central Australia, in 1980. Mrs Chamberlain was convicted in 1982 and imprisoned. Six years and five tons of paperwork later, the conviction was quashed.

Part III

Solutions

33

Searching for the Truth:

There Are No Fox-Hunters in Europe

My reading suggests that even those comparative lawyers who are critical of the French criminal law do accept that French courts are fair, and that the verdict reached is generally accurate.

— Justice James Burchett, Australian Federal Court, 1996

If Justice Burchett is right, the common law's position is untenable. In considering various solutions, it should be kept in mind that for the past 200 years the magic tricks have largely made it unnecessary to bribe judges, except perhaps in the Chicago of Jake (Greasy Thumb) Guzik and Murray (The Camel) Humphreys, and for them it was probably more a matter of principle than necessity. At least theoretically, a move to fact-gathering inquisitorial judges would carry a greater risk of attempts to corrupt judges. However, as in Europe, safeguards can be built into the system.

* * *

Members of the cartel, perhaps still afflicted with an "insular dislike of things foreign", assert that in France you are guilty until proved innocent. (In England, so the joke goes, you are innocent until proved Irish.) Justice Burchett's observation above refutes that assertion; it also destroys every argument for retaining the common law's nine magic tricks. If French courts are fair and their verdicts generally accurate, common law courts must be unfair and inaccurate.

The task is thus to get oppression, unfairness and high cost out of the common law and truth and justice into it. There are no perfect solutions; European systems are not perfect. Some European judges, for example, are not independent of the state, and suspects may be left in prison longer than most English-speaking countries would tolerate. But we must look to Europe to see if some combination of the better parts of the two systems may afford a workable solution. For the sake of completeness, there will be some overlapping in the chapters on European law.

European Law. European law starts with a number of advantages. It has never had a cartel; it has believed that truth is relevant to justice since 1215; it has been refining fact-gathering techniques, particularly since the end of the 18th century. It does not believe the law is a game like fox-hunting or that the trial is a theatrical performance. It believes that properly-trained judges, not detectives, should control the police investigation, and that properly-trained judges, not lawyers, should control the trials. It believes the judges should find out the truth for themselves. It believes there should be no magic tricks which conceal evidence, and that the verdict of the jury and judge should be scrutable. And, crucially, European law believes that a proper adversary system, i.e. one which protects the suspect without interfering with the truth, should operate at the pre-trial investigation as well as at the trial.

In French courts in 100 fairly serious cases judge and jury are thoroughly convinced of the guilt of 90; 10 per cent are given the benefit of the doubt. In the most serious cases the figure is 95. In summary then, in a "fair and generally accurate" inquisitorial system, perhaps 10 guilty get off and something approaching zero innocent go to prison, whereas in common law countries perhaps one per cent of those in prison are innocent while 80 per cent of the guilty get off.

Mechanics. The mechanics of inquisitorial criminal trials vary to some extent, but they are generally simplicity itself by comparison with the "stupefying unreality" of a common law trial. A trained judge controls the trial and the fact-gathering for him or herself and the jury, who sit on the bench with him or her. There is no such thing as a plea of guilty; that would prevent the judge and jury finding out the full facts for themselves. There are no magic tricks; the judge does not conceal relevant evidence from him or herself and the jurors; the accused's evidence is relevant.

Adversarial. It is sometimes said that an inquisitorial system is non-adversarial, and European criminal law is less adversarial than its commercial law. Nonetheless, their criminal trials are adversarial except in terms of control of the trial. Lawyers appear for the accused, the prosecution (the people) and the victim; they advance their clients' interests by making submissions and suggesting questions to the judge. The difference is that they cannot ask questions directly; that might obscure the truth as it does in the common law system.

Goalposts. The judge examines the witnesses in a neutral way; he does not shift the goalposts from the accused to the victim. The standard of proof amounts to the same as the common law "beyond a reasonable doubt", but is expressed in a way jurors can understand: they and the judge have to be "intimately, thoroughly convinced", and they have to give reasons for their verdict.

Cost. As for cost, an international Bar Association conference in Melbourne in 1994 was told that a French trial costs about a third or a half that of a common law trial. This means that the French system convicts at least four times as many serious criminals as the common law system at perhaps half the cost. If the common law was a public company, the 1597 million shareholders would dismiss the three million directors at the annual general meeting.

Bosselmann. A former German judge, Klaus Bosselmann, is an associate professor at Auckland University's law school. Robert Mannion reports him as saying (in Mannion's summary) that "a good measure of any legal system is how well it is trusted by the community it serves. Europe has its own *causes celebres* but by comparison with common law countries there is a very high level of public confidence in court decisions. A population of more than 800 million seems to produce fewer cases involving serious doubt than New Zealand [pop. 3.5 million] has managed in the past few years. That confidence also translates into how lawyers are regarded. Lawyers in common law countries rank very low in polls on public respect (third from the bottom – narrowly above sharebrokers and politicians in New Zealand). In Europe, lawyers are highly regarded – although the law is not seen as such a lucrative career ... But what system would [Professor Bosselmann] prefer to face a serious criminal charge in? If he were innocent, he says, he would rather be in Europe, because there are more safeguards against misguided prosecutions. If he were guilty? Well, 'you have more hope here'."

Cowdery. Nicholas Cowdery QC, Director of Public Prosecutions in NSW, says: "The fundamental difference between the adversarial and inquisitorial systems in criminal proceedings may be illustrated by the statement that in the former the accused is a party to the proceedings – in the latter he or she is the subject of them. In civil proceedings in the adversarial system a party brings an action which is opposed by another party – in the inquisitorial system the claim has precedence over the parties ..." Cowdery quoted G. Van Kessel (*Adversary Excesses in American Criminal Trials*, 67 Notre Dame LR 403) as stating: "In terms of the fundamental differences between the two systems, surely there is nothing sinister or presumptively unfair in a procedure which depends upon an 'inquiry' into the facts by a neutral and informed judge rather than upon presentation of evidence by interested 'advocates' to an unprepared fact finder."

Mason. Sir Anthony Mason, Chief Justice of the High Court of Australia 1987-95, noted in March 1994 that the common law may produce injustice, and asked: "Are we prepared to make more radical changes to the common law adversary system that would bring it closer to the civil law system?"

Ziegert. Professor Alex Ziegert, head of the department of jurisprudence at Sydney University, pointed to a problem and the solution in 1997. He said the development of the adversary system in the 18th century had "profound consequences for legal practice in all proceedings", including a diminished "facilitative role" for the judge, removal of "a holistic perspective on legal proceedings", the introduction of "a high degree of technicality into proceedings, like the law of evidence, the hearsay principle, etc", and "it split artificially the court into a doubtful 'tribunal of facts' (the jury) and 'tribunal of law'. As a consequence, this type of procedural communication could only be maintained with a high degree of invoking traditions and myths rather than rational arguments, opposing the reforms which continental European legal systems, without the dominance of an organised legal profession, underwent in the past 150 years ... It appears from this discussion that as far as the further development of Australian law is concerned the office of a judge is of prime importance ... it would seem that the future of this office does not lie in further traditionalist hedging but in a move forward to professional (career) judges and to the conversion of passive jury members into active judges."

As Professor Ziegert seems to be suggesting, many of the common law's problems can be cured by restoring the role of fact-gatherer to the judge and by a change in geography: moving the jury from the side of the court to the Bench.

Truth-Driven Tribunals. The cartel argues that the common law is culturally too ingrained for a modified adversarial transplant, but common law countries already have several allegedly truth-driven tribunals which purport to use European techniques, e.g. inquests, commissions of inquiry, administrative appeal tribunals. The problem is that many have been lawyerised and adversarialised. Judge Richard Posner says that by 1960 in the US "potentially rival systems of regulation and dispute resolution, such as the administrative process and arbitration, which the judiciary and the legal profession had once fought, had been successfully lawyerised and were no longer a threat".

That no doubt applies in other common law countries, certainly in Australia; cheerily addressing me as Whitton QC, the Hon Andrew Rogers QC, former chief judge in commercial law in the NSW Supreme Court, said tribunals were intended to be inquisitorial but are now often chaired by lawyers and are much more adversarial. He said lawyers had managed "to create confusion where none existed", and that this is "putting up the costs tremendously".

In an address at a National Administrative Law Forum in Canberra in May 1997, I noted that common lawyers tend to be afflicted with the malady and offered some proposals to get tribunals back on the truth track:

1. Members of tribunals should be part of a specialised profession wholly divorced from the common law.

2. Aspiring professional members should be taught techniques of cross-examination and the judicial function, including weight to be given to evidence. Until then, common lawyers on the tribunal should not have a vote on the decision.

3. Tribunals should have trained investigators similar to the French *juge d'instruction*.

4. If common lawyers are allowed to appear for parties at the tribunal, they should be restricted to suggesting questions and making submissions. They should not be allowed to obscure the truth by cross-examination.

34

European Techniques

... the traditional inquisitorial trial is essentially a process of public confirmation of the results of the investigation.

– Bron McKillop, 1994

For data on European inquisitorial techniques I have largely relied on Bron McKillop, senior lecturer in law at Sydney University, Michael Mansfield QC and Sir Ludovic Kennedy. McKillop's *Inquisitorial Systems of Criminal Justice and the ICAC: A Comparison* (November 1994; folio 54 pp.: ICAC, Box 500, GPO Sydney 2001, Australia) is an account of how the systems work in France, Germany, Italy, and Scotland. He also examines the Grand Jury system in the US.

McKillop is also the author of *Anatomy of a French Murder Case*, in which he takes a case through from investigation to trial, and compares the procedure with common law procedures for a similar case. He told me in November 1997: "The quality of investigation in France is superior to ours: they're trying to get to the bottom of it, and there is judicial supervision. Most of the work is done by police, but they know how far they can go."

The data itself suggests how both European and common law systems could be improved. McKillop first gives the general characteristics of European systems. Basically, the procedure is seen as an inquiry into historical truth. Much of the work goes into the investigation; the trial relies to some extent on paper (the dossier) with some oral evidence, whereas in common law countries "orality" at the trial is the major focus. In Europe prosecutor as well as defence can appeal against the verdict.

Beccaria. In the 18th century the European system became more reasonable; the English system became less so. It appears that torture, given up by English judges in the 17th century, was still used in Italy in the 18th. Cesare, Marchese de Beccaria (1735 or 1738-94), jurist and philosopher, published the widely influential *On Crime and Punishments* in 1764. It denounced torture and capital punishment and advocated prevention of crime by education. In 1791 he was appointed to a board to reform the judicial code.

Code Napoleon. Among evil psychopaths, Bonaparte (1769-1821) ranks with Josef Stalin (1879-1953) and Adolf Hitler (1889-1945), but perhaps the lasting effects of his legal reforms to some extent compensate for his mass murders. He appointed a commission of four in 1800 to codify French private law. The Justice Minister, Jean-Jacques Cambeceres (1753-1824), had a major role in the final draft in 1804 known as the Code Napoleon, a name also given to

Bonaparte's four other codes, the Code of Civil Procedure 1807, the Commercial Code 1808, the Code of Criminal Procedure 1811 and the Penal Code 1811. The code imported from England the notion of a jury. The Code Napoleon is still in force. It had a strong influence on countries briefly under his control, Holland and Belgium, parts of Germany, Spain and hence on Latin American countries.

The Judge. Bron McKillop says: "Judges on the continent are especially trained for their work . The judiciary is a career service, commencing in specialised judicial training schools after graduation as lawyers and normally involving progression from lower to higher echelons on satisfactory performance, ability and approval of superiors. Most judges in France and Italy, having done a few years as examining magistrates, would be fully familiar with how a dossier is put together and would understand and accept its importance in the criminal justice process."

The presiding judge dominates the proceedings. He has studied the dossier and works off it during the trial. He interrogates the accused and the witnesses he feels it is necessary to call. He also receives requests for supplementary questions the prosecutor and defence counsel would like him to put. Judicial personalities vary; some are bureaucratic, letter-of-the-law types like common law judges, but some are prepared to go beyond the dossier in their search for the truth. The second type would seem to be closer to the spirit of European law. Thus McKillop: "There are presiding judges who are intolerant of any departure in the evidence at trial from the depositions in the dossier, especially of accused seeking to resile at trial from admissions made during the investigation; and there are presiding judges who question the accused and the witnesses dispassionately, with minimal use of leading questions, and who are prepared to probe matters possibly helpful to the accused even beyond the record contained in the dossier."

Judicial Independence. Judges in common law countries have been nominally independent of the state since 1701, but it appears they have never been independent of lawyers or the cartel. The reverse is the case in European countries: some judges are not independent of the state, but they are independent of lawyers: there is no cartel. And, as noted, they are trained professional judges; common law judges are untrained amateur judges. It is surely preferable to have trained judges who are independent of both state and lawyers.

The Accused. The accused is seen as a valuable source of information in the search for truth and he/she generally accepts this despite a right of silence. His life, character and previous convictions are investigated and presented at his/her trial.

Defence Counsel. The common law adversary system operates only at the trial. The European adversary system operates at both the pre-trial investigation and at the trial. The suspect's lawyer can do anything to assist his client's interests. Most importantly, he can use the dossier and his own inquiries to demonstrate his client's innocence at the pre-trial stage. At the trial, he can suggest questions but he is not allowed to cross-examine witnesses.

Victim. The victim is generally able to be represented at the trial by a lawyer with the task of pursuing damages or preparing the way for a civil action. If lawyers appeared for victims at common law trials, their objections might be able to spare the victim some of the brutality of adversary cross-examination, and they would have the merit of protecting the victim and the community from the effects of a slack prosecution.

The Trial. McKillop says trials in Germany tend to be discontinuous, "bit by bit, in instalments, over a long time", and that this allows "for conclusions to be drawn slowly ... rather than quickly, considerately rather than impressionistically". However, "the traditional inquisitorial trial is essentially a process of public confirmation of the results of the investigation. The process has been described as an appeal from the dossier or as an audit of the dossier, the evidence at the trial having been 'pre-cooked' and the outcome of the trial 'pre-destined'." He says attempts have recently been made in Germany and Italy, without much success, to have evidence at the trial the sole basis for decision. Evidence at the trial is not recorded in the dossier. This seems wrong.

Jurors (Lay Judges). The French jury sits only in the court hearing the most serious charges (*cour d'assises*). The nine jurors sit with the three judges, but they are not allowed to see the dossier, just as common law juries are not allowed to see the transcript. Both practices seem wrong.

Bonaparte believed the Italians were not ready for jury trial at the start of the 19th century. Jurors were introduced into Germany after 1848 and in Italy a little later. McKillop says: "The Fascists abolished the jury in 1931 but today jurors sit in Italy in the *corte d'assisse* and function in a similar way to the jurors in the French *cour d'assises*."

The German jury was abolished by the Weimar Republic in 1924, but semi-professional lay judges, or assessors (*schoffen*), now sit in the lower criminal court, and two lay judges sit with three judges in the higher criminal court.

Although juries are a relatively recent phenomenon in Europe, McKillop says they are perceived as meaningfully democratic and there is no real movement to abolish them.

Standard of Proof. A doubt must be resolved in favour of the accused; McKillop says there is probably no real difference between beyond a reasonable doubt and the European "conviction of guilt", e.g. the French *in time conviction* and the German *freie uberzeugung*. There may be no difference in the standard but, as noted, there is a difference in the formula: the English is negative and confusing, whereas French jurors should have no trouble in understanding their obligation to be "intimately [thoroughly] convinced".

Appeal Courts. European criminal justice systems insist on quality control: trial results automatically go up to appeal courts for review; unlike common law systems, the prosecutor as well as the defence can make the case that the verdict was wrong. The review is comprehensive; the dossier helps the appeal court to scrutinise the lower court's reasoning, application of the law and findings of fact. A drawback is that the evidence of witnesses at the trial is not reviewed because it is not recorded in the dossier.

*　*　*

Summary: In brief, the differences between European law and the common law may be summarised thus:

European systems are investigative; they seek the truth; a judge supervises the pre-trial investigation; they have an adversary system at the pre-trial and trial; the defence lawyer can examine the dossier at the pre-trial; a judge gathers the facts at the trial; the jury sits with the judge; lawyers are not allowed to question witnesses; evidence is not concealed.

Common law systems are accusatorial; they do not seek the truth; police supervise the pre-trial investigation; there is no adversary system at the pre-trial investigation; defence lawyers are not allowed to examine the police running sheets; lawyers gather the facts at the trial; an extreme adversary system operates at the trial; lawyers cross-examine witnesses; evidence is concealed.

35

The Pre-Trial Investigation 1: France, Japan, Belgium

Perhaps one of the most important aspects of this [French] system is that every single piece of information relating to the case – witness statements, forensic reports, the juge's instructions to the police and their response – are all included in the dossier and the defence lawyer has access to it.

– Michael Mansfield QC, 1993

Mansfield QC is attracted to the French version of the adversary system because the defence lawyer has access to the dossier. The lawyer can see how the case is running and if his client is innocent he has the chance to point to evidence that will put the *juge* right at an early stage. In common law countries, the adversary system does not exist at the pre-trial stage, and police and prosecution can get locked into a false position with innocent suspects.

Mansfield continues: "Both parties are playing with exactly the same cards and should the case eventually go to court, the prosecution's case will be based on the information in the dossier and nothing else. Defence lawyers will have the same dossier and there will be no surprises, no secret witnesses, no last-minute evidence presented on the first day in court and, equally as important, nothing is secretly excluded from evidence which doesn't fit the prosecution's case. The withholding of information, together with uncorroborated confessions, has been a regular theme in Britain's appalling record of miscarriages ...."

The Juge. France is littered with signs saying: **WHY NOT BE A JUDGE?** This means there is no cartel in France. Nor should there be: as previously noted, lawyering is lawyering; judging is judging. Michael Mansfield says the French magistrature has two branches: "sitting" judges and "standing" judges. The sitting judges sit in the courtroom (with the jury) and are "in theory at any rate, independent of the executive and legislative powers and their independence is guaranteed by the President of the Republic".

The other group, the Prosecutors, stand when they appear in court. The *juge d'instruction* and the public prosecutor come into this category. Mansfield says the Prosecutors are appointed for three years to one court but can remain longer; "to uphold the principle of independence, a *juge d'instruction* can't be moved except at their own request. The prosecutor doesn't have this protection".

Career Structure. Mansfield says the career structure starts at the National Schools for Magistrates in Bordeaux and Paris; anyone under 27 with a suitable degree from university can apply to become one of the 250 students accepted as *auditeurs de justice* each year. The course lasts 2 1/2 years; one year is spent in class and one in court learning the functions of judge and prosecutor. The *auditeur* spends the other six months with police, the *gendarmerie*, the Bar, prisons and even private companies.

In cases of serious crime – murder, manslaughter, rape, armed robbery – which carry long terms of imprisonment, the police investigation is supervised by a trained *juge d'instruction*, literally judge of the investigation. The rank is akin to a magistrate; it can be translated as examining magistrate. Half are women. Their task is to find out what happened, not to get a conviction. They can get forensic help from experts independent of the state, and they reconstruct the crime as soon as possible, but do not rush to a conclusion. There is no committal hearing.

The suspect is questioned by the *juge*, not the police, in the presence of his/her lawyer. He/she has a right of silence but usually speaks; an inference can be drawn from a refusal. There is no such thing as a plea of guilty; the *juge* and later the trial judge and jury have to find out the truth for themselves, and in any event the French understand, as common lawyers apparently do not, that deranged people can plead guilty to anything, including murder.

Miscarriages. Ludovic Kennedy noted in 1989 that the idea of judges supervising the police investigation was favoured by Sir Peter Imbert, then head of the Metropolitan Police [Scotland Yard], and by Lord Scarman, a former Law Lord. He said: "Had such an official been present to interrogate the Guildford Four, it would not have taken him long to find that they had no case to answer ... The elimination of police malpractices combined with the rigorous investigations of the *juge* and the accused having to give an account of him or herself at all stages are factors built into the system to bring about a correct verdict. I think it probable that if there had been an examining magistrate investigating the cases of Timothy Evans, James Hanratty, Patrick Meehan, the two in the Luton case, Margaret Livesey, George Long, the Guildford Four, the Maguire Seven, and the Birmingham Six, not one of those unfortunates – in addition to scores of others – would have come to trial, let alone have been convicted."

Moreover, Kennedy said, "in cases where juries are suspicious of police evidence (and I'm told that an increasing number are), [supervision by an investigating magistrate] would prevent the acquittal of the guilty. And thirdly, if the questioning is fair and non-partisan, there can no longer be any reason for retaining the suspect's right to silence".

A Stroke of the Pen. Kennedy said appointing examining magistrates to interrogate suspects in all serious cases is "not only desirable but also practicable. It would require no more than an extension of existing legislation".

Mansfield. Michael Mansfield QC said in 1993: "It is important to remember the difference in approach between our police-operated system of investigation and that of a *juge d'instruction*. In the latter case the search is for truth and not guilt ... She [Catherine Samet, a *juge*] maintains that her first and most important dedication is to human rights and lawyers are aware of this. They rely on the *juge d'instruction* because they have confidence in the position and the ideals which the holder of that position represents."

He says it would be naive to pretend that the system is without faults and free from outside pressures; there had been recent examples in which political interference was exerted for *juges* to drop cases which could embarrass the government.

A Juge Speaks. "However," Mansfield said, "Catherine Samet is fairly sanguine about it. [She said]: 'Indirectly I come under the prosecutor and when the prosecutor hands a case over to me, he or she can instruct me not to follow a particular line of investigation. The prosecutor is accountable to the Ministry of Justice and has political considerations. But once I am in charge of investigation I can do more or less what I wish and there is often more than one way of getting the same result. There can also be indirect pressure and it is important and quite possible to ignore this if it is not legitimate. But sometimes it is a question of doing what you can rather than what you want ... Mostly you can withstand political pressure but in the end you can only expect of people what they are'." It seems clear that the French could learn from the independence of common law judges from the executive.

Juge Samet also said: "I have no desire to be a police woman because my principal aim is to guarantee a person's rights. If anything I am an academic. What motivates me most of all is my love for people and criminals are men and women, members of our society. In my office I see them cry, I see them laugh, I see them suffer in prison. People are very complicated and I never forget this. Someone can do something horrible but for a very pure reason and I will try to get at this reason, I try to understand them. Despite my title, my role is not to judge them but to understand them. I believe in justice and I believe in a democracy which works. I try to uphold the three pillars of the French constitution – Liberty, Equality, Fraternity – and to that you could add human rights."

The Dossier. Perhaps the greatest safeguard against a miscarriage is the *juge's* dossier on the case. Into it goes every piece of information in favour of the suspect as well as the evidence against him. McKillop says: "The pursuit of the truth is regarded as paramount ... In all investigations exculpatory as well as inculpatory matter is required to be investigated so that the whole truth of the matter may be revealed. All aspects of an investigation, substantive and procedural, are recorded in a dossier which is under the control of the prosecutor. Defence counsel has the right to inspect the dossier at all times."

The dossier has four parts:

Pieces de fond: a record of the investigation including the first police report, depositions of the accused and witnesses, experts' reports, surveillance.

Detention preventive: a record of the accused's pre-trial detention, if any.

Renseignements et personalite: the accused's history, background and prior convictions.

Pieces de forme: a record of warrants, orders, directives.

There are three main types of pre-trial investigation:

Flagrant Offences (*L'Enquete Flagrante*): for *delits* (offences carrying two months to five years) and crimes carrying five years or more, detected while being committed or recently. A prosecutor supervises the judicial police (detectives responsible to prosecutors or investigating judges). Police can arrest and detain (*garde a vue*). The detained person is entitled to confidential legal advice for 30 minutes at the beginning of the detention, and has a right to a medical examination and a visit by a family member. The prosecutor may question suspects without a lawyer but records the results. He may order the suspect to be taken before a *juge* who can order further detention for up to four days, and he can send it to another *juge* who can order long-term detention.

Preliminary Investigation (*L'Enquete Preliminaire*): for unflagrant offences which do not require an examining magistrate: driving offences, fraud, *contraventions* carrying up to two months or a fine.

Judicial Investigation (*L'Information Judiciare or L'Instruction Criminelle*): for all crimes and *delits* nominated by the prosecutor. A *juge* conducts the investigation with extensive powers to detain, to search and seize, to interrogate the suspect and the witnesses, to arrange a reconstruction of the event and for witnesses to confront the defendant, to obtain independent experts, to make background inquiries about the defendant (*personalite*), and to delegate the investigation to the judicial police. The procedure is supposed to be secret but non-lawyers involved generally leak to the press in cases of public interest.

Committal for Trial: In a case of major crime, the *juge* remits the case to three judges (the *chambre d'accusation*) for decision as to whether the defendant is sent for trial before the *cour d'assises*.

* * *

As Sir Ludovic Kennedy notes, it requires no more than a stroke of the pen to use the *juge* to prevent oppression and miscarriages in common law countries. Common lawyers and civil libertarians, usually so stentorian about civil rights, are not at the forefront of demands that a trained judge supervise police investigations, question suspects and build up a dossier to which defence lawyers have access and input. Are the lawyers more focussed in getting the guilty off rather than keeping the innocent out of prison? Are civil liberties groups silent because they have been lawyerised?

Japan

Japan's pre-trial inquisitorial procedure is a worry. Nicholas Cowdery QC, of Sydney, went to Japan in 1993 at the invitation of the Japanese Federation of Bar Associations to inquire into Japan's pre-indictment custody system on behalf of the International Bar Association (IBA). He presented his 72-page report to the 25th IBA conference in Melbourne in October 1993.

Cowdery said Japan's justice system made "a mockery" of rights to silence and to a lawyer, even though both allegedly existed. He said suspects could be held in police cells for 23 days and routinely interrogated without being made aware of their rights. He said confessions were often extracted by physcial and psychological force, and that this led to innocent persons confessing to crimes which carried the death penalty.

He said that in 1992 Japan had a conviction success rate of 99.995 per cent and that about 95 per cent were based on signed confessions. He said the emphasis on confessions meant that charges against guilty criminals were often not laid because they refused to confess.

CPR. Japan's inquisitorial system is clearly not a good model, but the right to silence and a lawyer also allegedly exist in common law countries. New York police cars are stamped with the letters CPR. They stand for Courtesy, Professionalism, Respect, but there are no doubt other interpretations. After a fracas at a nightclub, Abner Louima, 30, formerly of Haiti, was brought into the 70th Precinct at Flatbush early on August 9, 1997. He says he was sodomised with a toilet plunger and the instrument was then forced into his mouth and broke several teeth.

Belgium

Nor is Belgium's system a good model; the investigating magistrates are rather like judges in common law countries: they are not trained and they are appointed by politicians.

Stephen Bates reported in November 1997: "It is becoming apparent that the Belgian magistracy, which is responsible for investigating crimes, and the country's police forces – there are three separate ones – simply cannot cope. They have not solved a major crime for years ...

"You don't have to be much of a lawyer, indeed it pays not to be, to be appointed to the job by local politicians. You can just be a party hack and what you get out of the job is a low salary (about £14,000 a year, but opportunities for graft) ... When a written examination was introduced for potential magistrates a year or two back, it was so successful that there was soon a shortage of candidates to fill the vacancies ... When a committee condemned Benoit Dejemeppe, the chief magistrate of Brussels, as incompetent recently, they were told that was not a good enough reason to sack him. Brussels itself has 74 magistrates coping with 350,000 crimes a year. That is an average of 13 a day each theoretically requiring investigation, report and prosecution. No wonder two-thirds of cases never get to court and those which do can take five years."

36

The Pre-Trial Investigation 2: Italy, Germany, Scotland, the US

Data on pre-trial investigations in other European countries and Scotland and the US largely relies on Bron McKillop's study for the NSW Independent Commission Against Corruption.

Italy

> *Gambino: ... with these new laws [investigating judges] won't be able to do anything.*
>
> *Anon: They'll go pick beans.*

– Mafia conversation, 1988

Mussolini. Bonaparte's Criminal Code was the basis of Italian criminal procedure until 1930, when *"porco fascisti"* in the government of Benito Mussolini (1883-1945), proclaimed a new code which, McKillop says, "strengthened the position of the prosecuting authority as representative of the executive power and weakened the position of the accused". This remained in force even after 1948, when Italy adopted a constitution which provided for civil rights, including a right to defence counsel from the start of criminal proceedings and a requirement that arrests be by judicial warrant.

An Adversary System. An attempt was made in 1989 to change from the inquisitorial adversary system to the common law's extreme adversary system. McKillop says: "[The Italian system] has recently tried to swing radically from an inquisitorial to an accusatorial/adversarial system and this does not seem to have worked."

Barker QC. Nonetheless, some common lawyers see the attempt as confirming the superiority of their system: the heirs of Pope Innocent III and the Lateran Council have at last come to their senses. Ian Barker QC, the man who, as it were, got the dingo off, wrote (*The Australian*, February 11, 1997): "In [*Trial by Voodoo*] he expresses admiration for systems such as the inquisitorial procedure adopted by the Italians in 1865. As it happens, under Mussolini the Italian system became a paradigm of the procedures advocated by Whitton. But typical of the book is that Mr Whitton's Italian researches stopped in 1865. *Trial by Voodoo* is silent about Italy's 1989 *Codici Di Procedure Penale*, expressly based in large measure on the Anglo-American adversarial model." I am of course hugely in the debt of the distinguished common lawyer for pointing this out, and hasten to repair the omission.

Tortora. Some in Italy no doubt believed that an adversary system would improve civil rights; Alexander Stille notes that Naples judges made a ghastly error in the 1983 case of Enzo Tortora, a television host who was falsely accused by two highly suspect criminals of dealing in drugs during his investigation of organised crime in Naples. Tortora was held at length in prison without bail and died of cancer while trying to exonerate himself.

The Camel Lives. Italian lawyers may also have seen more money in an adversary system, but the key factor in clipping the judges' wings seems to have been that the Mafia judged it would enhance their chances of escaping justice. The ghostly hand of Murray (The Camel) Humphreys may thus be discerned in the events that resulted in the attempt to introduce the system. The following chronology is largely from Alexander Stille's *Excellent Cadavers*.

Falcone and Borsellino. Judge Giovanni Falcone and Judge Paolo Borsellino were two of the four investigating magistrates who formed a new anti-Mafia pool in Palermo, Sicily, in November 1983. Falcone issued 366 arrest warrants against Mafiosi in September 1984. The Palermo maxi-trial opened in February 1986 with 475 defendants, 117 of them fugitives. The trial proceeded until December 1987.

A Warning to Andreotti. In June 1987, national elections were held for a new Italian Parliament. A Mafia informer, Francesco Mannoia, later told Judge Falcone that the Mafia organised a movement of votes away from Giulio Andreotti's Christian Democrats as a warning that they "had not found a way of stopping the anti-Mafia investigations of the judges of Palermo". The votes generally moved to the Radical Party, which had championed defendants' rights and had received heavy contributions from Mafia bosses – even Luciano Leggio, boss of the Corleone Mafia family but then in Palermo's Ucciardone prison, asked for a Radical Party card – and the Socialist party, which had attacked the power of the judges. The Socialists nearly doubled their vote in Palermo, a Christian Democrat stronghold.

Referendum. In November 1987, a referendum sponsored by the Socialist and Radical parties was passed. It limited the power of the judges, and allowed them to be sued for damages for errors of judgment, a petrifying thought for common law judges afflicted with the malady.

Anti-Mafia Pool Dismantled. In December 1987, the maxi-trial ended with 344 convictions and 114 not guilty. In July 1988, Borsellino publicly denounced the dismantling of the Palermo anti-Mafia pool.

Criminal Code. The legislature discussed changes to the criminal code designed to greatly limit the power of judges to arrest and hold suspects in prison. On September 20, 1988, US agents tapped a conversation in Sicilian dialect in the Cafe Giardano in Brooklyn between a heroin-dealer, Joe Gambino, and an anonymous man just back from Palermo:

Anon: Now they've approved the new law, now they can't prosecute as they did in the past ... They can't arrest people when they want. Before they do, they have to have solid proof, they have to convict first and arrest later.

Gambino: Oh, so it's like here, in America.

Anon: No, it's better, much better. Now these bastards, the magistrates and cops, can't even dream of arresting anyone the way they do now.

Gambino: The cops will take it up the ass. And [Falcone] won't be able to do anything either? ... They'll all take it up the ass.

Anon: Yeah, they'll take it in the ass.

Three days later, Gambino talked to another anonymous caller:

Gambino: They tell me the new code has been passed in Italy.

Anon: It's better than the American law ... the evidence has to be overwhelming ... the prosecutors can go —— themselves ...

Gambino: Yeah, but with these new laws they won't be able to do anything.

Anon: They'll go pick beans.

Andreotti became Prime Minister of Italy for the sixth time on July 23, 1989. The new Criminal Procedure Code came into effect on October 24, 1989. In February 1991, the Supreme Court released 42 of those convicted at the maxi-trial, including Michele (The Pope) Greco. Justice Minister Claudio Martelli, having consulted with Falcone, had them re-arrested, and the Supreme Court President, Corrado Carnevale, was obliged to step down. The Supreme Court, minus Carnevale, upheld the Palermo maxi-trial convictions on January 31, 1992.

Falcone Assassinated. The Mafia assassinated Salvatore Lima, Andreotti's man in Palermo, on March 12 and Judge Falcone on Saturday, May 23, 1992. This was seen as the death of the Italian state; Parliament called for a day of mourning. On the Monday, after Falcone's funeral, Parliament elected Oscar Scalfaro as President. On June 8, he issued a presidential decree, later ratified by legislation, substantially modifying the 1989 Criminal Code to allow for a partial return to the 1930 Code. McKillop says: "The modifications ... were said to be necessary because the new Code was ineffective against the Mafia." The Mafia assassinated Judge Borsellino on July 19, 1992.

Andreotti Charged. On March 27, 1993, Palermo prosecutors accused Andreotti of collusion with the Mafia. The Christian Democrat Party formally dissolved itself in July 1993 and re-emerged as *Il Partito Popolare* ...

* * *

McKillop examined the 1930 code and the 1989 code and the 1992 changes.

1930. An examining judge controlled investigations for most cases tried in the higher courts. He had the duty and the power to make any inquiry necessary to ascertain the truth, including evidence for and against the suspect. The investigation was recorded in a file, the dossier, for use at the trial. Inquiry measures were originally kept secret from the defence but from 1948 the defence was given access to most details.

Crimes within the jurisdiction of the lowest court (the *Pretura*), were summarily investigated by the judge (*Pretore*) who was also the prosecutor. McKillop says this was an anachronistic inquisitorial form: the investigator, prosecutor and judge were the same person.

The interrogation of the suspect was and is integral to the process. The suspect, who could have a lawyer present, was advised of a right to remain silent but rarely exercised it. The interrogator was obliged to elicit and pursue matters relevant to the suspect's defence. In practice police did the questioning before and after arrests and generally in the absence of a defence lawyer.

1989. The 1989 code eliminated the examining judge and the use of the dossier at trial so it could be "oral" and initiated plea-bargaining on the US model. The *Pretore* no longer had an investigative and prosecuting function; a separate prosecutor was introduced. Investigations were now to be carried out by judicial police and prosecutors under the passive supervision of a new judicial officer, the pre-trial judge, who authorised telephone tapping and arrests.

1992. The judicial police were given greater powers of investigation and were made less subject to control by prosecutors. The dossier reverted to its earlier important role to allow depositions of witnesses to be used at trial instead of oral evidence.

Germany

The former West German system has applied throughout Germany since West and East Germany were reunited after 1989. The examining magistrate was abolished in 1975 in West Germany. The prosecutor now has theoretical control over all aspects of an investigation but in practice the police (*Kriminalpolizei*) initiate and develop investigations. Witnesses are usually examined by police on a voluntary basis, but the prosecutor can oblige them to attend.

Police can detain a suspect until the next day, but pre-trial detention and search generally require a judicial warrant, and cannot be longer than six months without review by a judge of a higher court. The prosecutor must examine the accused before a formal charge (*Anklage*) is filed; any matter raised in his favour must be investigated "so that the whole truth can be discovered".

The prosecutor can have an accused examined by a judge. He has no right to be legally represented during his examination, but the prosecutor may, "and often does", allow it. The results of the investigation are recorded in a dossier (*Akte*) to which defence counsel has access, but only at the end of the investigation. The dossier goes to the trial court.

Committal for Trial. The prosecutor moves that the case go to the court competent to hear it; that court decides whether it will hear it. The accused can object, on factual or legal ground, to the court hearing his case.

Scotland

Scotland's legal system had historical links with France's, but the Scottish system has now basically been common lawyerised. The remaining inquisitorial features are:

The Procurator Fiscal. The procurator fiscal is descended from the French *procureur* (prosecutor), and is responsible, either personally or via police, for the investigation of all crimes in his district, for examining all witnesses for major trials, and for investigating sudden or suspicious deaths, fires, explosions, and complaints against the police.

The Judicial Examination. This was revived by the Criminal Justice (Scotland) Act of 1980. The suspect is brought before the sheriff and questioned by the procurator-fiscal in the presence of his lawyer. He is not obliged to answer, but the prosecutor and judge can comment on that at his trial. The judge, but not the prosecutor, can also comment if he fails to give evidence at the trial.

McKillop notes: "The right to comment in these two situations can be regarded as a type of inquisitorial pressure on an accused to contribute to the ascertainment of the truth of matters before the court."

The US Grand Jury

> It is a grand inquest, a body with powers of investigation and inquisition, the scope of whose inquiries is not to be limited narrowly by questions of propriety or forecasts of the probable results of the investigation, or by doubts whether any particular individual will be found properly subject to an accusation of crime.

> – US Supreme Court, *Blair v United States* (1919)

Writing of the grand jury's role in colonial America, R. Younger said (*The People's Panel: The Grand Jury in the United States 1643-1941*): "Grand juries acted in the nature of local assemblies: making known the wishes of the people, proposing new laws, protesting against abuses in government, performing administrative tasks, and looking after the welfare of their communities."

The modern US grand jury is used to produce indictments (written accusations that someone has committed a crime) and as an investigative body, e.g. the Watergate break-in and cover-up. In both functions it operates inquisitorially rather than adversarially. It thus has the same problem as its rough equivalents in other common law countries, Royal Commissions of inquiry and standing commissions on corruption and organised crime, i.e. subsequent trial jurors will hear much less evidence because the trial is subject to common law rules for concealing evidence.

Judges summon, empanel, instruct and supervise grand jurors. They sit to hear matters on a regular basis over a period of weeks or months. There are usually 23 members, with 16 as a quorum; a bare majority, 12, is enough to indict. The only persons allowed to be present are the grand jurors, lawyers for the government, the witness, an interpreter and a stenographer or operator of a recording device. The suspect, his counsel and counsel for the witness are excluded from the proceedings. Only the jurors are present when they deliberate or vote. A breach of secrecy is punishable as a contempt of court.

The grand jury only hears evidence against the suspect. McKillop says it is accepted that prosecutors have "a large measure of control over proceedings before modern grand juries", and that "a grand jury indictment is little more than a rubber stamp for the prosecutor's decision to prosecute": in 1976 federal grand juries returned some 23,000 indictments against 123 "no bills" (a decision not to proceed); in the 12 months to September 30, 1984, they returned 17,419 indictments against 68 no bills.

As noted, prosecutors can offer, and grand jurors can indict on, evidence that will not be admissible at trial. McKillop says it is argued that "inadmissible evidence usually has probative [tending to prove guilt] value that assists in the grand jury's proper function which is investigative and not adjudicative, and that evidentiary rules are designed to ensure fairness in an adversary proceeding and the grand jury is not adversarial".

The investigative function is generally confined to misconduct by public officials. It can compel witnesses to attend and produce documents, but they can object on grounds such as the first, fourth and fifth amendments but the Supreme Court usually finds in favour of the grand jury. Witnesses must give evidence but it cannot be used against them. If they still refuse to answer they can be imprisoned until the expiration of the grand jury, but for no more than 18 months. Witnesses now have to be told of the general purpose of the inquiry, and whether they are "targets". There are suggestions that grand juries have been used to harass dissidents.

The US grand jury has obvious defects: insufficient fairness and adversarial help for witnesses and suspects. Nonetheless, with the inclusion of a trained judge and increased protection for suspects, it appears to offer a stronger basis for a truth-driven criminal justice system than any other in the common law world.

37

The Trial: France, Germany, Italy

I rely largely on analyses by Bron McKillop and Ludovic Kennedy for data on French trials and McKillop for material on trials in Germany and Italy.

France

French criminal courts, from the bottom up, are:

Tribunal de Police: a single judge deals with offences (*contraventions*) punishable by fine or a maximum of two months in prison.

Tribunal Correctionel: deals with offences (*delits*) drawing a fine or prison terms from two months to five years. In more serious cases, three judges preside and their decision has to be unanimous; in less serious cases, a single judge does the work.

Cour d'Assises: deals with offences (*crimes*) carrying penalties from five years to life. It consists of a president and two other judges and nine lay persons (*jures*). A guilty verdict requires a majority of at least 8-4; the sentence requires a simple majority of 7-5. Ludovic Kennedy says: "Some, I know, think that the proximity of judges and jurors makes the jurors susceptible to judicial influence, but it is also said that they are made to feel less the detached observers they are under the adversary system and more a responsible and integral part of the trial process."

Cour d'Appel: hears appeals from the police court and the *tribunal correctionel*. Three judges hear appeals by prosecutor and accused on facts and law. The appeal is usually by way of a complete rehearing.

Cour de Cassation: The ultimate appeal court. It can consist of nine, 15 or 35 judges and hears appeals on law only. A successful appeal results in retrial.

Advantages. Ludovic Kennedy notes the advantages: "The inquisitorial approach which began with the investigations of the *juge* is continued in the court of trial; which means that the questioning of witnesses is not done by partisan counsel but by the presiding judge, counsel's role being limited to opening and closing speeches, though at any time they may ask the presiding judge to put questions they think he has omitted to put.

"This method has several advantages. Firstly, it avoids the pseudo-dramatic atmosphere of the adversary system trial. One reason why you see so few third rate courtroom dramas emanating from countries with the inquisitorial system is that the system, being essentially low key, simply does not lend itself to that kind of thing.

"Secondly, the questioning of witnesses in a quiet, firm but non-partisan way is often more productive of a fruitful response than by the employment of a more committed approach. Thirdly, the system saves time for it obviates the need for prosecution and defence to cover, often at tedious length, the same ground; and this also can be less confusing for the jury.

"And lastly the trial itself does not come grinding to a halt, as so often happens in Britain, when the jury are shuffled out of court so that the judge can decide what is or is not admissible evidence. In a system whose object is to find the truth, there is very little evidence – so long as it is relevant – that is not admissible.

"Another attractive feature of the French system is the way in which expert witnesses are treated. In Britain prosecution and defence each produce their own tame psychiatrist or pathologist and by skilful questioning along narrow lines, invariably make them seem to contradict each other. In France it is the custom of the court to call as many expert witnesses as the court or counsel may require and by painstaking eliciting of information try, wherever possible, to reach a consensus. This is surely a more effective method of reaching the truth than the adversary approach, which can be both humiliating for the expert witness as well as puzzling for the jury." Kennedy says the conviction rate is around 90 per cent in the *Tribune Correctionel* and about 95% in the *Cour d'Assise*.

Germany

Criminal courts in Germany are organised on a state (*land*) basis but apply federal law and procedure.

Amtsgericht: the local court, the lower of the two courts. It has one professional judge when hearing less serious cases. For more serious cases it is called the *Schoffengericht* and has one professional judge and two lay judges.

Landgericht: the district court, the higher court. It has three professional judges and two lay judges. For the most serious crimes, it is called the *Schwurgericht*. Lengthy or complex trials, particularly in the *Landgericht*, may proceed in stages over weeks or months.

Majority. A two-thirds majority is required for any decision against the accused in both courts. Thus, in the lower court one lay judge must support any conviction and two lay judges can secure an acquittal. In the higher court, two-thirds is 3.3; it presumably requires four of the five for a conviction.

No Guilty Pleas. As in France, there are no guilty pleas as such, but in an uncontested minor case there can be a species of plea-bargaining: the prosecutor can propose a specific penalty, or "penal order" (*strafbefehl*). If approved by a judge, it may be accepted or rejected by the defendant. If he rejects it, the case proceeds.

Takeover Attempts. It appears that German lawyers have been making bids for at least partial control of trials for more than a century, but that thus far the judges, unlike 18th century common law judges, have resisted them. The principles of orality and immediacy are supposed to ensure that the decision is based directly on the live evidence by witnesses, including the accused, and not on the dossier.

A Dead Letter. Orality and immediacy were supposed to be reinforced by provision for adversary examination and cross-examination of witnesses; the prosecutor and defence counsel could jointly ask the presiding judge that he/she leave the examination of witnesses to them.

However, McKillop says: "This provision has become a dead letter. The presiding judge continues to do most of the questioning, based on depositions in the dossier, including the questioning of the accused at the outset of the trial." The presiding judge also decides, on the basis of the dossier, which witnesses to call. Depositions of people who are absent can be read, and a deposition can be used to contradict oral evidence, e.g. an accused who resiles from a confession before a judge. Thus, says McKillop, "the dossier ... continues to play an important role at the German criminal trial."

Verdict. As in France, after addresses by prosecutor and defence counsel, the prosecutor recommends a specific punishment. A two-thirds majority of the professional and lay judges is necessary for a guilty verdict and they must have a "free conviction" (*freie uberzeugung*) of guilt. The accused must be given the benefit of any doubt. The decision is read out by the presiding judge; detailed written reasons are later prepared by the professional judges.

Appeals. The accused can appeal against a guilty verdict, and the prosecutor can appeal against an acquittal. But if the appellate court substitutes a conviction for an acquittal it can only impose the minimum penalty prescribed by law.

Lay Appeal Judges. Lay judges sit on all the appeal courts except the highest, the state and federal Supreme Courts. Appeals from the decision of a single judge are heard by two lay judges and one professional judge; appeals from a decision by a professional judge and two lay judges are heard by three professional judges and two lay judges.

Italy

The Italian courts are:

Pretura. This is the lowest court, presided over by a single professional judge, the *Pretore*. He/she has jurisdiction over crimes with a maximum penalty of three years.

Tribunale. This court is composed of three professional judges and has jurisdiction over certain defined crimes, such as financial crimes and crimes by the press. It also has jurisdiction over crimes not dealt with in the *Pretura* and the *Corte d'assisse*.

Corte d'assisse. This court has a President and other professional judges plus six lay judges who must have at least a basic secondary education. They have jurisdiction over defined serious crimes, including crimes against the state.

McKillop says in theory Italian trials are based on orality (oral evidence in open court) and immediacy (judgment based on perception and evaluation of the oral evidence), but in practice the trial consists of the reception of written summaries of evidence from the pre-trial investigation, "and so is little more than a public confirmation of the secret investigation phase".

The President or the *Pretore* may question the accused and witnesses to confirm their depositions, but this seems the exception rather than the rule. The court clerk prepares summaries of the trial proceedings, including the evidence given. All parties, including the victim, or civil party (*parte civile*), have a right to a closing address; McKillop says these are generally the liveliest part of the trial.

Verdict. The professional and lay judges reach the verdicts, including liability, penalty, damages, restitution and costs, in private and announce them in open court. The verdicts must be supported by reasons. The principle of personal conviction (the French *in time conviction*) applies.

Appeals. A decision during the pre-trial investigation not to proceed to trial is open to appellate review. Appeals are a rehearing on the evidence in the file. Appeals from the *Pretura* go to the *Tribunale*; appeals from the *Tribunale* go to the Court of Appeal, which consists of three professional judges. Appeals from the *Corte d'assise* go to the *Corte d'assisse d'appello*, composed of a President, who is a judge of the *Corte de Cassation* (the highest court of appeal), another professional judge and six lay judges, who must have at least a full secondary education.

Judge Carnevale. Alexander Stille notes "the trend of Italy's Supreme Court, which seemed to overturn every mafia conviction it encountered. In a strange quirk of fate, all organised crime cases had become the almost exclusive province of one rather enigmatic judge, Corrado Carnevale – known as *l'ammazza-sentenze*, 'the sentence-killer'. Although Italy's Supreme Court is divided into several sections, it was decided that all organised crime cases should be heard by the 'first section' of the Supreme Court, of which Carnevale, the sentence-killer, was President.

"Considered by some a 'fifth column' of the mafia, but by others a judicial purist, the only thing certain about Carnevale is that in case after case he set free convicted mafiosi, frequently on the most slender of technicalities. Mistakes in form, mistakes in filing dates and other seemingly superficial errors led to the undoing of major prosecutions ...

"Under growing political pressure, the Italian Supreme Court agreed [in 1991] to change the bizarre system that had given Carnevale, the 'sentence-killer', a virtual monopoly on organised crime cases: rather than being funnelled automatically to the First Section of the Supreme Court, the cases would now be assigned randomly among the seven sections of the court. Although the judiciary is supposed to be entirely independent, it has always been

– for good or ill – highly sensitive to political pressure. For years, the parties in power had defended Carnevale as a judicial 'purist', now he found himself under fire from the same quarters ... Looking into Carnevale's record on the bench, the Ministry of Justice found evidence that he had engaged in a serious breach of judicial ethics, failing to withdraw from a case in which he had substantial economic interest. Feeling the heat of disciplinary proceedings, Carnevale asked to withdraw from the panel that reviewed the appeal of the maxi-trial. When the Supreme Court announced its verdict on January 31, 1992, the result was overwhelmingly favorable to the prosecution."

38

A Summary of Possible Criminal Solutions

... the system of administering justice is in crisis ...

– Justice Sir Gerard Brennan, Chief Justice High Court of Australia, 1996

Sir Gerard said in September 1996 that the justice system was in crisis as governments cut spending and litigation was restricted to the wealthy, business and those receiving legal aid. Calling for an urgent improvement in efficiency, he said: "It is not an overstatement to say that the system of administering justice is in crisis."

Greater efficiency is easily achieved by getting judges to do more work and lawyers to do less. The solutions to the common law's problems of injustice, unfairness and general incompetence at protecting victims and the community are implicit in the foregoing chapters. Lawyers should be able to develop, relatively quickly, the outline of appropriate legislation to rectify the situation. The task is to decrease both Type A miscarriages, where the guilty get off, and Type B miscarriages, where the innocent are convicted. Some essentials:

Truth. As Judge Rothwax says: "Without truth there can be no justice." The community's representatives in legislatures must insist on that fundamental change.

The Cartel. It is necessary to dismantle the cartel to allow the judiciary to be truly independent. This can be done by separating judicial education from lawyer education.

The Judiciary: A six-fold increase in the judiciary is necessary to reduce the cost of justice and to improve its efficiency. (See chapter 40, Funding the Solutions.)

The Investigating Judge. The use of trained investigating judges to supervise the pre-trial investigation will heavily reduce Type B miscarriages, the conviction of the innocent.

The Dossier. Everything for and against the suspect goes into a dossier, which is available to the suspect's lawyer at all times. Evidence at the trial should go into the dossier and it should be available to the jury as well as the judge.

The Adversary System. The adversary system needs to be modified so that it protects the suspect's interests but does not interfere with the truth. The modified adversary system must be used at the pre-trial investigation as well as at the trial.

Victims. Victims should be part of the adversary system and should be represented at the trial.

The Jury. The jurors should sit on the bench with a trained judge and they should give their verdict and sentence together and their reasons. Some consideration should be given to having semi-professional lay judges tested for intelligence, common sense and fairness.

Rules for Concealing Evidence. The rules should all be abolished as being inconsistent with the search for truth and unnecessary now that the jurors are conferring with the judge.

Appeal Courts. Lay judges should be part of appeal courts. The community's lawyer, the prosecutor, should be able to appeal against the verdict as well as the accused's lawyer.

Standard of Proof. Should be in a positive form, i.e. the judge and jury should be thoroughly convinced. The benefit of the doubt should go to the accused.

Note. It may be thought the malady will still be a short-term problem when the common law gives way to the common sense and the magic tricks are eliminated. That is, current judges will still find it hard to rid their minds of the rules for concealing evidence until new judges are properly trained in a truth-based system. However, Justice Harry Gibbs seems to have been unique in not suspending the rules of evidence. Other judges in charge of inquiries seem to have no trouble in doing so; the problem only arises in the report. And at a trial under the new regime, jurors will tell the judge what the facts mean.

39

Solutions to the Agonies of Civil Litigation

Managerial Judging. The buzz words in common law civil litigation are judicial "case management" and "managerial" judging. This is a way of fiddling at the margins, of giving the appearance of something being done. It avoids the real issue, which is the necessity for judges to take back control of the trial in the interests of truth, justice and less costly litigation.

Lawsuit Abuse. Data in this book suggests that criminal law is a fraud on the community, but most readers' direct experience of the law, either privately or as company executives, will be through the ruinously costly agonies of civil litigation, which perhaps reached their logical conclusion in the US. The civil rights violin can rarely have been played with such creativity as by Robert Lee Brock, of Virginia. Bill Tammeus reported in *The New York Times* in April 1995 that Brock, having sued himself for US$5 million, told Judge Rebecca Beach Smith: "I partook of alcoholic beverages in 1993, July 1st. As a result I caused myself to violate my religious beliefs. This was done by my going out and getting arrested." He claimed he had violated his own civil rights by getting arrested and because he had no income in prison he asked the State of Virginia to pay him the money he would owe to himself. Judge Smith found the claim and relief sought were "totally ridiculous"; she dismissed the suit as frivolous, but the Government was expected to pay the bill for the Brock trial.

Tammeus commented: "Frivolous? If everything frivolous in US jurisprudence were thrown out, half the lawyers and judges would be out of work. Frivolity – if history is any guide – is one of the founding principles of the US legal system. Indeed, to find frivolity, hilarity or just plain nonsense, you need look no further than the O.J. Simpson trial or the John Wayne Bobbitt case."

California, home of hopeful causes, holds a Lawsuit Abuse Awareness Week. Sue Williams noted a few of the more outrageous examples in the Sydney *Sun-Herald* of October 5, 1997:

- A student fell from a window while exposing his rear to passers-by. He tried to sue the university for negligence.
- A surfer sued another surfer for taking his wave.
- A prisoner whose ice cream melted before he could eat it claimed violation of his civil rights.

The cures for the problems of civil litigation are similar but not quite the same as for criminal law; I append some notes largely from Professor John Langbein's *The German Advantage in Civil Procedure* (1985). Aspects of it are also relevant to the common law adversary system in criminal law; his harpoon is mostly deployed in voluminous footnotes.

Adversary Systems. Professor David Luban says Langbein advocates the abolition of the adversary system. In fact, Langbein advocated the retention of the adversary system in a modified form. Thus: "My theme is that, by assigning judges rather than lawyers to investigate the facts, the Germans avoid the most troublesome aspects of our practice. But I emphasise that the familiar contrast between our adversarial procedure and the supposedly nonadversarial procedure of the Continental tradition has been grossly overdrawn.

"To be sure, since the greater responsibility of the bench for fact-gathering is what distinguishes the Continental tradition, a necessary (and welcome) correlative is that counsel's role in eliciting evidence is greatly restricted. Apart from fact-gathering, however, the lawyers for the parties play major and broadly comparable roles in both the German and American systems. Both are adversary systems of civil procedure.

The German Adversary System. "There as here, the lawyers advance partisan positions from first pleadings to final arguments. German litigators suggest legal theories and lines of factual inquiry, they superintend and supplement judicial examination of witnesses, they urge inferences from fact, they discuss and distinguish precedents, they interpret statutes, and they formulate views of the law that further the interests of their clients. I shall urge that German experience shows that we would do better if we were greatly to restrict the adversaries' role in fact-gathering."

Overview. Langbein first gives an overview of German civil procedure. He says there are two fundamental differences between

German and Anglo-American civil procedures. First, it is the judge rather than the parties' lawyers who mainly gathers and sifts evidence, but the lawyers keep careful watch on his work. Second, the judge gathers and evaluates evidence over a series of hearings, as many as necessary; there is no distinction between pre-trial and trial, between discovering evidence and presenting it.

The proceedings start with a lawyer making a complaint on behalf of a plaintiff. The complaint lays out the key facts, a legal theory, and asks for a remedy. Supporting documents are attached or indicated, and helpful witnesses are identified. The defendant does the same. The judge examines the material and sends for public records. He now has the beginning of a dossier; all subsequent evidence-gathering and submissions go into the dossier, and it is continuously open to inspection by the lawyers.

Initial Hearing. The judge calls a hearing and possibly some of the witnesses. He may be able to resolve the case by discussing it with the lawyers and their clients and suggesting avenues of compromise. If the parties persist, he will act as examiner-in-chief of the witnesses. Counsel for either party may then pose additional questions, but in Germany "counsel are not prominent as examiners." If the method were to be used in common law countries, any additional questions should be asked by the judge to prevent lawyers using a technique of cross-examining in ever-decreasing circles so that the last answer must be that black is white.

Judge Controls Sequence. In Anglo-American procedure, the lawyers choose what aspects of the "plaintiff's case" and the "defendant's case" they will put before a passive and ignorant judge. These concepts are unknown in Germany; the judge ranges over the entire case, "constantly looking for the jugular – for the issue of law or fact that might dispose of the case".

No Theatre. The German approach has been called the "conference method" of adjudication. The tone is of a routine business meeting. It lessens tension and theatrics and encourages compromise and settlement. The loser pays system also encourages settlement before judgment.

Summaries. Common law incentives are towards expansiveness: lawyers are paid by the hour and court reporters by the page. The German incentive is the other way: evidence is rarely recorded verbatim; the judge pauses from time to time to dictate a summary into the dossier, and the lawyers can suggest improvements. The summaries are useful for quick refreshers at later hearings, for the written judgment and for the appeal court.

No Rules for Concealing Evidence. In civil litigation, judges sit without a jury and they function without the common law rules of evidence (such as hearsay) that exclude probative evidence.

Expertise. There are no "saxophones"; if there is a technical problem, the judge, in consultation with the lawyers, selects the expert or experts and defines their role.

Lawyers' Role. The lawyers can comment orally or in writing when the judge has heard witnesses or procured other evidence. They can thus suggest further proofs or advance legal theories. "Thus," says Langbein, "non-adversarial proof-taking alternates with adversarial dialogue across as many hearings as necessary. The process merges the investigatory function of our pretrial discovery and evidence-presenting function of our trial."

Witnesses. German lawyers nominate witnesses who may be favourable to their client, but they rarely have contact with them outside the court. Contact is both a serious ethical breach and self-defeating: German judges explicitly express doubts about the reliability of witnesses who have discussed the case with counsel or who have been sighted consorting unduly with the client.

The Common Law Adversary System. By way of contrast, Langbein quotes Judge Marvin Frankel (*The Search for Truth: An Umpireal View*, 1975) on the effects of the Anglo-American adversary system: "It is the rare case in which either side yearns to have the witnesses, or anyone, give *the whole truth*." (Frankel's emphasis.) And Jerome Frank (*Courts on Trial: Myth and Reality in American Justice*, 1949): "[The witness] often detects what the lawyer hopes to prove at the trial. If the witness desires to have the lawyer's client win the case, he will often, unconsciously, mold his story accordingly. Telling and re-telling it to the lawyer, he will honestly believe that his story, as he narrates it in court, is true, although it importantly deviates from what he originally believed."

Langbein says: "Cross-examination at trial – our only substantial safeguard against this systematic bias in the testimony that reaches our courts – is a frail and fitful palliative. Cross-examination is too often ineffective to undo the consequences of skillful coaching. Further, because cross-examination allows so much latitude for bullying and other truth-defeating stratagems, it is frequently the source of fresh distortion when brought to bear against truthful testimony.

"As a leading litigator [Hanley, *Working the Witness Puzzle*, 1977] boasted recently: 'By a carefully planned and executed cross-examination, I can raise at least a slight question about the accuracy of [an adverse] witness's story, or question his motives or impartiality'."

He quotes Judge Frankel again: "The litigator's devices, let us be clear, have utility in testing dishonest witnesses, ferretting out falsehood, and thus exposing the truth. But to a considerable degree these devices are like other potent weapons, equally lethal for heroes and villains."

Langbein says: "No less a critic than Jerome Frank was prepared to concede that in American procedures the adversaries 'sometimes do bring into court evidence which, in a dispassionate inquiry, might be overlooked.' This is a telling argument for including adversaries in the fact-gathering process, but not for letting them run it ...

[German] lawyers nominate witnesses, attend and supplement court questioning, and develop adversary positions on the significance of the evidence. Yet German procedure totally avoids the distortions incident to our partisan witness practice."

German Adversary System. Professor Langbein says: "Outside the realm of fact-gathering, German civil procedure is about as adversarial as our own. Both systems welcome the lawyerly contribution to identifying legal issues and sharpening legal analysis. German civil procedure is materially less adversarial than own own only in the fact-gathering function, where partisanship has such potential to pollute the sources of truth. Accordingly, the proper question is not whether to have lawyers, but how to use them; not whether to have an adversarial component to civil procedure, but how to prevent adversarial excess. If we were to incorporate the essential lesson of the German system in our own procedure we would still have a strongly adversarial civil procedure. We would not, however, have coached witnesses and litigation-based experts."

Inequality of Counsel. Germans call it *Waffenungleichheit*, literally, inequality of weapons. Langbein says: "In a fair fight the pugilists must be well matched. You cannot send me into a ring with Muhammad Ali if you expect a fair fight. The simple truth is that very little in our adversary system is designed to match combatants of comparable prowess, even though adversarial prowess is a main factor affecting the outcome of litigation.

"Adversary theory thus presupposes a condition that adversary practice achieves only indifferently. It is a rare litigator in the United States who has not witnessed the spectacle of a bumbling adversary whose poor discovery work or inability to present evidence at trial caused his client to lose a case that should have been won. Disparity in the quality of legal representation can make a difference in Germany, too, but the active role of the judge places major limits on the extent of the injury that bad lawyering can work on a litigant. In German procedure both parties get the same fact-gatherer – the judge.

Witnesses Appear Once. In Germany, a witness is usually examined only once. Langbein says: "Contrast the American practice of partisan interview and preparation, pretrial deposition, preparation of trial, and examination and cross-examination at trial. These many steps take their toll in expense and irritation."

Incentives Against Judicial Sloth. An argument in favour of the Anglo-American adversary system is that at least the private lawyers who control the trial are presumably giving the fact-gathering their best efforts on behalf of their clients, whereas the danger of the judge as fact-gatherer is that he may be a lazy bureaucrat. *Please read "she or he" for "he", etc.*

The Germans are aware of this and design the judicial career in ways that promote diligence and excellence. The German judge is not an elderly ex-lawyer who has succumbed to sloth or to a less staccato existence; he begins his professional career as a judge. in 1983 there were 17,000 judges in West Germany in a population of 61,306,700 or one judge for every 3606 people. The young jurist, along with future lawyers, has several years of university legal education. He then sits a state examination and becomes an apprentice for 2 1/2 years as a clerk: for judges in civil and criminal courts, in the prosecutor's office, and in a lawyer's office. He sits a second state examination. The careers of the jurist and the lawyer then diverge.

Langbein says: "The judiciary is a prized career: influential, interesting, secure and (by comparison with practice at the bar) prestigious and not badly compensated." Only those with the best examination results have any chance of becoming judges.

A judge typically begins in his late 20s. He is on probation for five years; after that he must be either dismissed or given tenure. He starts either in the lower court, *Amtsgericht*, or as a junior member of the *Landgericht* (LG), where he is guided by experienced judges. His work is overseen and evaluated throughout his career through several levels of judicial office and salary grades. His lifelong personnel file has an "efficiency rating" based on his rate of moving cases, his rate of reversal by higher courts, and on subjective evaluation.

The Judge as Crook. In Chicago, nonetheless, Langbein said, as things stood in 1985 he would have qualms about putting his civil action in the hands of a fact-gathering judge in the area where he then lived, Cook County, Illinois, where judges were elected on political slates constructed by people like Jake Arvey and Richard Daley. Langbein quotes an unpublished 1983 speech by Justice Seymour Simon, of the Illinois Supreme Court, in which he said the criterion for getting on the slate was "not learning and experience in the law [or] academic bakground and legal achievements", but instead "for their loyalty to the political party".

There appeared to be a deal of stamina in the Chicago culture of such bagmen and fixers as Jake (Greasy Thumb) Guzik (1887-1956) and Murray (The Camel) Humphreys (1899-1965). Jay Robert Nash says Moscow-born Guzik, a Capone operative from 1924, "was nicknamed Greasy Thumb for the amount of bribe money he paid to politicians and crooked policemen. He operated from a table at St Hubert's Old English Grill and Chop House, receiving bagmen from local police precincts and city hall". Guzik took the Fifth Amendment at the Kefauver organised crime hearings in 1951 on the ground that his answers "might discriminate against me". Nash says "he continued greasing important palms until his death of a heart attack on 21 February 1956 at his table [lamb chops and moselle] at St Hubert's restaurant." The Camel's view of judges has already been noted: "The difference between guilt and innocence in any court is who gets to the judge first with the most."

Langbein said: " ... while decent people do reach the Cook

Country bench in surprising numbers, events have shown that some of their colleagues are crooks. If my lawsuit may fall into the hands of a dullard or a thug, I become queasy about increasing his authority over the proceedings." A career judiciary would help break down that culture.

Judgment. Having gathered the facts and heard the adversaries' views, the judge decides the case in a written judgment that must contain full findings of fact and must give the reasons for his application of the law.

Appeal Courts. Appeal courts do not presume the first judgment was correct. They hear the case from the beginning. The process is economical because of the original judge's succinct summaries. The appellate judges will call in witnesses if they feel demeanour is a factor.

Case Management. Common law judges are trying to move civil litigation along by way of "case management". They have pre-trial conferences to identify the key issues and try to promote settlement. In this way the judges are taking back a measure of control of the trial and are moving it in the direction of the German system. But the lawyers still control the adversary system.

Conclusion. Professor Langbein concludes: "Regardless of where managerial judging is headed for the future, it has already routed adversary theory. I take that as further support for the view ... that adversary theory was misapplied to fact-gathering in the first place. Nothing but inertia and vested interests justify the waste and distortion of adversary fact-gathering. The success of German civil procedure stands as an enduring reproach to those who say that we must continue to suffer adversary tricksters in the proof of fact."

40

Funding the Solutions

... it is contrary to the public interest that, for repeat litigants, the costs of litigation should remain tax deductible.

— Justice Geoffrey Davies, 1997

A study is needed of the economics involved in the common law and inquisitorial systems. Kathryn Cronin, in charge of the Australian Law Reform Commission's inquiry into the efficacy of the common law adversarial system in civil litigation, says the situation is complicated because in Germany, for example, some of the people they call judges are people Australians would call tribunal members. The International Bar Association has asked its members round the world to work on the economic cost of litigation in their countries. This useful data is expected to be in hand in 1998. Meanwhile, here are some preliminary notes.

Crime is estimated to cost a small country like Australia $13,000,000,000 a year. What is laughingly called the criminal justice system costs taxpayers $6,000,000,000, most of it wasted if 80 per cent of the known guilty in medium to serious cases get off and one per cent of those in prison are innocent. That is not justice, or anything like it. A French trial costs a third to a half that of a common law trial, and puts off the street 90 per cent of the known guilty in medium to serious cases, and much less frequently convicts an innocent person.

How many judges would be needed for an inquisitorial system? We can get a line on that from the German system. In 1983, West Germany had 17,000 judges in a population of 61,306,700, i.e. one judge for every 3606 people. In March 1997, Australia had a population of 18,492,000 and so would need 5128 judges to be on a par with West Germany. As at November 13, 1997, Australia actually had 863 members of the judiciary, including magistrates. It would thus need another 4265. In the first instance, these can come from retrained members of the existing 27,000 solicitors and barristers, and eventually from judges trained from law school.

It seems reasonable to compensate judges rather more generously for actually doing, for the first time, the work of fact-gathering and investigating the truth. (Some might disobligingly say that raising their calling above that of journalism and selling used cars should be recompense enough.) Perhaps an average of $200,000 a year would be an appropriate emolument. This would take salaries up from something like $130,000,000 a year to $1025,800,000 a year, and there would be additional overheads. The premises need not be grandiose; as we have seen, the German approach to civil litigation is more like a conference than a trial. They also need investigative help and perhaps semi-professional lay judges (jurors).

The cartel says governments in common law countries would refuse to pay for the extra judges. They do not say this is because the cartel is highly influential in those countries' governments; they say rather that governments would find it too costly. If so, part of the solution is simple: hidden subsidies for lawyers could be transferred to funding the extra judges. Thus:

The average taxpayer provides a hidden subsidy to law firms via their clients: most of their legal fees are tax-deductible. For example, Justice Geoffrey Davies, of the Queensland Court of Appeal, said in July 1997 that the Australian Law Reform Commission made "a rough estimate" in April 1997 that "about $700 million may be claimed as deductions from assessable income for legal costs incurred in litigation by businesses each year ... If it is, as I think, in the public interest to provide economic incentives to resolve disputes by means less labour-intensive than litigation, it is contrary to the public interest that, for repeat litigants, the costs of litigation should remain tax deductible."

The $700 million could be transferred to funding the extra judges and their overheads and staff. The lawyers would barely miss it; their gross income in 1996 was $5600,000,000, and their profit was $1750,000,000. Businesses would not lose: the battery of lawyers they now pay to do the fact-gathering in commercial actions will be costing them something like $2500 an hour: two barristers $1500 an hour, three solicitors $1000 an hour; $100,000 a week. The fact-gathering judge, by contrast, is working for them at $100 an hour, or $4000 a week.

Ordinary citizens would also find it a lot cheaper if a judge did the fact-gathering with a couple of lawyers watching to see he did it right, rather than having a clutch of lawyers doing the fact-gathering and a judge passively wondering what they were going to produce.

In any event, what is the price of justice? As Melbourne lawyer Mel Barnett says, we don't have a justice system; all we have is a legal system.

Part IV

The Only Obstacle to Truth and Justice
in Civil and Criminal Trials

41

How the Cartel Obstructs Reform

In England, the reason for the failure of all efforts at a rational codification of law were due to the successful resistance against such rationalisation offered by the great and centrally organised lawyers' guilds, a monopolistic stratum of notables from whose midst the judges of the High Court are recruited ... they successfully fought all moves towards rational law which threatened their material position."

– Max Weber, 1915

As we have seen, the common law has major problems of legitimacy, truth, intimacy, the malady, a defective jury system, injustice, unfairness, inaccuracy of verdict, cost, etc., etc. We have also seen that there are practicable solutions. So how has it survived for eight centuries? More particularly, how has it survived since defence lawyers invented the extreme adversary system and the rules for concealing evidence 200 years ago?

Two Centuries of Obstruction. Jeremy Bentham made his first criticism of the law in 1776. The cartel withstood his, Dickens' and others' complaints about its evils for a century. Justice Ipp notes the response: "Annoyance over the impudence of lay criticism gradually changed to resentment as the attacks increased in frequency and bitterness, and this in time gave place to serious apprehension and alarm."

Justice Ipp notes an 1826 report in *The Westminster Review*: "[although] the delay, vexation, and expense of English judicature [are very largely avoidable, yet] so successful have been the artifices of lawyers that Englishmen have hitherto almost universally believed the assertion of Sir William Blackstone that these inconveniences are the price we *necessarily* pay for the benefits of legal protection." Even after O.J. Simpson, Lindy Chamberlain, the Menendez boys, and the Birmingham Six, there are still remnants of that belief today.

The cartel also resorted to Leigh Mallory's "because it's there" defence. Justice Ipp notes an 1831 assertion in *The Legal Observer*: "For the last 250 years [i.e. since about the time Justice Dyer fraudulently tried to invent the privilege against self-incrimination] the complaints against the present system have been continual and unvaried, [yet] the Court of Chancery and its machinery ... has remained nearly the same in every particular. It is obvious therefore that ... the supposed evils ... cannot after all have been very enormous or they would not have been thus endured." This overlooks the fact that the cartel had a major influence in Parliament.

Bleak House, published in monthly instalments from March 1852 to September 1853, is, according to *The Cambridge Guide to Literature in English*, "Dickens's merciless indictment of the Court of Chancery and its bungling, morally corrupt handling of the endless case of *Jarndyce v Jarndyce* ..."

Fiddling at the Margins. In the end, the cartel's serious apprehension and alarm led to Lord Selborne's Judicature Act of 1873 and another in 1875. Roundell Palmer, Lord Selborne (1812-1895), a hymn-writer, was an MP 1861-72, Solicitor-General 1861, Attorney-General 1863-1866, and Lord Chancellor 1872-1874 and 1880-1885. His Judicature Act did some fiddling at the margins; some courts were abolished and others (Chancery, Queen's Bench, Common Pleas, Exchequer, Probate, Divorce and Admiralty) were shuffled under one roof, the Supreme Court of Judicature, consisting of a High Court of Justice and a Court of Appeal. (A Court of Criminal Appeal was not established until 1907.)

The magic tricks remained intact, but Lord Selborne's Judicature Act gave the appearance of something being done. This placated outsiders, but David Rose quotes the German lawyer and sociologist, Max Weber (*Economy and Society*, 1915), as stating: "In England, the reason for the failure of all efforts at a rational codification of law were due to the successful resistance against such rationalisation offered by the great and centrally organised lawyers' guilds, a monopolistic stratum of notables from whose midst the judges of the High Court are recruited ... they successfully fought all moves towards rational law which threatened their material position."

Max Weber is echoed by Professor A.A.S. Zuckerman, of Oxford University. As quoted by Justice Sackville, Professor Zuckerman "sees the profession as having an historically proven capacity to undermine reforms when it is in their financial interest to do so. [He] cites contemporary reports suggesting that costs and delays increased significantly following the great procedural reforms effected by the Judicature Acts of 1873 and 1875".

Vanity Fair. Morris L. Cohen notes an essay on what probably amounted to the inner cartel by "Jehu Junior" in the December 5, 1891 issue of an English weekly magazine, *Vanity Fair* (1868-1914). Cohen says it was illustrated by a cartoon, *Bench and Bar*, said to be by Spy (Sir Leslie Ward, 1851-1922). It shows the Lord Chancellor, Lord Halsbury (1823-1921), who was later largely responsible for the Criminal Evidence Act of 1898, and some 40 judges and lawyers.

Jehu Junior on Justice: "Of all the wares and merchandises that are sold in this *Vanity Fair*, there is none more rightly held in high esteem than Justice; which though it be a very costly article here, has yet been famous throughout the world for many a century."

On judges: "These are some of the Judges who are now dispensing justice at exceeding cost and with incredible delay, yet very skilfully, in this *Vanity Fair*."

On lawyers: "These are specimens of those who fatten while their clients are ruined. They work well, and no fair or better specimens, nor more knowing of the law, which they make more complicated as they go; in recompense for which they have promoted a very beautiful system by which their clients are allowed no more access to them than is needed for the payment of their high fees ..."

Runciman. A century after Lord Selborne's Judicature Acts, a series of gross miscarriages of justice came to a climax in the freeing of the Birmingham Six. The Home Secretary, Kenneth Baker, who was not a lawyer, announced in 1991 a Royal Commission into the criminal justice system, including the "possibility of an investigative role for the courts before and during a case". As noted, this was clearly an instruction to the inquiry chairman, Viscount Runciman, 57, to consider a change to the European method of judges investigating the truth before and during the trial.

The Legal Bureaucracy. The great and good Lord Runciman, a businessman and sociologist, wrote a book about Max Weber's sociology, so he should have known something about how the cartel would respond: the legal bureaucracy, as avid for power as any other element of the cartel, likes to run inquiries of this sort on rails to suit its own agenda, and they like to control the report.

However, with very great respect, Lord Runciman does not appear to have been as sharp as the Hon Gerald Fitzgerald QC, who was given the job of inquiring into police and political corruption in Queensland in 1987. I note in *The Hillbilly Dictator* that Fitzgerald insisted on independence from the legal bureaucracy, and that the bureaucrats "fell to biting the carpet" when they "found they were to be cut out of the administration of the inquiry ..."

In the event, the cartel appears to have overwhelmed Lord Runciman; David Rose notes that "virtually all the Commission's witnesses came from one or other part of the existing system. All had a strong vested interest in its remaining essentially the same". Runciman reported that "hardly any of those who gave evidence to the Commission suggested that the system in another jurisdiction should be adopted in England and Wales".

Rose notes: "The alternative to the adversarial model is an 'inquisitorial' system, in which the objective search for truth becomes an avowed public purpose, not a by-product generated by chance. In the halcyon days of 1991, as Home Secretary Kenneth Baker established the Royal Commission, there was widespread speculation that a radical shift in this direction might emerge.

France and Germany. "One of the Commission's first acts was to order research into two nearby jurisdictions which broadly follow inquisitorial principles, France and Germany. The authors of this study [Leonard H. Leigh and Lucia Zedner, *A Report on the Administration of Criminal Justice in the Pre-Trial phase in France and Germany*, Her Majesty's Stationery Office, 1992] reached several immediately striking conclusions.

"First, they found that in neither country was it likely that miscarriages of justice such as the Guildford or Birmingham cases would occur. Second, in contrast to the stratified and often vexed relationship between the different actors in the criminal process in England, on the continent this relationship was marked by 'a high degree of confidence, and of co-operation and mutual trust'. Finally, public confidence in both systems remained high in their respective countries, and in the German case the conviction rate was as high as 90 per cent."

Rose went on: "It is not the intention here to advocate the wholesale adoption of the French or German model. Both, as the Royal Commission study made clear, have their disadvantages, notably long delays before trial during which a suspect may spend an unacceptably long time in custody.

"But the Royal Commission elected not even to consider whether it might be possible to adapt and improve existing inquisitorial methods. It dealt with the matter of basic procedural structures in just six paragraphs of a 261-page report, saying: 'Every system is the product of a distinctive history and culture, and the more different the history and culture from our own, the greater must be the danger that an attempted transplant must fail'."

The answer to that is provided by Dr R.M. Jackson, Professor of the Laws of England at Cambridge. As noted above, he says: " ... the machinery of justice in England has to be seen in its peculiar historical setting. It must not be regarded as a logical structure designed round basic principles. Procedures and practices led to a 'contest' conception of trial ... but this gives it no special sanctity."

Viscount Runciman would have done well to also order research on the origin of England's criminal justice system. He may have found that the cartel's insular dislike of Europe in the 13th century and the machinations of defence lawyers and the poltroonery by judges in the 18th were major factors in the "distinctive history and culture" that produced the absence of truth, fairness and justice in the system.

* * *

The Legal Mind-Set. Justice Geoffrey Davies says: "... lawyers and judges ... have been raised with the belief that our system is, if not perfect, as near to it as humans can devise ... our system operates unfairly ... it is the mind-sets of lawyers and judges which are the greatest impediments to change aimed at increasing its fairness."

Former Justice Michael Manifold Helsham said lawyers do not have the faintest idea how an inquisitorial system works. Mention the Lateran Council to a common lawyer or judge and he will look at you blankly. George Santayana said: "Progress, far from consisting in change, depends on retentiveness ... Those who do not remember the past are condemned to repeat it."

Civil Libertarians. The contribution of civil libertarians to obstructing reform should not be overlooked. Plucknett says the English Government had to withdraw legislation abolishing trial by battle in Massachusetts in 1774 when it was opposed by people who claimed it was "a great pillar of the constitution". Trial by battle was successfully claimed by an alleged murderer, Abraham Thornton, in England in 1817. Plucknett notes that even Lord Eldon was prepared to lend his name to its abolition by statute in 1819, but this "obvious reform" was "most curiously ... opposed by the radicals, who believed that the liberty of the subject was being thereby attacked".

Judicial Obstruction? Truth and justice require a moderation of the extreme adversary system and the abolition of the rules for concealing evidence, but in 1994 a lawyer suggested that judges have the power to overrule legislation they believe is unfair to the accused. Since most of the rules purport to be about fairness, judges might thus attempt to overrule their abolition. Thus:

In 1981, the NSW Parliament sought to protect girls and women who complained of sexual assault; Section 409B of the Crimes Act stopped defence lawyers from badgering them about their sexual history. But in August 1994 Judge Shillington accepted an argument from a lawyer, Timothy Game, that this could prevent a fair trial of his client who was charged with a serious sexual assault against a schoolgirl. Judge Shillington ordered a permanent stay of the proceedings, i.e. the accused would never be brought to trial on that charge.

Judge Shillington said: "Mr Game's submission is that in effect the accused's case would be placed in a straight jacket and it would be completely unreal if the material proscribed by the Act were not capable of being put before the tribunal of fact. Having considered these matters it seems to me that this is a fair summary of the situation."

In the circumstances of the case, it appeared that Judge Shillington's view was correct. On the other hand, and leaving on one side the fact that it is merely risible to describe a common law trial as a tribunal of fact, the community's case is also completely unreal and placed in a straight jacket in all rape trials because the jury cannot hear evidence of the alleged rapist's sexual history.

As noted, the reasonable solution is for the judge to question the complainant and accused in a neutral and unthuggish way, and to discuss the two sides of the story with his juror colleagues on the bench. But Stephen Odgers, a Sydney academic and appellate lawyer, discerned in Judge Shillington's decision the seed of a grave constitutional contest between judges and legislators. He said the decision reflected recent High Court rulings that trials must be fair to the accused; it followed that judges may overrule any legislation they think is unfair, and free the accused without trial. "Inevitably," Odgers said, "the courts and the government will come into conflict – a conflict the courts are likely to win."

That sounded like the cartel throwing down the gauntlet to the community: telling its representatives in Parliament not to mess with rules that purport to be about fair trials for the accused, i.e. Magic Tricks 4-8, the right of silence, the rules against pattern evidence and hearsay, the *Christie* discretion, and the formula for the standard of proof. It appeared to follow that if Australian legislators at last enacted RICO-type legislation to allow jurors to hear of patterns of behaviour, judges would turn organised criminals loose on the community on the ground that the legislation was unfair to them.

The problem for Odgers' thesis is that the community, which pays for the legal system, has a legitimate expectation that trials will be fair to everybody: the accused, the victims and the community itself. And Justice Geoffrey Davies pointed out at the NSW Legal Convention in November 1996: "There is now, in my view, an imbalance in favour of accused persons and against the interests of the community." It follows that trials are not fair, and cannot be fair until judges and/or legislators redress the bias against victims and the community.

Noting Justice Davies' view and Odgers' suggestion that judges would win the battle if Parliament enacted legislation they thought unfair to the accused, I observed (*The Australian*, January 9, 1997): "I'm not sure [Odgers is] right. Elected representatives of the people can hardly accept the implication that judges alone know what is fair, or would even, with very great respect, recognise a fair trial if they fell over one. Nor can High Court judges have said the last word on fair trials until they redress the unfairness to the community noted by Justice Davies. And the Parliament has the power to dismiss judges for misconduct; if judges persist in letting accused go free without trial, Parliament might construe that as a refusal to sit, or a perversion of justice."

NSW's first law officer, Attorney-General Jeffrey Shaw QC, took up Odgers' gauntlet, if such it were, in an article (*The Australian*, January 20, 1997). He wrote: "Whitton has validly questioned whether courts should 'stay' rape trials simply because the NSW Parliament has prohibited the cross-examination of complainants about prior sexual history. He makes the forceful point that it is difficult to characterise a trial as 'unfair' if it is being conducted in accordance with the rules laid down by Parliament. Indeed the High Court has upheld that very proposition in *Grills v The Queen*, a decision reported in the December 1996 issue of *The Australian Law Journal*, where the judges clearly rejected the argument that "a court may decline to exercise its jurisdiction to try a criminal case because it forms the view that a law enacted by the Parliament is unfair."

This means that Australian legislators can eliminate rules that make trials unfair to victims and the community without having to resort to dismissing judges for misconduct. However, it might have to come to that in other common law countries; the law lords, for example, apparently felt free, in the interests of "justice", to undermine legislation on contempt by affront.

Privilege. Lawyers' clients have a privilege that makes lawyers immune from prosecution if they refuse to disclose discussions with them. Reporters' sources have no such privilege, but Lord Salmon, dissenting in *British Steel Corporation v Granada* (1981), adopted without qualification Lord Denning's formula: " ... the public has a right of access to information which is of public concern and of which the public ought to know. The newspapers are the agents, so to speak, of the public to collect that information and to tell the public of it. In support of this right of access the newspapers should not in general be compelled to disclose their sources of information."

Lord Scarman, former Law Lord, referred in a letter to *The Times* in 1987 to "the more fundamental law providing the right of the public to access to information ... and the public right of free speech, of which the freedom of the Press is an important constituent. Old ingrained habits die hard. We are not yet able to abandon the traditional emphasis of our law on private rights ..."

Lord Salmon and Lord Scarmon are in a minority; judges usually insist that disclosure of the identity of the reporter's client is necessary for the administration of justice. A Sydney lawyer, Kerrie Henderson, notes that in *Cojuangco* (1988) the Australian High Court said non-disclosure could not be allowed because "there is a paramount interest in the administration of justice which requires that cases be tried by courts on the relevant and admissible evidence".

Henderson said: "The call to 'the interests of justice' asserts the primacy of the legal system as a social institution – the High Court's 'paramount interest in the administration of justice' – and in so doing also reinforces the standing of the courts and the judiciary as the organs through which that paramount interest is expressed. Such powerful tools are rarely voluntarily weakened ..."Except, as we saw, when the judges let defence lawyers take over trials.

Contempt. The source is sacred, but judges reel in affront when reporters respectfully decline to name them. The affront derives from the mediaeval notion of contempt: God appointed the king; the king appointed the judge; any affront to the judge was thus by extension an affront to God, and would therefore attract immediate retaliation pending eternal damnation. For example, Oliver Cyriax says a thief named Noy was convicted at Salisbury Assizes in 1631. The trial was presumably nasty, brutish and short; Noy threw a "brickbat" at Judge Richardson but missed. Retaliation was instant: the judge first had the instrument of the contempt, Noy's hand, cut off and displayed on a gibbet, and then had him hanged in view of the court. The deity presumably remained inscrutable.

More than three centuries later judges effectively subverted the will of Parliament concerning reporters and contempt, and upheld the private right to revenge over the public right to information. In the 1970s, a public utility, British Steel, was making large losses; Granada television revealed mismanagement via leaked documents. British Steel sought disclosure of the source in order to fulfil its express intention to "dismiss or reprimand or harass" him or her. In *BSC v Granada* (1981), judges, but not Lord Salmon, said Granada must disclose the source.

Contempt of Court Act 1981. The decision was so outrageous that Parliament brought down the Contempt of Court Act 1981. Section 10 said: "No court may require a person to disclose, nor is any person guilty of contempt of court for refusing to disclose, the source of information contained in a publication for which he is responsible unless it is established to the satisfaction of the court that disclosure is necessary in the interests of justice, national security, or for the prevention of disorder or crime."

The clear intention was to allow reporters to do their work in the public interest without risk of going to prison, but the Act brought the law into collision with the other power blocs, Parliament and Press; judges seemed to think that they, rather than Parliament, should decide when reporters must disclose the source. In Section 10, "may" and the three exceptions gave the judges a discretion, and hence power; speaking to the Bill, the Lord Chancellor, Lord Hailsham, said: "What are the interests of justice? I suggest that they are as long as the judge's foot."

Tisdall. In the 1983 Tisdall case, law lords admitted that a document leaked by Sarah Tisdall to *The Guardian* was innocuous in terms of national security; it merely revealed that the Minister for Defence, Michael Heseltine, had misled the House. The name of the informant thus could not be "necessary" for national security, but the judges ruled that *The Guardian* must hand it over. The organ felt obliged to do so; Ms Tisdall got six months in prison.

Warner. In the 1987 Jeremy Warner case, Warner, whose source had disclosed information about insider trading, argued that he did not have to reveal his sources because this was not "necessary" in the interests of justice. In what amounted to a contempt of the English language, the law lords said "necessary" might mean "useful". Warner was fined £20,000 with £100,000 costs for refusing to disclose his source's identity.

This meant that lawyers for revenge-seekers could argue that almost anything might be useful for justice, national security, or the prevention of disorder or crime, and that the source therefore had to be named.

Goodwin. William Goodwin's 1990 case was effectively the end of Section 10. Goodwin was given some information about a private company, and rang the company to check it. The company got an injunction to prevent publication, and demanded that Goodwin hand over notes that might disclose the name of his informant.

Lord Bridge. Until then, it had been accepted that "in the interests of justice" meant in a case actually proceeding, but Lord Bridge, 73, who had summed up for a conviction in the Birmingham Six case in 1974, now claimed it could merely refer to the wish of a private company to discipline a disloyal employee although "no legal proceedings might be necessary to achieve this end".

Lord Bridge said that for a journalist to put himself above [the law lords' interpretation of] the law whenever he disagreed with a court's decision was "a doctrine which directly undermined the rule of law and was wholly unacceptable in a democratic society". Goodwin might think that the law lords put themselves above the law in their gutting of the Contempt of Court Act 1981.

Decisions by the House of Lords are binding on other English courts. The Tisdall, Warner and Goodwin decisions suggest that judges will always hold that the private right of revenge takes precedence over the public right to information and free speech, and that judges will require disclosure of the source in every conceivable situation. The law lords had thus returned to judges the power they held on affront before the 1981 Act, i.e. the power of instant retaliation they enjoyed in mediaeval times.

Law Lords Overturned. However, in 1996 judges in the European Court of Human Rights voted 11-7 that the order for Goodwin to reveal his source and the fine for refusing to do so were a violation of his right to freedom of expression.

The Cartel as Laggard. Perhaps we can give the last word to a member of the inner cartel who represents the community in its unequal contest with the law, NSW Director of Public Prosecutions, Nicholas Cowdery QC. He said in his address, *Justice In Pursuit of Lawyers*, at the St James Ethics Centre in August 1997: "Lawyers, especially those in private practice, have generally been dragged along in the wake of reforms to the legal system designed to assist in the attainment of justice ... Some have embraced it with feeling. Generally lawyers closest to the lay community – lawyers dispensing legal aid or community legal assistance and those in government service – have most ardently pursued the notions of truth and justice, while many others have hung back. As corporations, Bar Associations and, to a slightly lesser extent, Law Societies have been the greatest laggards.

"Why? Surely it cannot be that the pursuit of justice is not for lawyers? ... I fear that the corporate Bar's view of its independence ... has been narrowed to introspection and self interest, excluding allegiance to the system of justice as a whole. Solicitors on the other hand have often allowed their allegiance to their clients to become obedience and servility (but at a price).

" ... Lawyers in private practice ... work for profit. This is of course a perfectly legitimate desire and an acceptable goal for any worker, but damage occurs when profit becomes an unreasonable need or pursued out of greed. In the way our private legal profession operates both of these can occur on a grand scale. They are promoted by the structure and governance of our profession which perpetuate inefficiencies that are expensive to service; our exaggerated self-image; the adversarial system of litigation inherited from England; many rules of procedure that are socially counter-productive and deflect our attention from the end of achieving justice in its proper sense ...

"I acknowledge that it would be unfair to tar every lawyer with the same corporate brush. Many individuals selflessly devote their time and energies to the service of others above and beyond the call of duty and I specifically acknowledge them – but they are a minority. In some individual practitioners, by contrast, there develops a hearty disrespect for the system that causes them to deliberately or unconsciously prey on it at the expense of the community as a whole. Under their influence the processes of justice themselves can eventually become distorted.

"What is the purpose of a lawyer? Should we simply give up? Is it time now to emulate Astraea, the Greek goddess of justice, who returned to Olympus in defeat when the world became so wicked that Zeus sent a destructive flood, and became the star Virgo in the heavens?

"Earlier this century Sir Patrick Hastings [1880-1952], English Attorney-General [1924] wrote: 'With all its possible defects, English justice is the best thing that is left to us. If I could give one word of advice to the great minds who will be chosen to control our destinies, I would suggest to them that, with all the changes they will be called to make, they should leave our Law alone.'

"But it is no longer valid – if it ever was – to equate justice with law ... The Duc de la Rochefoucauld wrote that "Love of justice in most men is no more than the fear of injustice"; but to a lawyer love of justice is, or should be, the love of a lifetime. Is it being spurned?

"... Our professional associations, regrettably, seem almost completely reactionary in their corporate attitudes. Whether they intend it or not, they are very often perceived as selfish, elitist (in the worst sense of the word) and unreasonably self-protective. They are inward-looking and insensitive to others. If their actions benefit other than their members, it is almost by unavoidable accident. They are essentially parochial and mean-spirited...

"The pursuit of justice is a necessary aspect of government, hence (in part) the constitution of the judiciary as the third arm of government. The just rule of law is a requirement for the peaceful co-existence of the state and the citizen and for orderly peace between citizens. In general terms the dedication of lawyers to that end is deeply suspect. We can speculate whether or not it has always been so and whether or not it is wholly the fault of the lawyers. Records of selflessness and community service on the part of Barristers, in particular, are few and far between. Certainly there are such stories, but when they are found they seem to be outstandingly exceptional. Is this an accurate reflection of life?

"... The mind-set of lawyers – that they have to win the case for the client ... is the greatest obstacle to change, to increased fairness and the legal system's pursuit of truth and justice. We cannot expect lawyers to change unless the environment in which we are required to work changes.

"Perhaps we might start not by abandoning but by reforming the adversarial system. Obviously it is not possible to start again with an entirely new system; but incremental change, borrowing from other systems, should be under active contemplation. The Australian Law Reform Commission has started the process. In the criminal jurisdiction in this state a healthy sign is the reference by the

223

Attorney-General to the Law Reform Commission earlier this month of the issues embraced by the so-called right of silence."

David Bennett, president of the NSW Bar Association, said Cowdery's speech was "facile and silly", and that he did not understand Cowdery's motivation; Patrick Fair, president of the NSW Law Society, said the speech was "jaundiced". But what Cowdery seems to be saying is that the 1600 million people in common law countries are entitled to a system which delivers truth and justice. We may suspect that, whatever their misgivings, common lawyers and judges will find it intensely liberating to at last be dealing in truth. The new millennium offers an appropriate time to begin. Meanwhile, the malady lingers on.

Epilogue

How to Get a Frottist off Murder and other Jokes: Warm Afternoons in Boston

Dr Peter James, geologist, historian, novelist and Rugby international, wrote a book, *In Place of Justice*, about Brisbane's National Hotel inquiry, in 1974. In 1997 he wrote a novel called *The Glopmakers* ($A15, 6 Admiralty Towers, Howard Street, Brisbane 4000, Australia). Characters include Mr Justice Squander, his stepson, Dr Hugo (Piggy) Throwback, of the Forensic Department, and Premier D.O. de Rant. Dr James has kindly given me permission to quote some material relative to oppression by the leviathan state.

In what may be an echo of Lord Goddard (see chapter 19: The Goddard Rule), or some old scandal closer to home, he writes: " ... the real truth was that Mr Justice Squander's worries were alcoholled. He was first unveiled, as it were, during a provincial court sitting after workmen had removed, along with the courtroom clock, a panel of polished wood from the front of his bench. No one had appraised Mr Justice Squander of this.

"Thus, when he took his seat of judgement on that notable occasion, and leafed through some legal documents on the bench with his right hand, the waiting counsel for the defence and prosecution, the Bailiff, the policeman on duty, half of the jury and not a few of the spectators, were privileged to see – all framed in the missing panel of wood – His Honour's left hand hoisting up the legal gown, unzipping the fly of his charcoal grey strides and gently fondling the wrinkled and hairy genitalia within: comfort for his hangover ...

"The judge's aide, a pretty young recent graduette, spotted what was going on and moved in front of the missing panel to spread her own gown wide, like Batman, until His Honour was able to restore his dignity. Mr Justice Squander restored his dignity further, following the luncheon adjournment, by giving the smirking accused the maximum sentence with hard labour, for what was little more than petty larceny. More, he went on to voice his public regret that the gallows had been discarded as a form of punishment in Our Part of the Nation, since it meant a down-grading of the total spectrum of sentences available to the bench ..."

Dr Throwback later examined Mr Justice Squander's prostrate body behind the bench and pronounced him not dead but drunk. Forced to retire, he became involved in an international paedophile ring and murdered his wife when she surprised him accommodating a shoe fetish. Perhaps in an echo of 10 Rillington Place (see chapter 29: How the Innocent Don't Get Off), he bricked up her body in the cellar along with child victims of snuff movies. He also resorted to frottage (touching) on council buses, and had to escape headlong when girls complained. This led to the discovery of the bodies in the cellar; the splash in *The Daily Switch* was: **The Afternoon of the Flashing Jogger**. An inquest was held. James continues:

"Well, ha ha, people had said when they first read the startling news, who would believe a man could be ignorant of the fact that his wife's body was down in his own cellar? Well, as it turned out, the legal system would believe it. Mr Squander's solicitor was helpful in this regard. He proffered as evidence a Statutory Declaration that Mr Squander no longer went down into his cellar since he had given up drinking wine, which was two or three years previously. Indeed, the last time Mr Squander had visited his cellar was when he had his cellar appraised for sale so he could clear it out to rent to a movie company, and Mrs Squander was hale and hearty then, in the blossom of health, making arrangements for her extended tour of Europe.

"On the matter of the flashing jogger, Mr Squander's solicitor pointed out that his client had been in bed since breakfast on the day of the flashing jogger with his impending heart attack; any one might have entered and left the Squander household on that day without his knowledge. To suggest his client had any association with a man who had run amok on a council bus was stretching the limits of imagination. More likely it was someone who had a record of urban terrorism or something like that, the solicitor continued.

"Mr Squander's solicitor had slapped a couple of writs on the gutter press for their insinuations, which put such sensitive matters *sub-judice* and allowed proceedings to proceed in earnest. Mr Justice Squander's solicitor produced a string of witnesses for the coroner on the matter of the council bus frottist, allowing confusion to creep in and perhaps true judgement to creep out. The frottist was described as 165 cm tall and 185 cm tall; as weighing 50 kg and weighing 100 kg; as being 20 years of age and over 40 years of age; as both white and slightly black; as both tattooed and clean skin."

The police framed an unemployed Sri-Lankan as the frottist-paedophile-murderer. James goes on: "To top it all, [the Sri-Lankan] could not even own up to his crimes. Pathetically, when he came to trial, he proffered his passport as evidence that he was not even in the country when Mrs Squander went to meet her maker. But that argument fell flat on its face when his passport was presented in court and found to have several pages taken out. The Sri-Lankan interjected to say that the pages were all present when he tendered the document to the police and he got quite a reprimand from the judge for his interruption – not only for his contempt but also for implying that the police had tampered with the pages of his passport, which was obviously against the law. The judge drew the court's attention to a paragraph in the Passport Act which stated that very clearly. Anyway, a review of the time of Mrs Squander's death by the Forensic department brought the date forward quite a lot and nullified that particular argument of the Sri Lankan's.

"I knew a lot of people were looking forward to the formal sentencing of the Sri-Lankan, hoping such cases would help to bring back the gallows. It was therefore something of a disappointment to them when the man constructed his own personal gallows in custody and hanged himself. I knew several who suggested that this cowardly way of avoiding his debt to society was no more than a poor attempt to avoid a bad finish ...

"So, when it was all over, Mr Justice Squander was able to pursue, with some righteousness, some of the writs taken out by his solicitor against the gutter press, sending the proprietors of a couple of them to the wall. All's well that ends well, said the ladies at my wife's bridgefests ..."

Warm Afternoons in Boston

On an ancillary but rather different note, former Justice James Staples, author of the clearly accurate statement: "We need less law and more justice in our courts", advises that *The Lawyer's Journal*, published by the Massachusetts Bar Association, "recently [September 1977] saw fit to record the following questions (and answers) put to witnesses during examination and cross-examination." I prefer to think the lawyers were not victims of the malady, merely of stuffy courtrooms on drowsy afternoons. Thus:

Doctor, how many autopsies have you performed on dead people? – *All my autopsies are performed on dead people.*

"Now, doctor, isn't it true that when a person dies in his sleep he doesn't know about it until the next morning?"

Do you recall the time when you examined the body? – *The autopsy started around 8.30 pm.*

And Mr Dennington was dead at the time? – *No, he was sitting on the table wondering why I was doing an autopsy.*

You were shot in the fracas? – *No, I was shot midway between the fracas and the navel.*

"Was it you or your younger brother who was killed in the war?"

Are you qualified to give a urine sample? – *I have been since early childhood.*

"Did he kill you?"

So the date of conception [of the baby] was August 8th? – *Yes. And what were you doing at the time?*

"How far apart were the vehicles at the time of the collision?"

She had three children, right? – Yes
How many were boys? – None.
Were there any girls?

"Were you present when your picture was taken?"

"You were there until the time you left, is that true?"

How was your first marriage terminated? – By death.
And by whose death was it terminated?

Mr Slattery, you went on a rather elaborate honeymoon, didn't
you? – I went to Europe, sir.
And you took your new wife?

Can you describe the individual? – He was of medium height and
had a beard.
Was this a male or a female?

"How many times have you committed suicide?"

All your responses must be oral, OK? What school did you go to?
– Oral.

Doctor, before you performed the autopsy, did you check for a
pulse? – No.
Did you check for blood pressure? – No.
Did you check for breathing? – No.
So then it is possible that the patient was alive when you began
the autopsy? – No.
How can you be so sure, doctor? – Because his brain was sitting
on my desk in a jar.
But could the patient have still been alive nevertheless? – It is
possible that he could have been alive and practising law
somewhere.

Sources mentioned in the text:

Anonymous, (1992), *The Concise Dictionary of National Biography – From Earliest Times to 1985*, 3 vols, Oxford: OUP.

Baker, J.H. (1990), *An Introduction to English Legal History*, London: Butterworths.

Bates, Stephen (1997), *A Country to Die For*, The Spectator, 15 November 1997.

Burchett, J.C.S. (1996), *Comment on Paper by P. Newman J. on the Investigating Judge in the Civil Law System*, Conference of Supreme and Federal Court Judges, Darwin, January 1996.

Callinan, I.D.F. (1988), *Commissions of Inquiry*, Legal convention, Hobart.

Chan, Janet and Barnes, Lynne (1995), *The Price of Justice? – Lengthy Criminal Trials in Australia*, Sydney: Hawkins.

Cohen, Morris L. (1992), *Law: The Art of Justice*, New York: Hugh Lauter Levin Associates Inc.

Cowdery, Nicholas (1997), *Justice in Pursuit of Lawyers*, Sydney: St James Ethics Centre, 26 August 1997.

Crowley, Dr Michael J. (1994), *The Impact of Psychological Expert Testimony in Child Sexual Abuse Cases*, unpublished thesis, University of Tasmania.

Cyriax, Oliver (1996), *The Penguin Encyclopedia of Crime*, London: Penguin.

Davies, Geoffrey (1995), *A Blueprint for Reform*, paper, Australian Legal Convention, September 27, 1995

Davies, Geoffrey (1997), *Fairness in a Predominantly Adversarial System*, conference, Beyond the Adversarial System, Brisbane July 10, 1997.

de Bono, Edward (1991), *I Am Right – You Are Wrong*, Penguin: London.

Downie, Leonard (1976), *The New Muckrakers – An Inside Look at America's Investigative Reporters*, Washington: New Republic.

Falcone, Giovanni and Padovan, Marcelle (1991), *Men of Honour – The Truth About the Mafia*, London: Fourth Estate.

Forbes, J.R.S. (1987), *Similar Facts*, Sydney: The Law Book Company.

Forbes, J.R.S. (1992), *Evidence in Queensland*, Sydney: The Law Book Company.

Gilbert, Michael (ed, 1986), *The Oxford Book of Legal Anecdotes*, Oxford: OUP.

Gleeson, Murray (1997), *Who Do Judges Think They Are?*, Sydney: Sir Earle Page Memorial Oration, 22 October 1997.

Goldrick, J.V.P. (1983), *The "Australia" Court-Martial of 1942*, Armidale: unpublished thesis, Master of Letters, University of New England.

Henderson, Kerrie (1992), *The Cojuangco Case and Disclosure of Journalists' Sources*, Brisbane: Australian Studies in Journalism.

Ipp, Justice David (1995), *Reforms to the Adversarial Process in Civil Litigation*, Sydney: The Australian Law Journal.

Irons, Peter (1994), *Brennan vs. Rehnquist: The Battle for the Constitution*, New York: Alfred A. Knopf.

Jacobs, James B., with Panarella, Christopher and Worthington, Jay, (1994) *Busting the Mob: United States v Cosa Nostra*, New York University Press.

James, Peter (1974), *In Place of Justice*, Brisbane: Refulgence.

James, Peter (1990), *The Sundown Murders*, Brisbane: Boolarong.

James, Peter (1997), *The Glopmakers*, Brisbane: Boolarong.

Jackson, R.M. (1977), *The Machinery of Justice in England*, Cambridge: Cambridge University Press.

Kennedy, Ludovic (1989), *The Advantages of the Inquisitorial over the Adversary System of Criminal Justice*, address to the Howard League of Penal Reform, 15 November 1989.

Kennedy, Ludovic (1991), *Truth to Tell*, London: Black Swan.

Kirby, Michael (1995), *Crime in Australia – Change and Continuity*, Australian Institute of Criminology symposium, June 1995.

Landsman, Stephan (1988), *Readings on Adversarial Justice: The American Approach to Adjudication*, St Paul: West Publishing Co.

Langbein, John H. (1985), *The German Advantage in Civil Procedure*, Chicago: The University of Chicago Law Review, Fall 1985.

Langbein, John H. (1994), *The Historical Origins of the Privilege Against Self-Incrimination at Common Law*, Michigan Law Review, March 1994.

Langbein, John H. (1996), *Historical Foundations of the Law of Evidence: A View from the Ryder Sources*, New York: Columbia Law Review, June 1996.

Luban, David (1997), *Twenty Theses on Adversarial Ethics*, conference, Beyond the Adversarial System, Brisbane, July 10-11, 1997.

McKillop, Bron (1994), *Inquisitorial Systems of Criminal Justice and the ICAC: a Comparison*, Sydney: ICAC.

McKillop, Bron (1997), *Anatomy of a French Murder Case*, Sydney: Hawkins.

Mannion, Robert (1997), *Putting our legal system on trial*, Wellington: The New Zealander, January 22, 1997.

Mansfield QC, Michael (1993), *Presumed Guilty – The British Legal System Exposed*, London: Heinemann.

Marks, Hon Mr Justice K.H., (1984), *"Thinking up" about the Right of Silence and Unsworn Statements*, Melbourne: Victorian Law Institute Journal, April 1984.

Marnham, Patrick (1988), *Trail of Havoc – In the Steps of Lord Lucan*, London: Penguin.

Moffitt, Athol (1985), *A Quarter to Midnight – The Australian Crisis: Organised Crime and the Decline of the Institutions of State*, Sydney: Angus & Robertson.

Nash, Jay Robert (1992), *World Encyclopaedia of Organized Crime*, London: Headline.

O'Reilly, Gregory W. (1994), *England Limits the Right of Silence and Moves Towards an Inquisitorial System of Justice*, Journal of Criminal Law & Criminology, Northwestern University School of Law.

Pannick, David (1987), *Judges*, Oxford: OUP.

Pannick, David QC (1992), *Advocates*, Oxford: OUP

Plucknett, Theodore F.T. (1956), *A Concise History of the Common Law*, London: Butterworth & Co.

Posner, Richard A. (1995), *Overcoming Law*, Cambridge (Mass.): Harvard University Press.

Roden, Adrian (1989), *A Delicate Balance: The Place of Individual's Rights in Corruption Investigations*, Canberra: Australian Government Printing Service.

Rose, David (1996), *In The Name of the Law – The Collapse of Criminal Justice*, London: Cape.

Rothwax, Judge Harold J. (1996), *Guilty – The Collapse of Criminal Justice*, New York: Random House.

Sackville, Ronald (1997), *The Civil Justice System – The Processes of Change*, Brisbane: Beyond the Adversarial System conference July 10-11, 1997.

Samuels, Gordon (1996), *Reinventing the Courts*, NSW Legal Convention, November 1, 1996

Sexton, Michael and Maher, Laurence W. (1982), *The Legal Mystique*, Sydney: Angus & Robertson.

Sifakis, Carl (1987), *The Mafia Encyclopedia - From Accardo to Zwillman*, New York: Facts on File.

Stille, Alexander (1995), *Excellent Cadavers - The Mafia and the Death of the First Italian Republic*, New York: Pantheon.

Stone, Julius and W.A.N. Wells (1991), *Evidence - Its History and Policies*, Sydney: Butterworths.

Stewart, Donald (1983), *Report: Royal Commission of Inquiry into Drug Trafficking [Mr Asia]*, Canberra: Australian Government Publishing Service.

Sutherland, James (1975), *The Oxford Book of Literary Anecdotes*, Oxford: OUP.

Victorian Community Council Against Violence (1995), *Bringing It Together – A Victim Support Strategy*, Melbourne: conference May 18-19, 1995.

Watson, Ray and Purnell, Howard,. (continuous updating), *Criminal Law in New South Wales, Volume 1 Indictable Offences*, Sydney: The Law Book Company.

Whitton, Evan (1989, 1993), *The Hillbilly Dictator*, Sydney: ABC Books.

Whitton, Evan (1994), *Trial by Voodoo – Why the Law Defeats Justice and Democracy*, Sydney: Random House.

Ziegert, K.A. (1995), *The Political Fitness of a Legal System: English Law, Australian Courts and the Republic*, Sydney: Sydney Law Review.

Ziegert, K.A. (1997), *The Flow & Functions of Legal Procedures – Comparative Observations on the Operations of Courts and Tribunals in Australia, Denmark, Germany and Sweden*, Department of Jurisprudence, University of Sydney.

Zuckerman, A.A.S. (1989), *The Principles of Criminal Evidence*, Oxford: The Clarendon Press.

Index

Note. Alphabetical order is letter-by-letter. Unless stated otherwise, references are to common law versions of trials, adversary system etc. Inquisitorial systems generally, and specifically in Belgium, France, Germany, Italy, Japan, Scotland, United States (Grand Jury), are noted in a separate section beginning on page 252.

251

Inquisitorial Systems

General